# BRIDGES IN CHINA

# 中国桥梁

## 1949—2024

人民交通出版社股份有限公司
北 京

## 编辑委员会

**名誉主任**　黄镇东
**主任委员**　项海帆
**副主任委员**　邓文中　凤懋润
**委　　员**　郑皆连　林元培　王景全　秦顺全　杨永斌
　　　　　　陈政清　张喜刚　包琦玮　邵长宇　徐恭义
　　　　　　韩振勇　顾安邦　韩　敏　刘正光　牛　斌
　　　　　　肖汝诚　周世忠　葛耀君

## 编 写 组

**主　　编**　葛耀君
**副 主 编**　肖汝诚　孙利民　李国平　徐　栋
**分章负责人**
学习与探索　葛耀君　朱乐东　杨詠昕
追赶与自主　肖汝诚　贾丽君　孙　斌
发展与图强　孙利民　夏　烨　阮　欣
创新与提高　李国平　沈　殷　操金鑫
攀登与超越　徐　栋　徐利平　刘　超
**特邀翻译**　Paul Gauvreau
**其他参编人**　方根深　宋超林　芦旭朝

## 编辑统筹

**策划编辑**　孙　玺
**责任编辑**　卢俊丽
**文字编辑**　陈虹宇　李　敏
**美术编辑**　周逸斐

## Editorial Committee

| | | | | | |
|---|---|---|---|---|---|
| **Honorary Chairman** | Huang Zhendong | | | | |
| **Chairman** | Xiang Haifan | | | | |
| **Vice-chairman** | Deng Wenzhong | Feng Maorun | | | |
| **Members** | Zheng Jielian | Lin Yuanpei | Wang Jingquan | Qin Shunquan | Yang Yongbin |
| | Chen Zhengqing | Zhang Xigang | Bao Qiwei | Shao Changyu | Xu Gongyi |
| | Han Zhenyong | Gu Anbang | Han Min | Liu Zhengguang | Niu Bin |
| | Xiao Rucheng | Zhou Shizhong | Ge Yaojun | | |

## Compilation Board

| | | | | |
|---|---|---|---|---|
| **Compiler-in-chief** | Ge Yaojun | | | |
| **Deputy Compiler-in-chief** | Xiao Rucheng | Sun Limin | Li Guoping | Xu Dong |
| **Compilers** | | | | |
| *Learning and Searching* | Ge Yaojun | Zhu Ledong | Yang Yongxin | |
| *Chasing and Independence* | Xiao Rucheng | Jia Lijun | Sun Bin | |
| *Development and Strengthening* | Sun Limin | Xia Ye | Ruan Xin | |
| *Innovation and Improvement* | Li Guoping | Shen Yin | Cao Jinxin | |
| *Climbing and Surpassing* | Xu Dong | Xu Liping | Liu Chao | |
| **Contributing Translator** | Paul Gauvreau | | | |
| **Other Contributors** | Fang Genshen | Song Chaolin | Lu Xuzhao | |

## Managing Editor

| | | |
|---|---|---|
| **Sponsoring Editor** | Sun Xi | |
| **Editor in Charge** | Lu Junli | |
| **Processing Editor** | Chen Hongyu | Li Min |
| **Art Editor** | Zhou Yifei | |

# 序　言

桥梁作为交通基础设施的重要构成和工程技术成就的重要标志，是一个国家科技水平和综合国力的重要体现。自1949年中华人民共和国成立以来，在中华民族伟大复兴的壮丽征程中，伴随中国经济社会的持续快速发展，中国的交通基础设施建设取得了举世瞩目的巨大成就。截至2023年末，中国的公路总里程已达到542万公里（包括18.5万公里高速公路）、铁路总里程15.9万公里（包括4.5万公里高速铁路），公路桥梁110万座（其中特大桥梁约9千座）、铁路桥梁9.5万座。经过75年的建设，公路桥梁和铁路桥梁的数量分别是新中国成立之初的7倍和20倍左右，双双成为世界第一，中国已经成为名副其实的桥梁大国。

中华人民共和国成立之初，中国没有钢结构焊接技术，没有预应力混凝土技术，没有一条贯通大江南北的交通大动脉。就是在这样的基础上，中国的桥梁建设开启了由弱到大到强的光辉征程。经过前30年的学习和探索，掌握和发展了预应力混凝土技术，研发了梁桥和拱桥的经济桥型和施工技术，建成了特大桥梁——武汉长江大桥和南京长江大桥。20世纪最后20年，积极跟踪国外大跨度桥梁建设先进技术，坚持自主建设大跨度斜拉桥和悬索桥，并取得了巨大的成功，先后创造了斜拉桥、混凝土梁桥和混凝土拱桥跨径的世界纪录。进入21世纪后，在前10年的发展与图强中，继续拓展大江、大河和高山峡谷上大跨度桥梁建设，并走向海洋研发长大跨海桥梁建设技术，多座拱桥、梁桥、斜拉桥和跨海大桥的跨度或长度都创造了新的世界纪录；在第二个10年的创新与提高中，不断提升桥梁连续跨越能力，开拓了多主跨斜拉桥、悬索桥和拱桥建设技术，提升了桥梁技术水平和品质，开始与国际先进水平并跑、领跑；在最近5年的攀登与超越中，中国更加注重桥梁技术创新、品质提升和生态环境，引领了世界桥梁品质和技术发展。经过75年的发展，在全世界已经建成的跨径前十的各类桥型中，梁桥有5座、拱桥有7座、斜拉桥有7座、悬索桥有5座在中国，特别是中西部地区的峡谷大桥体现了中国式现代化的伟大成就。在国际桥梁与结构工程协会已经颁发的32个"杰出结构奖"桥梁项目中，中国获得了其中的7项。中国75年的桥梁建设成就，尤其是大批超级桥梁工程的自主建设，标志着中国已由桥梁建设大国逐步成为桥梁建设强国。

2024年是中华人民共和国成立75周年。我们特别遴选了75年间各个发展阶段的75座代表性桥梁制成画册，以反映中国桥梁技术的创新与突破，展现中国桥梁75年间的卓越成就与非凡跨越。

这75座桥梁，不仅是中国桥梁不同时期的代表之作，更是中国从贫穷落后走向繁荣昌盛的见证，是中国人民"逢山开路，遇水架桥"奋斗精神的象征，闪耀着实干兴邦、大国崛起、民族复兴的时代光辉，是中华民族现代文明的重要标志。

75年来，中国桥梁工程发展取得了举世瞩目的成就，已成为推动国际桥梁技术进步和科技创新的新动力，而这一切，离不开中国桥梁工程师的奋发图强与杰出贡献，以及国家强大的装备制造能力。在此，谨以此书向那些为中国桥梁建设作出杰出贡献的前辈们，以及所有参与中国桥梁建设的工程师、设计施工人员以及相关工作者表示敬意，是他们的辛勤付出和智慧创造，使得中国桥梁能够在世界桥梁舞台上大放异彩。

75年来，中国建成了交通大国，交通成为中国现代化的开路先锋。当前，中国正全力以赴加快建设交通强国，到2035年基本建成交通强国，到2050年全面建成交通强国。而中国地质地貌复杂多样，西部高山峡谷遍布，东部大江大河横贯，东南沿海海湾海峡宽阔，要在960万平方公里的土地上织就一张中国式现代化的交通运输网络，桥梁（隧道）至关重要。这必将对中国桥梁建设提出更高的要求和挑战。在新的征程上，中国桥梁建设必将继续追求卓越，推动技术创新，致力于绿色、智能、可持续的桥梁建设新理念，更加注重设计美学、研发原创技术、强化建设质量，积极参与国际交流和竞争，为推动世界桥梁技术进步贡献新的中国力量。

*黄镇东*

2024年2月

Bridges, as crucial components of transportation infrastructure and significant indicators of engineering and technological achievement, reflect a country's scientific and technological level and its comprehensive national strength. Since the founding of the People's Republic of China in 1949, as part of the magnificent journey toward the great rejuvenation of the Chinese nation, China has witnessed sustained and rapid development in its economy and society. This development has led to globally recognized monumental achievements in transportation infrastructure construction. By the end of 2023, China's total road mileage had reached 5.42 million kilometres, including 185,000 kilometres of expressways, and its total railway mileage stood at 159,000 kilometres, including 45,000 kilometres of high-speed railways. The country boasts 1.1 million road bridges, including approximately 9,000 major bridges and 95,000 railway bridges. After 75 years of construction, the number of road and railway bridges has increased approximately 7-fold and 20-fold, respectively, compared to the numbers at the inception of the People's Republic of China, making China the world leader in both categories. China has truly become a bridge-building superpower.

At the founding of the People's Republic of China, the country had no steel structural welding technology, no prestressed concrete technology, and no major transportation artery connecting the country from north to south. From such beginnings, China's bridge construction embarked on a brilliant journey from weakness to strength. After the first 30 years of Learning and Searching, China mastered and developed prestressed concrete technology, designed economical bridge types and developed construction techniques for beam and arch bridges, and built major bridges such as the Wuhan Bridge over the Yangtze River and the Nanjing Bridge

# FOREWORD

over the Yangtze River. In the last two decades of the 20th century, the years of Chasing and Independence, China actively followed advanced technologies developed abroad for the construction of long-span bridges, insisted on independently building long-span cable-stayed and suspension bridges, and achieved great success, setting world records for the span of cable-stayed bridges, concrete beam bridges, and concrete arch bridges. Entering the 21st century, the first decade of which were the years of Development and Strengthening, China continued to expand the construction of long-span bridges over major rivers, high mountains, and gorges, and ventured into the sea to develop technologies for long-span sea-crossing bridges, thus setting new world records for the span or length of arch bridges, beam bridges, cable-stayed bridges, and sea-crossing bridges. In the second decade of the 21st century, the years of Innovation and Improvement, China continuously improved the continuous spanning capability of bridges, developed the construction technology of multi-span cable-stayed bridges, suspension bridges, and arch bridges, and elevated the technical level and quality of bridges. During this period, China began to run and even lead at the most advanced international level. The most recent five years are characterized by Climbing and Surpassing. During this period, China has placed greater emphasis on bridge technology innovation, quality improvement, and environmental sustainability, leading the world in bridge quality and technological development. After 75 years of development, China is home to many of the top ten longest span bridges in several types, including 5 beam bridges, 7 arch bridges, 7 cable-stayed bridges, and 5 suspension bridges. Of these, the bridges spanning deep gorges in China's central and western regions are particularly worthy examples of the great achievements of Chinese-style modernization. Of the 32 "Outstanding Structure Awards" for bridge projects issued by the International Association for Bridge and Structural Engineering, China has won 7. The achievements of 75 years of bridge construction in China, especially the independent construction of a large number of major bridges, signify that China has gradually transitioned from a major bridge-building country to a powerful bridge-building nation.

2024 marks the 75th anniversary of the founding of the People's Republic of China. To commemorate this milestone, a special selection of 75 representative bridges from various stages of development over the past 75 years has been compiled into this album. This collection aims to reflect the innovation and breakthroughs in Chinese bridge technology and showcase the remarkable achievements and extraordinary progress of the bridges in China over the last 75 years.

These 75 bridges not only represent the epitome of Chinese bridge engineering at different periods but also serve as a testament to China's journey from poverty to prosperity. They symbolize the enduring spirit of the Chinese people, who are determined to "cut through mountains and bridge waters" in their pursuit of progress. These structures shine with the glory of an era marked by hard work and national rejuvenation, embodying the rise of a great nation. They stand as significant markers of the modern civilization of the Chinese nation.

Over the past 75 years, bridge engineering in China has achieved remarkable success, becoming a new force driving the advancement of international bridge technology and scientific innovation. This progress could not have been achieved without the vigorous efforts and outstanding contributions of Chinese bridge engineers, as well as the country's strong manufacturing capabilities. This book is dedicated to those pioneers who have made significant contributions to the construction of bridges in China, as well as all the engineers, designers, construction workers, and related personnel involved in Chinese bridge construction. It is their hard work and creative intelligence that have allowed Chinese bridges to shine brightly on the world stage.

Over the past 75 years, China has been a country with vast transport infrastructure, and transport has become a frontier in China's modernization drive. China is currently making all-out efforts to accelerate its transformation into a country with great transport strength. By 2035, China aims to have firmly established itself in this endeavour, with the goal of fully achieving this status by 2050. Given China's complex and diverse geological and topographical features, including the high mountains and deep gorges in the west, the large rivers traversing the east, and the wide bays and straits along the southeastern coast, bridges and tunnels are crucial components in a modern transportation network crossing the country's 9.6 million square kilometers. This will undoubtedly place higher demands and challenges on bridge construction in China. On this new journey, Chinese bridge construction will continue to strive for excellence, drive technological innovation, and adhere to new concepts of green, intelligent, and sustainable bridge construction. There will be a greater focus on aesthetics, the development of original technologies, and the enhancement of quality. By actively participating in international exchanges and competitions, China is committed to contributing new strength to the advancement of global bridge technology.

**Huang Zhendong**

February 2024

# 目 录

## 1949 — 1979
### LEARNING AND SEARCHING  001  学习与探索

| | | |
|---|---|---|
| Introduction | 002 | 引言 |
| New Yi River Bridge of East Longhai Railway | 004 | 东陇海线新沂河桥 |
| Yaba River Bridge of Jingzhou Highway | 006 | 京周公路哑叭河桥 |
| Wuhan Bridge over Yangtze River | 008 | 武汉长江大桥 |
| Nanning Yong River Bridge | 012 | 南宁邕江大桥 |
| Wuling Wei River Bridge | 014 | 五陵卫河桥 |
| Hudai Bridge | 016 | 胡埭大桥 |
| Liaoyang Bridge over Taizi River | 018 | 辽阳太子河桥 |
| Liu River Bridge | 020 | 柳江大桥 |
| Nanjing Bridge over Yangtze River | 022 | 南京长江大桥 |
| Wulong River Bridge | 026 | 乌龙江桥 |
| Binzhou Highway Bridge over Yellow River | 028 | 滨州黄河公路大桥 |
| Juzizhou Bridge | 030 | 橘子洲大桥 |
| Taipei Guangfu Bridge | 032 | 台北光复桥 |
| Luan River Highway Bridge | 034 | 滦河公路桥 |

## 1980 — 1999
### CHASING AND INDEPENDENCE  037  追赶与自主

| | | |
|---|---|---|
| Introduction | 038 | 引言 |
| Chongqing Shibanpo Bridge over Yangtze River | 040 | 重庆石板坡长江大桥 |
| Jinan Bridge over Yellow River | 042 | 济南黄河大桥 |
| Tianjin Yonghe Bridge | 044 | 天津永和桥 |
| Panyu Luoxi Bridge | 046 | 番禺洛溪桥 |
| Shanghai Nanpu Bridge | 048 | 上海南浦大桥 |
| Jiujiang Bridge over Yangtze River | 052 | 九江长江大桥 |
| Shanghai Yangpu Bridge | 054 | 上海杨浦大桥 |
| Jiangjie River Bridge | 056 | 江界河大桥 |
| Shantou Bay Bridge | 058 | 汕头海湾大桥 |
| Hong Kong Tsing Ma Bridge | 060 | 香港青马大桥 |
| Humen Bridge over Pearl River | 064 | 虎门珠江大桥 |
| Wanzhou Bridge over Yangtze River | 066 | 万州长江大桥 |
| Jiangyin Bridge over Yangtze River | 068 | 江阴长江大桥 |

## 2000 — 2009
### DEVELOPMENT AND STRENGTHENING  071  发展与图强

| | | |
|---|---|---|
| Introduction | 072 | 引言 |
| Dan River Bridge | 074 | 丹河大桥 |
| Wuhu Bridge over Yangtze River | 076 | 芜湖长江大桥 |
| Shanghai Lupu Bridge | 078 | 上海卢浦大桥 |
| Runyang Highway Bridge over Yangtze River | 082 | 润扬长江公路大桥 |
| East Sea Bridge | 084 | 东海大桥 |
| Nanjing Dashengguan Bridge over Yangtze River | 086 | 南京大胜关长江大桥 |
| Chongqing Shibanpo Parallel Bridge over Yangtze River | 088 | 重庆石板坡长江大桥复线桥 |
| Caiyuanba Bridge over Yangtze River | 092 | 菜园坝长江大桥 |
| Hangzhou Bay Sea-crossing Bridge | 094 | 杭州湾跨海大桥 |
| Sutong Highway Bridge over Yangtze River | 096 | 苏通长江公路大桥 |
| Hong Kong Stonecutters Bridge | 100 | 香港昂船洲大桥 |

# INDEX

| | | | |
|---|---|---|---|
| Chaotianmen Bridge over Yangtze River | 104 | 朝天门长江大桥 | |
| Tianxingzhou Bridge over Yangtze River | 106 | 天兴洲长江大桥 | |
| Xihoumen Bridge | 108 | 西堠门大桥 | |
| Baling River Bridge | 112 | 坝陵河大桥 | |

## 2010 — 2019
## INNOVATION AND IMPROVEMENT　115　创新与提高

| | | |
|---|---|---|
| Introduction | 116 | 引言 |
| Beijing-Shanghai High-speed Railway Nanjing Dashengguan Bridge over Yangtze River | 118 | 京沪高铁南京大胜关长江大桥 |
| Jiaozhou Bay Bridge | 122 | 胶州湾大桥 |
| Danyang-Kunshan Grand Bridge | 124 | 丹昆特大桥 |
| Xinjiang Guozigou Bridge | 126 | 新疆果子沟大桥 |
| Wuhan Erqi Bridge over Yangtze River | 128 | 武汉二七长江大桥 |
| Aizhai Bridge | 130 | 矮寨大桥 |
| Hangzhou Jiubao Bridge | 132 | 杭州九堡大桥 |
| Taizhou Bridge over Yangtze River | 134 | 泰州长江大桥 |
| Bosideng Bridge over Yangtze River | 138 | 波司登长江大桥 |
| Jiashao Bridge | 140 | 嘉绍大桥 |
| Liupanshui-Panxian Expressway Bridge over Beipan River | 142 | 水盘高速北盘江特大桥 |
| Ma'anshan Bridge over Yangtze River | 146 | 马鞍山长江大桥 |
| Dongshuimen Bridge over Yangtze River | 148 | 东水门长江大桥 |
| Shanghai-Kunming High-speed Railway Bridge over Beipan River | 150 | 沪昆高铁北盘江特大桥 |
| Hong Kong-Zhuhai-Macao Bridge | 152 | 港珠澳大桥 |
| Nansha Bridge | 156 | 南沙大桥 |
| Beijing New Shougang Bridge | 158 | 北京新首钢大桥 |
| Pingtang Bridge | 160 | 平塘大桥 |
| Chongqing Egongyan Rail Transit Bridge | 162 | 重庆鹅公岩轨道大桥 |

## 2020 — 2024
## CLIMBING AND SURPASSING　165　攀登与超越

| | | |
|---|---|---|
| Introduction | 166 | 引言 |
| Shanghai-Suzhou-Nantong Highway and Railway Bridge over Yangtze River | 168 | 沪苏通长江公铁大桥 |
| Pingtan Strait Highway and Railway Bridge | 170 | 平潭海峡公铁两用大桥 |
| Wufengshan Bridge over Yangtze River | 172 | 五峰山长江大桥 |
| The Third Pingnan Bridge | 174 | 平南三桥 |
| Nanjing Jiangxinzhou Bridge over Yangtze River | 178 | 南京江心洲长江大桥 |
| Zangmu Bridge over Yarlung Zangbo River | 180 | 藏木雅鲁藏布大桥 |
| Zhoushan-Daishan Bridge | 182 | 舟岱大桥 |
| Phoenix Bridge over Yellow River | 184 | 凤凰黄河大桥 |
| Beikou Bridge over Ou River | 186 | 瓯江北口大桥 |
| Kinmen Bridge | 188 | 金门大桥 |
| Tian'e Longtan Bridge | 190 | 天峨龙滩特大桥 |
| Shenzhen-Zhongshan Link | 194 | 深中通道 |
| The Fourth Sea-crossing Bridge of Macao | 196 | 澳门第四条跨海大桥 |
| Huang Mao Hai Link | 198 | 黄茅海跨海通道 |
| Afterword | 200 | 后记 |

BRIDGES IN CHINA

1949

中 国 桥 梁

# 学习与探索
LEARNING AND SEARCHING

1979

# 引　言

中华人民共和国成立初期，百废待兴，经济十分困难。经过三年国民经济恢复时期后，1953年起中国开始实施第一个五年计划，而第二个五年计划遭遇了三年严重困难，随后不得不进入国民经济调整时期，紧接着就是"文化大革命"。

新中国成立后的第一个五年计划期间，中国从苏联引进了一批桥梁设计标准图，如T形和π形预制钢筋混凝土简支梁桥以及带挂梁的钢筋混凝土悬臂梁桥，推动了中国中小跨度钢筋混凝土梁桥的发展；由留苏学者和学生带回的当时苏联的预应力技术，特别是预应力锚具（柯罗夫金锚具），促成了中国第一座铁路预应力混凝土桥梁和第一座公路预应力混凝土桥梁的建成；在苏联专家的指导和帮助下，建造了万里长江第一桥——武汉长江大桥，贯通了中国第一条南北交通大动脉。

20世纪60年代初，中国处于三年困难时期，经济形势恶化，建筑材料匮乏，施工设备陈旧。尽管如此，中国的桥梁工程师在十分困难的条件下仍创造了一些符合当时国情的经济桥型和施工技术，例如轻型少筋的混凝土双曲拱桥，悬臂梁和T形刚构的悬臂施工方法等，特别是自力更生建成了第二座长江大桥——南京长江大桥，为交通事业发展做出了重要贡献。然而，中国桥梁界还是错过了国外20世纪60～70年代高速公路大发展的机遇，也失去了和外国同行进行技术交流和合作的机会，只能从少量国外文献资料中零星地了解到一些国际现代桥梁工程信息，在预应力技术、斜拉桥技术和计算机应用方面进行着默默的探索和研究。

新中国成立后的30年间，中国建成了一批公路和铁路桥梁，主要桥型为梁桥和拱桥，也有几座试验性的斜拉桥和悬索桥。本章选取了中国第一座铁路预应力混凝土桥梁和公路预应力混凝土桥梁，2座举世闻名的长江大桥，最早期和最具影响的双曲拱桥各1座，5座钢筋混凝土或预应力混凝土悬臂梁桥或T形刚构桥，第一座按10度地震烈度设防的预应力混凝土连续梁桥，连续钢桁梁黄河大桥和台湾地区斜拉桥等，代表了中国这一时期桥梁建设的技术水平和工程成就。

# INTRODUCTION

In the early days of the People's Republic of China, there were a thousand things to do, and the economy was confronted with significant challenges. Following three years of national economic recovery, the country embarked on its first Five-Year Plan in 1953. However, the second Five-Year Plan was met with the "Great Chinese Famine" which produced three years of serious difficulties and lead to a period of economic adjustment. This was closely followed by the "Cultural Revolution".

During the first Five-Year Plan following the establishment of the People's Republic of China, the country imported a series of bridge design standards from the Soviet Union, including designs for T-shaped and π-shaped precast reinforced concrete simply supported bridges, as well as reinforced concrete cantilever bridges with suspended girders. This significantly advanced the development of small to medium span reinforced concrete beam bridges in China. Prestressing technology from the Soviet Union, particularly the Kryukov prestressing anchor, brought back by the overseas scholars and students, led to the construction of the first prestressed concrete railway bridge and the first prestressed concrete highway bridge in China. With the guidance and assistance of Soviet experts, the first crossing of the Yangtze River, the Wuhan Bridge, was built. This vital link provided the first major north-south traffic artery in China.

In the early 1960s, China experienced three years of serious difficulties in which China's economic situation deteriorated. This produced a scarcity of building materials and outdated construction equipment. Despite these extremely difficult conditions, Chinese bridge engineers still managed to create economical bridge types and construction techniques compatible with the national situation at the time. Examples include lightweight, minimally reinforced concrete hyperbolic arch bridges and cantilever beams, and the cantilever construction method for T-shaped rigid frames. Notably, the self-reliant construction of the second bridge across the Yangtze River, the Nanjing Bridge, made a significant contribution to the development of China's transportation infrastructure. China's bridge engineering community had, however, missed the opportunity presented by the rapid development of highways in western countries during the 1960s and 1970s, and lost the chance for technical exchange and cooperation with international counterparts. Limited in their access to information from foreign literature, Chinese engineers worked hard to explore and conduct research in fields like prestressing technology, cable-stayed bridge technology, and computer applications.

During the first 30 years after the establishment of the People's Republic of China, a number of highway and railway bridges were constructed. The most common types were girders and arches. There were a few experimental cable-stayed and suspension bridges. This chapter focuses on several significant bridges that represent the technological advancements and engineering achievements of this period in China. It includes China's first railway and highway prestressed concrete bridges, two world-renowned Yangtze River bridges, the earliest and most influential hyperbolic arch bridges, five reinforced or prestressed concrete cantilever beam or T-shaped rigid frame bridges, the first prestressed concrete continuous beam bridge designed to withstand the seismic intensity scale of 10 degrees, a continuous steel truss bridge over the Yellow River, and a cable-stayed bridge in Taiwan region.

# 东陇海线新沂河桥

## New Yi River Bridge of East Longhai Railway

桥　　名：东陇海线新沂河桥
桥　　型：预应力混凝土简支双T梁桥
主跨跨径：23.9m
桥　　址：江苏省新沂市
建成时间：1956年
设计单位：铁道部大桥工程局
施工单位：铁道部丰台桥梁厂

东陇海线新沂河桥位于江苏省新沂市，全长691.7m，采用28跨23.9m跨径的后张法预应力混凝土双T形截面简支梁，是中国第一座铁路预应力混凝土桥梁。1955年，在铁道部铁道科学研究院、铁道部定型设计事务所和丰台桥梁厂完成了12m跨径后张法预应力混凝土梁的系统试验研究后，铁道部大桥设计事务所设计出了标准轨距、跨径23.9m的预应力混凝土铁路梁，由丰台桥梁厂预制，于1956年初架设到新沂河桥上。预应力混凝土双T形梁采用400级钢筋混凝土，苏联柯罗夫金式张拉锚固体系，每束由56~60根$\phi$5钢丝（极限强度1200MPa）组成，架设采用800kN双悬臂式架桥机。这种梁型成为随后32m以下跨径预应力混凝土铁路梁桥中应用最广泛的标准化定型结构，开创了我国预应力混凝土桥梁工业化大批量生产的道路，促进了预应力混凝土技术的迅速发展。

New Yi River Bridge of East Longhai Railway is located in Xinyi City, Jiangsu Province. The railway bridge has a total length of 691.7m and features 28 spans of post-tensioned prestressed concrete double-T beams with each span of 23.9m. It stands as the first railway bridge constructed using prestressed concrete in China. In 1955, following the completion of systematic experimental research on post-tensioned prestressed concrete beams with a span of 12m by the Railway Scientific Research Institute, the Standard Design Office and the Fengtai Bridge Factory of the Ministry of Railways, the Ministry of Railways Bridge Design Office developed a standardized design for prestressed concrete railway beams with a standard gauge span of 23.9m. Manufactured by Fengtai Bridge Factory, these beams were prefabricated and erected on the New Yi River Bridge in early 1956. The prestressed concrete double-T beams utilize 400 grade reinforced concrete and the Korofkin-type post tensioning anchorage system from the Soviet Union. Each bundle is composed of 56 to 60 $\phi$5 steel wires (with the ultimate strength of 1,200 MPa). The construction process involved in the use of an 800kN double cantilever launching gantry. This beam design subsequently became the most widely used standardized structure for prestressed concrete railway bridges with spans below 32m, marking a significant advancement in the industrialized mass production of prestressed concrete bridges in China. This development played a pivotal role in promoting the rapid evolution of prestressed concrete technology in China.

**Name:** New Yi River Bridge of East Longhai Railway
**Type:** Prestressed concrete simply supported double T-beam bridge
**Main span:** 23.9m
**Location:** Xinyi City, Jiangsu Province
**Completion:** 1956
**Designer(s):** Bridge Engineering Bureau of Ministry of Railways
**Contractor(s):** Fengtai Bridge Factory of Ministry of Railways

# 京周公路哑叭河桥

## Yaba River Bridge of Jingzhou Highway

哑叭河桥位于京周公路上，是一座单跨20m的公路桥梁，桥面宽度净7m，由6片后张法预应力混凝土装配式简支T梁组成，是中国第一座预应力混凝土公路桥梁。预应力混凝土T梁采用400级钢筋混凝土，预埋铁皮管道，每束预应力筋由43根ϕ5钢丝组成，苏联柯罗夫金式张拉锚固体系，采用600kN单作用千斤顶张拉，每片预制T梁的吊装质量为240kN。该桥的成功建设为中国预应力混凝土公路桥的设计与施工提供了宝贵的经验，为编制中国预应力混凝土桥梁的施工技术规程及其推广应用起到了促进作用。

2017年，京周公路哑叭河桥因为公路改线被拆除。

Yaba River Bridge is located on the Jingzhou Highway and is a single-span 20m highway bridge with a net deck width of 7m. It consists of six post tensioned prestressed concrete simply supported T beams and is the first highway prestressed concrete bridge in China. The prestressed concrete T beam uses 400 grade reinforced concrete, embedded iron pipes, each prestressed tendon consists of 43 ϕ 5 steel wires, and the Soviet Korovkin-type anchorage system. It is tensioned by a 600kN single-acting jack, and the lifting weight of each prefabricated T girder is 240kN. The successful construction of this bridge has provided valuable experience for the design and construction of highway prestressed concrete bridges in China, and has played a catalytic role in the preparation of China's prestressed concrete bridge operation procedures and their promotion and application.

In 2017, Yaba River Bridge of Jingzhou Highway was no demolished due to highway realignment.

桥　　名：京周公路哑叭河桥
桥　　型：预应力混凝土简支T梁桥
主跨跨径：20m
桥　　址：北京市房山区
建成时间：1956年
设计单位：交通部公路规划设计院，交通部交通科学研究院
施工单位：交通部第七工程局

Name: Yaba River Bridge of Jingzhou Highway
Type: Prestressed concrete simply supported T-beam bridge
Main span: 20m
Location: Fangshan District, Beijing
Completion: 1956
Designer(s): Transport Planning and Research Institute of Ministry of Transport, China Academy of Transportation Sciences
Contractor(s): Seventh Engineering Bureau of Ministry of Transport

# 武汉长江大桥

## Wuhan Bridge over Yangtze River

桥　　名：武汉长江大桥
桥　　型：连续钢桁梁桥
桥梁长度：全长1.67km，主跨跨径128m
桥　　址：湖北省武汉市
建成时间：1957年10月
设计单位：中铁大桥勘测设计院
施工单位：中铁大桥局集团有限公司

武汉长江大桥位于湖北省武汉市，从汉阳区龟山跨越长江到武昌区蛇山，桥梁全长 1.67km，是第一座跨越万里长江的公铁两用桥梁。

武汉长江大桥由 1156m 主桥、303m 汉阳侧引桥和 211m 武昌侧引桥组成。上层公路双向四车道宽 18m，设计速度为 100km/h，两侧人行道各宽 2.25m；下层双线铁路，设计速度为 160km/h。主桥为 3 联 3×128m 的全铆米字形连续钢桁梁，桁高 16m，主桁中距 10m，采用 A3q 钢制作，H 形截面。铁路部分引桥采用钢筋混凝土简支 T 梁，上层的公路部分采用柱式桥墩和钢筋混凝土连拱。主桥与引桥连接处，两侧各设有一座桥头堡，四座桥头堡均为钢筋混凝土框架结构。主桥连续钢桁梁首次采用伸臂安装法，在前方桥墩设置临时墩旁托架以减少伸臂长度 16m，安装历时 10 个月。首次采用直径 1.55m 的钢筋混凝土管柱作为主要桥墩基础，并制造了冲击式钻机，将管柱底基岩冲击成孔，嵌入岩层 2~7m 深，每墩用管柱 30~35 根，每柱承载力为 1910kN，采用导管法水下混凝土封底。

武汉长江大桥的成功建设，将京汉铁路和粤汉铁路连接起来，成为中国第一条贯通南北的大动脉，是中国桥梁建设的一个里程碑。在大桥的设计和施工等方面，得到了苏联专家的大力支持和帮助。

Wuhan Bridge over Yangtze River is located in Wuhan City, Hubei Province, crossing the Yangtze River from Turtle Mountain in Hanyang District to Snake Mountain in Wuchang District. The total length of the bridge is 1.67km, making it the first dual-use bridge for both highway and railway that spans the mighty Yangtze River.

Wuhan Bridge over Yangtze River consists of a main bridge of 1,156m, Han Yang side approach bridge of 303m, and Wu Chang side approach bridge of 211m. The upper deck has four highway lanes with a width of 18m designed for a speed of 100km/h, and pedestrian walkways on both sides, each with a width of 2.25m. The lower deck accommodates a double-track railway with a design speed of 160km/h. The main bridge is a continuous steel truss girder with a total of three spans, each measuring 128m, forming a riveted inverted " 米 " shape with a girder depth of 16m and a 10m central distance between the main trusses. It is made of A3q steel with an H-shaped cross-section. The railway approach bridge uses reinforced concrete simply supported T girders, while the highway approach bridge above the railway employs column-type piers and reinforced concrete continuous arches. On both sides of the connection between the main bridge and the approach bridges, there are bridge abutments, each constructed as a reinforced concrete frame structure. The installation of the continuous steel truss girder of the main bridge initially utilized an extending arm installation method. Temporary supports were set up on forward piers to reduce the length of the extending arm by 16m, and the installation process took 10 months. The foundation of the main piers firstly adopted a pioneering approach, using reinforced concrete pipe columns with a diameter of 1.55m. An impact drilling machine was designed to create holes in the rock at the bottom of the pipe columns, embedded at depths of 2m to 7m into the rock layer. Each pier included 30 to 35 pipe columns, each with a bearing capacity of 1,910kN, and an underwater concrete seal was applied using the tube jacking method.

The successful construction of Wuhan Bridge over Yangtze River connected the Beijing-Hankou and Guangzhou-Hankou railways, forming a major north-south artery in China and marking a milestone in Chinese bridge construction. The design and construction of the bridge received substantial support and assistance from experts from the Soviet Union.

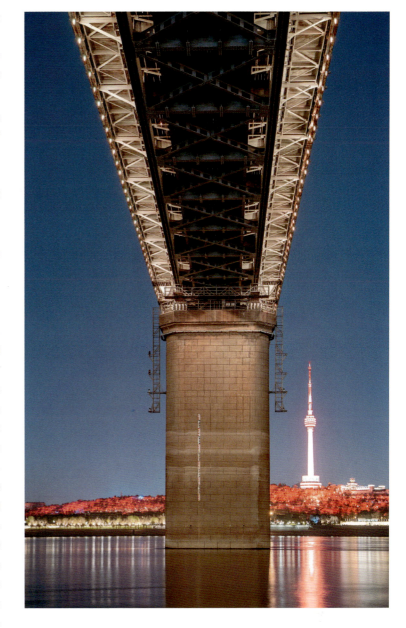

**Name:** Wuhan Bridge over Yangtze River
**Type:** Continuous steel truss girder bridge
**Length:** Total length 1.67km, main span 128m
**Location:** Wuhan City, Hubei Province
**Completion:** October 1957
**Designer(s):** China Railway Major Bridge Reconnaissance & Design Institute
**Contractor(s):** China Railway Major Bridge Engineering Group Co., Ltd.

# 南宁邕江大桥

## Nanning Yong River Bridge

| | |
|---|---|
| 桥　名： | 南宁邕江大桥 |
| 桥　型： | 钢筋混凝土悬臂箱梁桥 |
| 主跨跨径： | 55m |
| 桥　址： | 广西壮族自治区南宁市 |
| 建成时间： | 1964年7月 |
| 设计单位： | 广西壮族自治区交通厅，柳州铁路局，同济大学，广西壮族自治区地质局，广西壮族自治区建工局，南宁市建设局 |
| 施工单位： | 广西壮族自治区交通厅工程局，柳州铁路局，上海市基础工程公司 |

**Name:** Nanning Yong River Bridge
**Type:** Reinforced concrete cantilever box girder bridge
**Main span:** 55m
**Location:** Nanning City, Guangxi Zhuang Autonomous Region
**Completion:** July 1964
**Designer(s):** Transport Department of Guangxi Zhuang Autonomous Region, Liuzhou Railway Bureau, Tongji University, Geological Bureau of Guangxi Zhuang Autonomous Region, Construction Engineering Bureau of Guangxi Zhuang Autonomous Region, Building and Construction Bureau of Nanning City
**Contractor(s):** Engineering Bureau of Transport Department of Guangxi Zhuang Autonomous Region, Liuzhou Railway Bureau, Shanghai Foundation Engineering Company

南宁邕江大桥位于广西壮族自治区南宁市中心城区交通枢纽位置，以东北—西南方向跨越邕江，北连民权路、朝阳路和南宁火车站，南接江南区星光大道。大桥全长414.6m，主桥长394.6m，桥面总宽24m，包括共18m宽由双向共4条机动车道和2条非机动车道组成的车行道，以及两侧各3m宽的2条人行道。

该桥是中国城市桥梁最早采用闭口薄壁杆件理论设计的钢筋混凝土箱形截面悬臂梁桥，主桥共有7跨，两边跨采用单悬臂梁结构，跨径均为45m；中间5跨均采用带中央挂梁的双悬臂结构，每跨跨径为55m，挂梁长度23m，在当时居全国同类桥梁之首。上部结构主梁为双箱三室箱梁断面，简支在桥墩上，在双箱之间设置横隔梁以提高整体性。墩台处的横隔梁为刚接，其余均为简支横隔梁。下部结构北岸为埋置式桥台，南岸为U形桥台。桥墩采用双柱式，支承于分离式沉井基础上。1号墩和4~6号墩为筑岛及就地预制沉井基础，2号墩、3号墩因施工水位深达11m，采用预制双层薄壁钢筋混凝土浮运沉井。

南宁邕江大桥的建成结束了邕江南宁市区段的轮渡历史，并成为连接南宁中心城区邕江南北最为方便、快捷的主要过江通道，至今它仍然是邕江江南居民前往江北中心最主要的通道。

Nanning Yong River Bridge is located at a place of transportation junction in the downtown of Nanning City of Guangxi Zhuang Autonomous Region, and crosses Yong River in the northeast-southwest direction. It connects to the Minquan Road, and leads to Chaoyang Road and Nanning Railway Station in the north side, and links the Xingguang Avenue in Jiangnan District in the south side. The overall length of the bridge is 414.6m, and the main bridge length is 394.6m. The bridge deck is 24m wide and contains six carriageways in dual directions (four for motor vehicles and two for non-motor vehicles), and two 3m-wide sidewalks.

Among the urban bridges in China, this bridge is the first reinforced concrete cantilever box-girder bridge designed based on the theory of thin-walled closed cross-section bars. The bridge has seven spans, including two side spans of a single-cantilever girder structure with a length of 45m and five middle spans of a double-cantilever girder structure with a length of 55m including a 23m-long central hanging beam, which was the longest cantilever bridges in China at that time. The main girder of the bridge superstructure has a double-box cross section each with three cells, and are simply supported on the bridge piers. Transverse diaphragms were set between two boxes to increase the integrity of the main girder. The diaphragms at the bridge piers and abutments are rigidly connected to the boxes while the others are simply supported on the boxes. For the substructures, the north abutment is of buried type while the south abutment is of U-type, and the bridge piers are of double-columns type and are supported on the separate-caisson foundations. The caissons prefabricated in situ on the pre-built artificial islands were adopted for the foundations of the piers No.1, No.4 to No.6. The prefabricated double-layer thin-walled reinforced concrete floating caissons were used for the foundations of the piers No.2 and No. 3, because the water depth corresponding to the construction water level reached 11m at the locations of the two piers.

The completion of Nanning Yong River Bridge ceased the ferry history on the Yong River within the urban area of Nanning, and proved the most convenient and main river-crossing shortcut connecting the northern and southern sides of the Yong River in the Nanning central urban area, which is still the main passageway for the citizens living in the southern side of the Yong River going to the downtown in the northern side of the river.

# 五陵卫河桥
## Wuling Wei River Bridge

五陵卫河桥位于河南省安阳市汤阴县，在汤阴至濮阳原窄轨铁路线上跨越卫河，是一座窄轨铁路桥梁。该桥是中国第一座采用平衡悬臂拼装施工法建成的预应力混凝土T形刚构桥，两个T构之间用啷筒式剪力铰连接，与岸边桥台采用水平滚动支座连接并配置压重，以避免支座产生负反力和桥台承受上拔力以及列车通过时岸端发生拍击现象。桥梁主跨为50m，两边跨各为25m，全长105.2m。桥面总宽4.5m，中央为铁路，两边各设1条宽0.75m的人行道。上部结构采用预应力混凝土箱梁结构，箱梁采用两侧带悬挑板的矩形单室单箱横截面，箱底宽2.72m，两侧挑臂板宽度均为0.89m，梁高从跨中的1.25m逐渐增加到桥墩处的2.50m。下部结构为重力式墩，基础采用就地钻孔灌注桩。

上部结构主梁每个悬臂分成10段，第1段在墩顶就地现浇，第2~10段预制吊装。全桥共36段预制箱梁，先采用地上滑移和船舶浮运相结合的方法逐块运至桥下，然后在桥墩两边对称地吊起，就位后再借助预应力钢束进行悬空拼接，直至两个T构全部完成。此时，跨中留有1.5m长的现浇合龙段，接着先安装啷筒式剪力铰，并根据由于拼装过程中累积误差而产生的两个悬臂实际高差和中线偏移量调整其位置和姿态，最后就地现浇混凝土以封装中间铰和完成合龙段。

20世纪80年代，桥上铁轨被拆除，桥梁改为乡村简易桥梁使用，2021年至2022年对该桥进行了加固改造，2023年1月恢复通车。

Wuling Wei River Bridge is located in Tangyin County, Anyang City, Henan Province, spanning the Wei River on the narrow-gauge railway line from Tangyin to Puyang. It is a narrow-gauge railway bridge. This bridge is the first prestressed concrete T-shaped rigid frame bridge in China that uses the balanced cantilever assembly construction method. The two T-shaped structures are connected by a pump-type shear hinge, and are connected to the abutments on the banks using horizontal rolling bearings and equipped with weights to avoid negative reaction force on the bearings and uplift force on the abutments, as well as slap phenomenon at the bank end when trains pass through. The main span of the bridge is 50m, with each side span being 25m, and the total length is 105.2m. The total width of the deck is 4.5m, with a railway in the center and one pedestrian path on each side with a width of 0.75m. The superstructure adopts a prestressed concrete box girder structure, with a rectangular single-chamber single-box cross-section with cantilevered slabs on both sides. The bottom width of the box is 2.72m, and the width of the cantilevered slabs on both sides is 0.89m. The beam depth gradually increases from 1.25m at the midpoint of the span to 2.50m at the pier. The substructure is a gravity pier with bored pile foundations.

The main girders of the superstructure are divided into 10 sections per cantilever, with the first section cast-in-place at the top of the pier and the second to tenth sections prefabricated for lifting. A total of 36 sections of precast box girders are transported under the bridge one by one by using the combination of ground skidding and ship's floatation, and then lifted symmetrically on both sides of the piers, and then suspended and spliced with the help of prestressing reinforcement until the two T-structures are all completed. At this time, there is a 1.5m long cast-in-situ close-up section in the middle of the span, and then the pump-type shear hinge is installed first, and its position and attitude are adjusted according to the actual depth difference between the two cantilever arms and the centerline offset caused by the accumulated errors in the assembly process, and finally the concrete is cast in-situ in order to encapsulate the intermediate hinges and to complete the close-up section.

In 1980s, this bridge was converted to a simple rural highway bridge by dismantling the railway tracks. This bridge was strengthened and retrofitted during 2021 and 2022, and reopened in January 2023.

---

桥　　名：五陵卫河桥
桥　　型：预应力混凝土T形刚构桥
主跨跨径：50m
桥　　址：河南省安阳市
建成时间：1965年4月
设计单位：河南省交通厅，同济大学，交通部交通科学研究院，上海公路工程研究所
施工单位：河南省交通厅

**Name:** Wuling Wei River Bridge
**Type:** Prestressed concrete T-shaped rigid frame bridge
**Main span:** 50m
**Location:** Anyang City, Henan Province
**Completion:** April 1965
**Designer(s):** Henan Provincial Department of Transport, Tongji University, China Academy of Transportation Sciences, Shanghai Highway Engineering Research Institute
**Contractor(s):** Henan Provincial Department of Transport

# 胡埭大桥

## Hudai Bridge

| | |
|---|---|
| 桥　　名： | 胡埭大桥 |
| 桥　　型： | 钢筋混凝土双曲拱桥 |
| 主跨径： | 55m |
| 桥　　址： | 江苏省无锡市 |
| 建成时间： | 1965年 |
| 设计单位： | 无锡县桥梁工程队 |
| 施工单位： | 无锡县桥梁工程队 |

**Name:** Hudai Bridge
**Type:** Reinforced concrete hyperbolic arch bridge
**Main span:** 55m
**Location:** Wuxi City, Jiangsu Province
**Completion:** 1965
**Designer(s):** Wuxi County Bridge Engineering Team
**Contractor(s):** Wuxi County Bridge Engineering Team

胡埭大桥位于江苏省无锡市胡埭镇，是一座钢筋混凝土双曲拱桥，跨径为55m，桥面宽度3m。

双曲拱桥是由中国无锡县桥梁工程队首创的一种新型拱桥，全世界第一座双曲拱桥是1964年4月建成的无锡市东亭桥。

双曲拱桥由钢筋混凝土拱肋、拱波、横梁或拉杆以及拱上建筑等组成，曲线形的拱肋与曲线形的拱波形成纵横双曲的拱圈结构。双曲拱桥施工中将结构化整为零，构件采用预制或分段预制，经拼装组合及现浇混凝土后集零为整。其中，拱肋由支架或无支架拼装后作为后续施工的拱架，其上砌置拱波和浇筑拱背混凝土，最后进行拱上建筑施工。拱肋可以采用矩形、倒T形、V形及箱形等截面，当跨径较小时也可将拱肋与拱波结合成整体波。双曲拱桥钢筋用量少，结构纤细轻盈，水平推力小，适宜在软土地基上建造。

胡埭大桥由原无锡县桥梁工程队的胡埭籍桥梁工程师苏松源负责设计和施工，仅仅花了4个月的时间就建成了这座曾经是全国跨度最大的双曲拱桥，而整座桥的造价只有3万元。胡埭大桥建成后，《人民日报》和《解放日报》等报刊先后刊登了有关消息和照片，1965年第12期《科技画报》的封面上刊登了该桥的彩色照片。该桥还被拍摄成"双曲拱桥"科教片，在全国放映。这一"世界桥梁的瑰宝"引起了国内外各界人士的关注，同济大学校长李国豪、中国科学院华罗庚、清华大学副校长张维以及苏联、英国、罗马尼亚、西班牙、日本、新加坡、菲律宾、泰国、印度尼西亚、阿尔巴尼亚、孟加拉国等22个国家和地区的代表团曾陆续前去参观考察。

Hudai Bridge is located in Hudai Town, Wuxi City, Jiangsu Province. It is a reinforced concrete hyperbolic arch bridge with a span of 55m and a bridge width of 3m.

The hyperbolic arch bridge is a new type of arch bridge pioneered by the Wuxi County Bridge Engineering Team in China. The world's first hyperbolic arch bridge was the Dongting Bridge in Wuxi City, completed in April 1964.

The hyperbolic arch bridge is constructed with reinforced concrete arch ribs, arch waves, cross beams, tension rods and spandrel structures. The curved arch ribs and arch waves form a longitudinal and transverse hyperbolic arch structure. During the construction of the hyperbolic arch bridge, the structure is modularized, and components are prefabricated in sections. After assembly and casting with ready-mixed concrete, the components are integrated into a whole. The arch ribs, assembled with or without supports, serve as the framework for subsequent construction. Arch waves are laid on top and concrete is cast on the arch back, followed by construction of spandrel structures. The arch ribs can have rectangular, inverted T-shaped, V-shaped or box-shaped cross-sections. For smaller spans, the arch ribs and arch waves can be combined into a unified wave. The hyperbolic arch bridge requires less reinforcement, has a slender and lightweight structure, exerts minimal horizontal thrust, and is suitable for construction on soft soil foundations.

Hudai Bridge was designed and constructed by Su Songyuan, a bridge engineer from the Wuxi County Bridge Engineering Team in Hudai. It took only four months to build this bridge, which was once the longest span hyperbolic arch bridge in the country. The total cost of the bridge was only 30,000 RMB. After completion, the People's Daily and the Liberation Daily, among other publications, published news and photos about the bridge. In 1965, the 12th issue of "Science and Technology Pictorial" featured a color photo of the bridge on its cover. The bridge was also featured in an educational film on hyperbolic arch bridges that was screened nationwide. This "treasure of world bridges" attracted attention from people around the world. Delegations from 22 countries and areas, including Tongji University President Li Guohao, Chinese Academy of Sciences member Hua Luogeng, Tsinghua University Vice President Zhang Wei, and representatives from the Soviet Union, United Kingdom, Romania, Spain, Japan, Singapore, Philippines, Thailand, Indonesia, Albania, Bangladesh and others, visited the bridge successively for inspection and study.

# 辽阳太子河桥

## Liaoyang Bridge over Taizi River

　　辽阳太子河桥位于辽宁省辽阳市,是中国最早的预应力混凝土T形刚构桥之一。全桥共有10跨,两个边跨跨径为27.6m,8个中跨跨径均为33m,全长325.9m,宽11m。

　　桥墩采用圆端形空心扁矩形截面,高9.75m。每个桥墩分四层用300号混凝土预制砌块逐层砌筑而成,并用预应力钢束与承台和预制的T构悬臂梁墩顶段固接成整体。承台和墩身腹腔用混凝土填芯,基础采用2排共16根直径为550mm的混凝土管桩。采用预应力桥墩不仅缩短了工期,还能确保桥墩在一侧桥孔破坏的情况下仍有足够强度和抗裂安全系数。T构悬臂梁由7片平行的预制Π形纵梁和横隔板组装而成,总长度为12m,两侧悬臂净长5.4m,采用预制吊装法施工,并通过湿接缝和预应力钢束与墩顶节段固结。每个桥孔中央挂梁长22m,也由7片纵梁和横隔板组成,每片纵梁沿纵向又分5段预制,然后借助钢导梁就位,通过预应力钢束拼接。挂梁的每片纵梁都通过滚动支座支承在设置在悬臂梁Π形纵梁端横隔板上的牛腿上。

　　在建设沈海高速公路(下行线)太子河桥(1990年建成)时,该桥主梁7片纵梁中的4片被拆除,桥面宽度缩减到约4.7m,而其桥墩则被完全保留,除了继续支承老桥剩余的桥面外,部分还用来支承新桥桥面。

| | |
|---|---|
| 桥　名: 辽阳太子河桥 | **Name:** Liaoyang Bridge over Taizi River |
| 桥　型: 带挂梁预应力混凝土T形刚构桥 | **Type:** Prestressed concrete T-shaped rigid frame bridge with suspended girder |
| 主跨跨径: 33m | **Main span:** 33m |
| 桥　址: 辽宁省辽阳市 | **Location:** Liaoyang City, Liaoning Province |
| 建成时间: 1965年 | **Completion:** 1965 |
| 设计单位: 辽宁省交通勘测设计院 | **Designer(s):** Liaoning Provincial Transportation Survey and Design Institute |
| 施工单位: 辽宁省交通厅公路工程局 | **Contractor(s):** Highway Engineering Bureau of transportation department of Liaoning Province |

Liaoyang Bridge over Taizi River is located in Liaoyang City, Liaoning Province, and is one of the earliest prestressed concrete T-shaped rigid frame bridges in China. The bridge has a total of 10 spans, with two side spans of 27.6m and eight middle spans of 33m, with a total length of 325.9m and a width of 11m.

The bridge pier adopts a round end hollow flat rectangular section, with a depth of 9.75m. Each bridge pier is divided into four layers and constructed layer by layer with 300-grade concrete precast blocks, and is fixedly connected to the pier cap and the pier top section of the prefabricated T-shaped cantilever beam as a whole using prestressed steel strands.

The bearing platform and pier body are filled with concrete, and the foundation is made up of 2 rows of 16 concrete pipe piles with a diameter of 550mm. The use of prestressed bridge piers not only shortens the construction period, but also ensures that they still have sufficient strength and crack resistance safety factor in the event of single span destruction. The T-shaped cantilever beam is composed of 7 parallel prefabricated Type Ⅱ longitudinal beams and transverse diaphragms, with a total length of 12m and a net length of 5.4m on both sides of the cantilever. It is constructed using prefabricated hoisting method and consolidated with the pier top section through wet joints and prestressed steel strands. The central hanging beam of each span is 22 meters long and also composed of 7 longitudinal beams and transverse diaphragms. Each longitudinal beam is prefabricated in 5 sections along the longitudinal direction, then placed in place with the help of steel guide beams, and finally spliced through prestressed steel strands. Each longitudinal beam of the hanging beam is supported by rolling bearings on the brackets set on the cross beam at the cantilever end of the Type Ⅱ longitudinal beam.

During the construction of Liaoyang Bridge over Taizi River (completed in 1990) on the Shenyang-Haikou Expressway (down line), 4 out of 7 longitudinal beams of the main beam were demolished, reducing the width of the bridge deck to about 4.7m, while its piers were completely preserved. In addition to continuing to support the remaining bridge deck of the old bridge, some of its piers were also used to support the new bridge deck.

# 柳江大桥
## Liu River Bridge

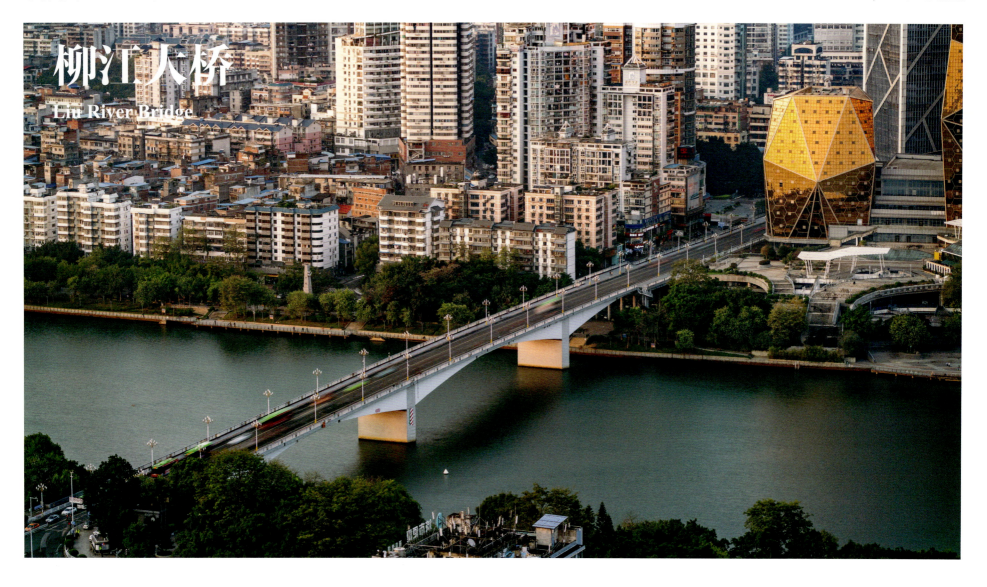

| | |
|---|---|
| 桥　名： 柳江大桥 | **Name:** Liu River Bridge |
| 桥　型： 带挂梁预应力混凝土T形刚构桥 | **Type:** Prestressed concrete T-shaped rigid frame bridge with suspended girder |
| 主跨跨径： 124m | **Main span:** 124m |
| 桥　址： 广西壮族自治区柳州市 | **Location:** Liuzhou City, Guangxi Zhuang Autonomous Region |
| 建成时间： 1968年10月 | **Completion:** October 1968 |
| 设计单位： 上海市政工程设计研究院 | **Designer(s):** Shanghai Municipal Engineering Design Institute |
| 施工单位： 上海市基础工程公司 | **Contractor(s):** Shanghai Foundation Engineering Company |

柳江大桥也称柳江一桥，位于广西壮族自治区柳州市中心城区，北起城中区龙城路，南接鱼峰区鱼峰路，是柳州第一座跨越柳江的公路大桥，结束了柳州靠浮桥和渡船过江的历史。该桥也是我国第一座采用悬臂浇筑法施工的预应力混凝土T形刚构桥。桥梁全长608.04m，主桥长408.19m，宽20m，由3个T形刚构和挂梁组成。主跨跨径为124m，两侧悬臂净长各44.5m，中间挂梁长25m。主梁采用双箱双室箱形截面和三向预应力配筋体系，用两套挂篮分别对称浇筑，两箱梁中间30cm纵缝现浇后，桥面板内横向施加预应力压紧，悬臂端设强大横梁将两组梁联结成整体。纵向预应力钢束共287根，其中直束113根，弯束174根，布置在顶板及承托内，钢束平弯后纵向下弯锚于腹板上。竖向预应力筋间距为30~60cm。

设计中计算了两组箱梁相对挠曲引起的错动力，并按封闭框架分析进行横向配筋。下部结构采用整体式桥墩，顺流向长28m，横流向宽14m。因当时有关这种桥型的设计和施工资料相当缺乏，故对悬臂梁的节段足尺模型进行了大量的试验研究。该桥桥面结构独特，施工工艺先进，荣获1978年全国科学大会奖。

Liu River Bridge, also known as the First Liu River Bridge, is located in the central urban area of Liuzhou City, Guangxi Zhuang Autonomous Region. It spans from Longcheng Road in Chengzhong District to Yufeng Road in Yufeng District. It is the first highway bridge across the Liu River in Liuzhou, putting an end to the historical reliance on pontoon bridges and ferries for river crossing. The bridge is also China's first prestressed concrete T-shaped rigid frame bridge constructed using the cantilever construction method. The total length of the bridge is 608.04m, with the main bridge measuring 408.19m in length and 20m in width. It consists of three T-shaped rigid frames and suspended girders. The main span is 124m, with each side cantilevering 44.5m and a 25-meter long central suspended girder. The main girders adopt double box double chambers box sections and a three-dimensional prestressing reinforcement system. They are cast symmetrically using two sets of hanging baskets. After the central 30cm longitudinal seam of the two box girders

being cast in place, transverse prestress is applied to the bridge deck, and a robust cross beam at the cantilever end connects the two sets of girders into a whole. There is a total of 287 longitudinal prestressing tendons, including 113 straight tendons and 174 curved tendons, arranged in the top plate and within the support. After lateral bending, the prestressing tendons bend longitudinally and are anchored to the web plate. The vertical prestressing tendons have a spacing of 30cm to 60cm. The design accounts for the relative deflection-induced dynamic force between the two sets of box girders and uses a closed-frame analysis for lateral reinforcement. The substructure uses an integral pier with a length of 28m along the flow direction and a transverse width of 14m. Due to the lack of design and construction data for this bridge type at the time, extensive experimental research was conducted on full-scale models of cantilever segments. The unique structure of the bridge deck and its advanced construction technology earned it the National Science Conference Award in 1978.

# 南京长江大桥

Nanjing Bridge over Yangtze River

| 桥　　名： | 南京长江大桥 | **Name:** Nanjing Bridge over Yangtze River |
| 桥　　型： | 连续钢桁梁桥 | **Type:** Continuous steel truss girder bridge |
| 桥梁长度： | 全长 4.589km/6.772km，主跨跨径 160m | **Length:** Total length 4.589km/6.772km, main span 160m |
| 桥　　址： | 江苏省南京市 | **Location:** Nanjing City, Jiangsu Province |
| 建成时间： | 1968 年 12 月 | **Completion:** December 1968 |
| 设计单位： | 中铁大桥勘测设计院 | **Designer(s):** China Railway Major Bridge Reconnaissance & Design Institute |
| 施工单位： | 中铁大桥局集团有限公司 | **Contractor(s):** China Railway Major Bridge Engineering Group Co., Ltd. |

　　南京长江大桥位于江苏省南京市，是一座公铁两用大桥，公路桥梁全长 4.589km，铁路桥梁全长 6.772km。

　　南京长江大桥由 1.576km 主桥、3.013km 公路引桥和 5.196km 铁路引桥组成。上层公路四车道宽 15m，两侧人行道各宽 2.25m；下层双线铁路宽 14m。主桥为 3 联 3×160m 的三跨全铆米字形连续钢桁架梁和 1 跨 128m 简支钢桁架梁，桁高 16m，主桁中距 14m，在支承处增设第三弦杆，高度增加至 30m，使用 16Mnq 钢制作。采用伸臂拼装法架设，在前方桥墩设置临时墩旁托架以减少伸臂长度；主桥共有 9 个桥墩，每个桥墩高 80m，每墩底部面积 400 多 m²，桥墩基础采用 4 种类型，包括重型混凝土沉井、钢沉井加管柱、浮式钢筋混凝土沉井和钢板桩围堰管柱。铁路引桥北岸 104 跨，南岸 48 跨，主要采用跨径 31.7m 预应力钢筋混凝土梁和直径 0.55m 钢筋混凝土管柱基础。公路引桥采用 34 跨双曲拱桥和 79 跨预应力混凝土 T 形梁，铁路引桥采用 159 跨 32.7m 预应力混凝土 T 形梁。

　　南京长江大桥是沟通中国南北交通的又一大动脉，是新中国第一座自主建造的大型桥梁，被看作是"自力更生的典范"和"社会主义建设的伟大成就"，获得了国家科技进步奖特等奖。

Nanjing Bridge over Yangtze River is located in Nanjing City, Jiangsu Province. It is a dual-use bridge for both highway and railway, with a total length of 4.589km for the highway bridge and 6.772km for the railway bridge. It is the first Yangtze River bridge constructed through self-reliance in China.

Nanjing Bridge over Yangtze River consists of a 1.576km main bridge, 3.013km highway approach bridge and a 5.196km railway approach bridge. The width of the four lanes on the upper highway bridge is 15m, and the width of the sidewalks on both sides is 2.25m. The lower railway bridge is 14m wide for double tracks. The main bridge consists of a continuous steel truss girder in a riveted inverted "米" shape with three spans, each measuring 160m and a single-span simply supported steel truss girder of 128m. The truss depth is 16m, and the central distance between the main trusses is 14m. A third chord is added at the support, increasing the depth to 30m. The main bridge is made of 16Mnq steel. The construction used the cantilever assembly method, with temporary supports on the front piers to reduce the cantilever length. There is a total of nine bridge piers, each measuring 80m high with a bottom area of over 400$m^2$. The pier foundations use four types, including heavy concrete caissons, steel caissons with pipes, floating reinforced concrete caissons and steel sheet pile cofferdams with columns. The railway approach bridge has 104 spans on the northern bank and 48 spans on the southern bank, mainly using prestressed concrete beams with a span of 31.7m and foundations with 0.55m diameter reinforced concrete columns. The highway approach bridge consists of 34 spans of reinforced concrete hyperbolic arch bridges and 79 spans of prestressed concrete T-beams. The railway approach bridge uses 159 spans of 32.7m prestressed concrete T-beams.

Nanjing Bridge over Yangtze River is a vital artery connecting the north and south traffic in China. It is the first long bridge in China constructed through self-reliance and is considered a "model of self-reliance" and a "great achievement in socialist construction". It has received the Special Prize of National Science and Technology Progress Award.

# 乌龙江桥
## Wulong River Bridge

|桥　　名：|乌龙江桥|
|---|---|
|桥　　型：|带挂梁预应力混凝土 T 形刚构桥|
|主跨跨径：|144m|
|桥　　址：|福建省福州市|
|建成时间：|1971 年|
|设计单位：|福建省 513 工程指挥部|
|施工单位：|福建省 513 工程指挥部|

**Name:** Wulong River Bridge
**Type:** Prestressed concrete T-shaped rigid frame bridge with suspended team
**Main span:** 144m
**Location:** Fuzhou City, Fujian Province
**Completion:** 1971
**Designer(s):** Fujian Provincial 513 Engineering Headquarters
**Contractor(s):** Fujian Provincial 513 Engineering Headquarters

乌龙江桥位于福建省福州市乌龙江下游峡口处，横跨乌龙江（又称峡江），是我国较早建成的一座大跨度预应力混凝土 T 形刚构桥。该桥全长 548m，主桥共 5 跨，跨径布置为 58m+3×144m+58m，桥面行车道宽 9m，两侧人行道各宽 1.25m。桥梁设计荷载为汽车—20，挂车—100。

乌龙江桥 T 形刚构之间采用长度为 33m 的简支挂梁相连接，T 形刚构与桥台之间用 6m 长的搭板相连。主梁宽 12m，采用双室箱形断面，顶板向两侧各悬挑 1.25m。中间两个 T 形刚构采用悬臂拼装法施工，两侧两个 T 形刚构采用悬臂浇筑法施工。乌龙江桥桥位所在地水文地质异常复杂，江中两个墩位平均水深 22m，水下 30m 深有砂砾覆盖层，基岩高低不平。虽然桥址情况复杂，但乌龙江桥仍然顺利完成了桥梁基础的建设，4 个桥墩中江畔两墩采用浅埋式扩大基础，江中两墩为钢板桩围堰管柱基础。在每天有两个正逆流向、潮差 5m 的情况下，由于采用围笼浮运、定位、管柱下沉以及插打钢板桩等技术，成功完成了桥墩工程。

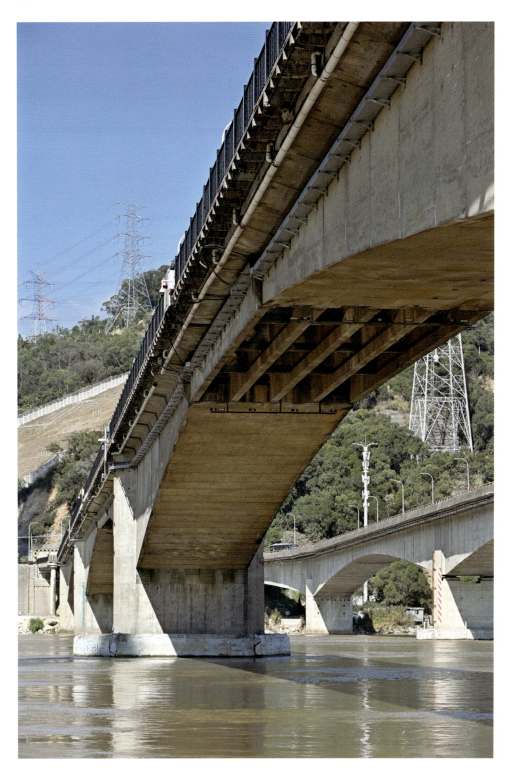

Wulong River Bridge is located at the downstream gorge of the Wulong River in Fuzhou City, Fujian Province. It is an early built long-span prestressed concrete T-shaped rigid frame bridge in China. The bridge has an overall length of 548m including a main bridge with five spans of 58m+3×144m+58m. The carriageway is 9m wide, with 1.25m wide sidewalks on both sides. The vehicle design load for this bridge is Truck-20, and Trailer-100.

Two T-shaped rigid frame are connected by a simply supported hanging beam with a length of 33m, and a 6m long approach slab is used to connect the T-shaped rigid frame to the bridge abutment. The main girder is 12m wide and has a cross-section of a double-cell box with its top plate overhanging 1.25m on each side. The two middle T-shaped rigid frames were constructed by cantilever assembling whilst the two side ones were built by cantilever casting. The hydrogeological condition at the bridge site is extremely complex. The average depth of the two piers in the river is 22 meters, and there is a sand and gravel covering layer at a depth of 30 meters underwater. The bedrock is uneven. Although the bridge site is complex, the bridge foundation was successfully treated during the construction process. Among the four bridge piers, two piers on the riverbank adopted shallow buried spread foundations, and tubular column foundations with steel sheet piling cofferdam were used for the two piers in the river. Despite the condition that flow direction changes twice a day with a tidal range of 5 meters, the bridge pier project was successfully completed due to the use of techniques such as cage floating, positioning, sinking of tubular columns, and insertion of steel sheet piles.

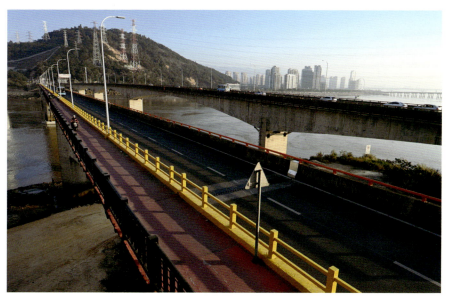

# 滨州黄河公路大桥

## Binzhou Highway Bridge over Yellow River

|桥　　名：|滨州黄河公路大桥|
|---|---|
|桥　　型：|连续钢桁梁桥等|
|主跨跨径：|112m|
|桥　　址：|山东省滨州市|
|建成时间：|1972年|
|设计单位：|山东省0016工程指挥部|
|施工单位：|山东省0016工程指挥部|

滨州黄河公路大桥原名北镇黄河公路桥，位于山东省滨州市，横跨黄河，是205国道滨州至博山高速公路的重要组成部分。全桥47跨，总长1.39km，桥跨自北向南为7×33m预应力混凝土梁、35×20m钢筋混凝土T梁、4×112m连续钢桁梁、1×10m钢筋混凝土板梁。建成时是黄河上最长的公路桥。桥梁设计荷载为汽车—15，挂车—80。

滨州黄河公路大桥桥面铺装沥青混凝土，总宽12m，行车道净宽9m，两侧人行道各1.5m。主桥为平行弦桁梁，铆接结构。全桥共有48个墩台，基础采用1.5m的钻孔灌注桩共150根，最长入土深度近百米，建成时为国内之最。南北两端的接线公路长4.78km，均用石砌护坡，两侧各设照明线、绿化带和栏杆。大桥南端建立了一座高45m颇为气派的桥标，在大桥北端建立了一座高30m的唐赛儿铜质雕塑，巾帼英雄跃马挥剑、气贯长虹，与滨州黄河公路大桥的伟岸气魄交相融合。

Binzhou Highway Bridge over Yellow River, formerly known as Beizhen Highway Bridge over Yellow River, is located in Binzhou City, Shandong Province and is an important component of the 205 National Highway from Binzhou to Boshan. The entire bridge has 47 spans, with a total length of 1.39km. From the north to the south, the bridge consists of 7×33m prestressed concrete girders, 35×20m reinforced concrete T-shaped girders, 4×112m continuous steel truss girders and a 10m reinforced concrete plate girder. It was the longest highway bridge across the Yellow River when it was completed. The vehicle design load for this bridge is Truck-15, and Trailer-80.

The bridge deck is paved with asphalt concrete, with a total width of 12 meters. The net width of the carriageway is 9 meters, and the sidewalks on both sides are 1.5 meters wide. The main truss is a riveted parallel chord truss girder. There are a total of 48 piers in the entire bridge, and 150 drilled cast-in-place piles with the diameter of 1.5m are used as the foundation. The longest soil penetration depth is nearly 100 meters, which set the record in China when it was built. The connecting road at the north and south ends of the bridge are 4.78km long, with stone slope protection and lighting lines, green belts, and railings on both sides. At the southern end of the bridge, a majestic 45m high landmark has been erected, while at the northern end, a 30m tall Tang Saier bronze sculpture has been erected, featuring the heroine leaping a horse, wielding a sword, shine brightly, blending with the majestic spirit of the Binzhou Highway Bridge over Yellow River.

**Name:** Binzhou Highway Bridge over Yellow River
**Type:** Continuous steel truss girder bridge etc.
**Main span:** 112m
**Location:** Binzhou City, Shandong Province
**Completion:** 1972
**Designer(s):** Shandong Provincial 0016 Engineering Headquarters
**Contractor(s):** Shandong Provincial 0016 Engineering Headquarters

# 橘子洲大桥

## Juzizhou Bridge

|桥　名：|橘子洲大桥|
|---|---|
|桥　型：|钢筋混凝土连续双曲拱桥|
|主跨跨径：|76m|
|桥　址：|湖南省长沙市|
|建成时间：|1972年9月|
|设计单位：|湖南省交通规划勘察设计院|
|施工单位：|湖南省公路局工程处|

橘子洲大桥原名长沙湘江桥，位于湖南省长沙市319国道上，跨越湘江。全桥总长1.532km，由主桥、引桥和支桥组成，设计荷载为汽车—20、挂车—100。桥面宽度为20m，按双向四车道城市快速路布置，其中行车道宽度14m，两侧人行道各宽3m。

橘子洲大桥的主桥为钢筋混凝土连续双曲拱桥，桥长1156m，跨径布置为8×76m+9×50m，两种跨径拱的矢跨比分别为1/8和1/6。主桥拱圈均采用钢筋混凝土等截面悬链线无铰拱，两种跨径拱的截面高度分别为1.3m和1.0m，由拱肋、拱波、填平层及拱板组合而成，横向采用8根拱肋、7片拱波。

拱上建筑采用半空腹式构造，空腹段为横向钢筋混凝土排架上支承圆弧拱腹孔。大桥采用双跨缆索吊装施工方法，一套设备分阶段吊装施工。主桥桥墩分别采用钢板桩围堰扩大基础、土围堰明挖扩大基础和沉井基础三种形式，直接嵌入红砂岩或钙质砂质页岩等岩盘。大桥东岸的4跨引桥为长度94m的无铰拱桥，采用钻孔灌注桩和挖孔灌注桩基础。主桥在8号墩南侧分出支桥，连通水陆洲，支桥为6跨30m和4跨20m的两铰桥，全长282m，桥面宽度8m，其中行车道宽6m、两侧人行道各宽1m，采用沉井基础。

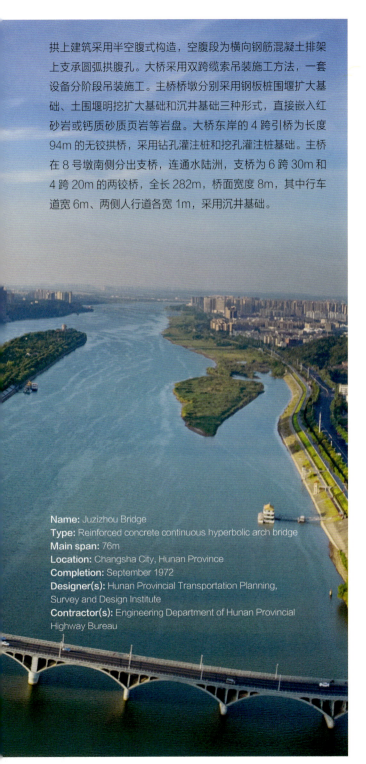

**Name:** Juzizhou Bridge
**Type:** Reinforced concrete continuous hyperbolic arch bridge
**Main span:** 76m
**Location:** Changsha City, Hunan Province
**Completion:** September 1972
**Designer(s):** Hunan Provincial Transportation Planning, Survey and Design Institute
**Contractor(s):** Engineering Department of Hunan Provincial Highway Bureau

Juzizhou Bridge, formerly known as Changsha Xiang River Bridge, is located on National Highway 319 in Changsha City, Hunan Province, spanning the Xiang River. The total length of the bridge is 1.532km, consisting of the main bridge, approach bridge, and branch bridge, with a design load of Truck-20 and Trailer-100. The bridge deck width is 20m, arranged as a two-way four-lane urban expressway with a carriageway width of 14m and sidewalks of 3m each on both sides.

The main bridge is a reinforced concrete continuous hyperbolic arch bridge, with a total length of 1,156m and a span arrangement of 8×76m+9×50m. The rise-span ratios for the two different arch spans are 1/8 and 1/6, respectively. The main bridge arch ring adopts reinforced concrete catenary fixed-end arch with constant cross section. The depths of the cross sections are 1.3m and 1.0m respectively, which are composed of 8 arch ribs, 7 arch waves, filling layers, and arch plates. The half-hollowed spandrel is composed of circular arches supported by transverse reinforced concrete bent frames. The bridge adopts a double span cable hoisting construction method, with the same set of equipment for phased hoisting construction. The main bridge adopts three types of foundation forms: steel sheet pile cofferdam expansion foundation, soil cofferdam open excavation expansion foundation and caisson foundation, directly embedded in rock formations such as red sandstone or calcareous sandy shale. The 4-span approach bridge on the east bank is a 94m-long fixed-end arch bridge, with drilled and excavated cast-in-place pile foundation. A branch bridge was built on the south side at the No. 8 Pier of the main bridge to connect the Shuiluzhou island. The branch bridge is composed of two-hinged arches of 6×30m and 4×20m, with a total length of 282m. The bridge deck width is 8m: the carriageway is 6m wide, and the sidewalks on both sides are 1m wide. Caisson foundations are used in the branch bridge.

# 台北光复桥
## Taipei Guangfu Bridge

  台北光复桥，位于中国台湾省台北市 114 号县道，是最早跨越新店溪连接板桥港与台北市的桥梁。原桥建成于 1933 年，1975 年光复桥重建，该桥总长 1.080km，桥面宽 20m，包括四条车行道（共 15m）及两侧人行道（各 2.5m），桥的两侧配备两条自行车牵引道连接堤外高滩地自行车道。

  台北光复桥主桥采用了多塔预应力混凝土斜拉桥的形式，4 跨 3 塔，最大跨径 134m，钢筋混凝土门形塔柱高 18m，辐射形索面斜拉索，每塔总计 8 根，桥面系统为 6 根 T 形预应力混凝土梁，红色外观简洁别致。

  Taipei Guangfu Bridge in Taiwan Province, China, located on No.114 County Road, is the first bridge that crosses Xindian Creek to connect Banqiao Port and Taipei City. The original bridge was built in 1933, and the new one was built in 1975. The total length of the bridge is 1.080km, with a deck width of 20m, including four-lane carriageway (15 meters in total) and sidewalks on both sides (2.5 meters each). Two bicycle traction tracks are equipped on both sides of the bridge to connect the high beach bike lanes outside the embankment.

  The main bridge adopts the form of a multi-tower prestressed concrete cable-stayed bridge, composed of 4 spans and 3 towers, with a maximum span of 134 meters. The reinforced concrete portal towers are 18m high, and each tower has 8 radiating stayed cables. The bridge deck system consists of 6 T-shaped prestressed concrete beams, with a simple and unique red appearance.

| | |
|---|---|
| 桥　　名： 台北光复桥 | **Name:** Taipei Guangfu Bridge |
| 桥　　型： 三塔四跨预应力混凝土斜拉桥 | **Type:** Prestressed concrete cable-stayed bridge with three towers and four spans |
| 主跨跨径： 134m | **Main span:** 134m |
| 桥　　址： 台湾省台北市 | **Location:** Taipei City, Taiwan Province |
| 建成时间： 1977 年 | **Completion:** 1977 |
| 建设单位： 台湾省"交通处公路局" | **Constructor(s):** "Highway Engineering Bureau, Communication Department " of Taiwan Province |
| 设计单位： 林同棪工程顾问股份有限公司 | **Designer(s):** T.Y. Lin Engineering Consultant Co., Ltd. |

# 滦河公路桥
## Luan River Highway Bridge

　　滦河公路桥位于河北省唐山市滦州市城关东郊，位于205国道上，跨越滦河，是国内第一座按10度地震设防的预应力混凝土连续梁公路桥。桥梁全长979.51m，上部结构由6联24跨连续梁组成，每联为4×40m的T形梁。每跨设4片主梁，桥宽9m。

　　滦河公路桥按预应力简支梁预制与安装，每联安装后，在中墩处用现浇横梁连接，而后进行负弯矩预应力筋张拉，构成4跨连续体系。下部结构中基础为钻孔灌注桩高桩承台，桩长30~40m，每根桩设计可承受570kN的地震水平力；桥墩分中墩、边墩两种，中墩18个，为钢筋混凝土实体墩，边墩5个，为空心墩；桥台采用混凝土U形桥台。

　　滦河公路桥按10度烈度进行抗震设计，并考虑纵横向与竖向综合设防。全桥分为6个独立"单元"设计，以避免一跨破坏而牵连全桥。主梁支承采用滑动盆式支座以形成漂浮体系；梁端与桥台间设有D型橡胶护弦，用以减震消能。

Luan River Highway Bridge is located in the eastern suburbs of Luanzhou County, Tangshan City, Hebei Province, on the 205 National Highway. It crosses the Luan River and is the first prestressed concrete continuous beam highway bridge in China to be fortified with a high seismic intensity of 10 degree. The total length of the bridge is 979.51m, and the upper structure consists of 6 continuous beams of 24 spans, each consisting of four 40m-long T-beams. Each span is composed of 4 main beams, with a bridge width of 9m.

Prefabrication and installation of the prestressed concrete simply supported beams were first carried out, then cast-in-place transverse beams were used to connect adjacent spans at middle piers, and negative moment region prestressed tendons were tensioned to form a four span continuous system. The foundations are drilled cast-in-place piles of 30~40 meters with elevated pile caps. Each pile is designed to withstand a seismic horizontal force of 570kN. There are two types of bridge piers: middle pier and end pier. There are 18 middle piers, which are reinforced concrete solid piers, and 5 end piers, which are hollow piers. The bridge abutment adopts a concrete U-shaped abutment.

Luan River Highway Bridge is designed for seismic resistance of 10 degree, considering the comprehensive fortification of longitudinal, transverse and vertical directions. The entire bridge is divided into 6 independent "units", in case one-span damage affects the entire bridge. The main girders are supported by sliding basin type bearings to form a floating system. A D-type rubber guard string is installed between the beam end and the bridge abutment for shock absorption and energy dissipation.

桥　　名：滦河公路桥
桥　　型：预应力混凝土连续梁桥
主跨跨径：40m
桥　　址：河北省唐山市
建成时间：1978 年
设计单位：交通部公路规划设计院
施工单位：交通部第一工程局

**Name:** Luan River Highway Bridge
**Type:** Prestressed concrete continuous girder bridge
**Main span:** 40m
**Location:** Tangshan City, Hebei Province
**Completion:** 1978
**Designer(s):** Transport Planning and Research Institute of Ministry of Transport
**Contractor(s):** First Engineering Bureau of Ministry of Transport

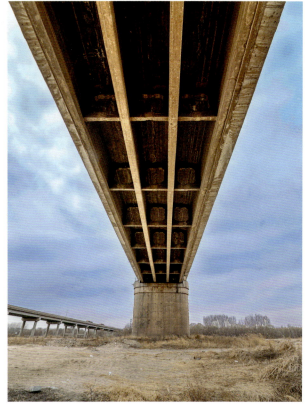

BRIDGES IN CHINA

# 1980

中 国 桥 梁

# 追赶与自主
## CHASING AND INDEPENDENCE

# 1999

# 引 言

随着改革开放历史新时期的到来，中国人民迎来了"科学的春天"。一方面全国经济开始复苏，交通作为先行官得到了各级政府的高度重视；另一方面，国外20世纪60~70年代的城市化建设和高速公路发展拉大了中国桥梁建设与国外的差距，全国桥梁界想要急起直追，追回失去的岁月，建设好自己的国家，为20世纪末实现四个现代化奋斗。

20世纪80年代，率先取得发展的是基于悬臂施工法的T形刚构桥，在冷拉粗钢筋和钢丝群锚体系技术支撑下，三向预应力混凝土桥梁跨径分别达到了带挂梁T形刚构的174m和连续刚构的180m。在前期试验性斜拉桥的基础上，预应力混凝土斜拉桥横空出世，而且在满足抗风和抗震设计要求的前提下，跨径增长到了260m，成为当时的亚洲之最，并且酝酿建设更大跨度的钢结构和钢-混凝土组合结构的斜拉桥。

20世纪80年代末，上海计划建设第一座跨越黄浦江的大桥，成为中国大跨度桥梁发展的一个重要机遇，在同济大学李国豪校长和项海帆教授的大力呼吁下，上海市政府做出了自主建设的英明决策。1991年上海南浦大桥的胜利建成，极大提振了中国桥梁界自主建设大跨度桥梁的信心和决心，两年后又建成了主跨602m的斜拉桥——上海杨浦大桥，创造了世界跨径纪录。90年代初，李国豪校长得知广东省将邀请英国公司带资施工虎门大桥后，再次吁请自主建设虎门大桥取得成功。1997年，中国顺利建成了主跨888m的悬索桥——虎门珠江大桥主航道桥以及创造世界跨径纪录的主跨270m的连续刚构辅航道桥。两年后又自主建成了跨径突破千米的悬索桥——江阴长江大桥。与此同时，中国大跨度拱桥建设也取得了长足的进步，先后建成了大跨度的钢结构拱梁组合体系、混凝土桁架拱桥和钢管混凝土劲性骨架混凝土箱形拱桥，其中，万州长江大桥创造了混凝土拱桥跨径的世界纪录。

20世纪最后20年，中国建成了一批大跨度桥梁，主要代表性桥型从梁桥和拱桥拓展到了斜拉桥和悬索桥，其中不乏具有世界先进水平的大跨度梁桥、拱桥和斜拉桥。本章选取了中国大跨度预应力混凝土梁桥3座（包括虎门大桥辅航道桥）、大跨度拱桥3座、斜拉桥4座和悬索桥4座。斜拉桥、梁桥和混凝土拱桥的跨径先后打破世界纪录，标志着中国大跨度桥梁建设步入了世界先进行列。

# INTRODUCTION

With the advent of the new era of the Reform and Opening-up in China, the Chinese people welcomed the resurgence in science and technology. On the one hand, the national economy began to recover, prioritizing investment in transportation which gained heightened attention from all levels of government. On the other hand, the urbanization and highway development in western countries during the 1960s and 1970s highlighted the gap in bridge construction between China and the rest of the world. The national bridge community was eager to catch up rapidly, reclaiming the lost years in an effort to build up the nation and strive towards the realization of the Modernizations of industry, agriculture, national defense and technology by the end of the 20th century.

In the 1980s, the T-shaped rigid frame bridge, based on the cantilever construction method, was among the first to achieve significant development in China. Supported by the technology of cold-drawn mild steel reinforcement and steel strand anchorage systems, the span of three-directional prestressed concrete bridges reached 174m for the T-shaped rigid frame with suspended girders and 180m for the continuous rigid frame. Building on the foundation of early experimental cable-stayed bridges, prestressed concrete cable-stayed bridges emerged, achieving spans up to 260m while meeting severe requirements for wind resistance and seismic design. This was the longest prestressed concrete cable-stayed bridge in Asia at the time. Additionally, there were plans to construct even longer-span cable-stayed bridges using steel and steel-concrete composite structures.

By the late 1980s, the first bridge crossing the Huangpu River in Shanghai was constructed, marking a significant achievement for the development of long-span bridges in China. Under the strong advocacy of Professor Guohao Li, President of Tongji University, and Professor Haifan Xiang, the Shanghai Municipal Government made a wise decision to undertake the construction independently. The successful completion of the Nanpu Bridge in Shanghai in 1991 greatly boosted the confidence and determination of the Chinese bridge community to build long-span bridges independently. This was followed two years later by the construction of the Yangpu Bridge, a cable-stayed bridge with a world-record span of 602m. In the early 1990s, upon learning that Guangdong Province planned to invite a British company to construct the Humen Bridge with foreign investment, Prof. Guohao Li once again advocated for independent construction. This effort was successful, and in 1997, the main channel of the Humen Bridge over the Pearl River, a suspension bridge with a span of 888m, was completed along with the world-record-breaking 270m span continuous rigid frame auxiliary channel bridge. Two years later, the Jiangyin Bridge over the Yangtze River, a suspension bridge with a span exceeding 1000m, was independently completed. Meanwhile, China also made significant progress in the construction of long-span arch bridges. Structural systems included long-span steel-concrete composite systems, concrete truss arch bridges, and concrete filled steel tube arch bridges. The Wanzhou Bridge over the Yangtze River set a world record for the span of concrete arch bridges.

In the last two decades of the 20th century, China constructed a series of long-span bridges, expanding from girder and arch bridges to include cable-stayed and suspension bridges, many of which reached a world-class level. This chapter highlights a selection of these remarkable structures: three long-span prestressed concrete girder bridges (including the auxiliary channel bridge of the Humen Bridge over the Pearl River), three long-span arch bridges, four cable-stayed bridges, and four suspension bridges. The spans of cable-stayed bridges, girder bridges, and concrete arch bridges successively broke world records, signifying that China's construction of long-span bridges had entered the forefront of global engineering achievement.

# 重庆石板坡长江大桥

## Chongqing Shibanpo Bridge over Yangtze River

重庆石板坡长江大桥，原名重庆长江大桥，位于重庆市市区，是连接渝中区与南岸区的过江通道，是长江中游第一座特大型城市公路桥。大桥北起石板坡立交，上跨长江水道，南至黄葛渡立交，全长1.12km，设双向四车道。

主桥为预应力混凝土T形刚构桥，主桥长1073m，宽21m，跨径布置为86.5m+4×138m+156m+174m+104.5m。主梁为双箱单室断面，两箱之间0.6m宽的顶板采用现浇预应力混凝土，利用横向预应力使两箱连成一体。主跨桥墩处箱梁高11m，边跨桥墩处箱梁高8m；挂梁跨径35m，为T形截面，跨中梁高3m。主梁采用三向预应力体系，纵向、横向预应力采用24根 $\phi5$ 高强钢丝，竖向预应力采用 $\phi28$ 的25MnSi冷拉粗钢筋。水中主墩基础采用双壁钢围堰加12根直径2.6m的钻孔灌注桩。

大桥采用新工艺进行深坑基础的嵌岩施工；在钻孔桩的施工中，组织试制大型牙轮钻机，一次试钻成功。墩身采用液压滑模施工。T构箱梁采用斜拉托架、斜拉挂篮施工，并首次采用箱梁滑模施工。重约1200kN的挂梁采用自制斜拉架桥机架设。

Chongqing Shibanpo Bridge over Yangtze River, formerly named Chongqing Bridge over Yangtze River, is located in the urban area of Chongqing City, connecting Yuzhong District and Nan'an District. The bridge is the first grand urban highway bridge in the midstream reaches of Yangtze River. The bridge starts from Shibanpo Interchange in the north, crosses the Yangtze River, then ends at Huanggedu Interchange in the south, with a total length of 1.12km and four lanes in dual directions.

The main bridge is a prestressed-concrete T-shaped rigid frame bridge with a length of 1,073m and a width of 21m. Its span arrangement is 86.5m+4×138m+156m+174m+104.5m. The main girder features a single-cell double-box cross-section. The part of top slab between the two boxes, with a width of 0.6m, was constructed with cast-in-situ prestressed concrete. Additionally, transverse prestressing has been employed to connect the two boxes. The depth of the main girder at the pier top in the main span and that in the side span are 11m and 8m, respectively. The suspended girder spans 35m, features a T-shaped cross-section, and has a depth of 3m at the span center. The main girder utilizes a three-dimensional prestressing system, incorporating 24 $\phi5$ high-strength steel wires in both the longitudinal and transverse directions, and $\phi28$ 25MnSi cold-drawn steel bars in the vertical direction. For the pier foundation in the river, a double-wall steel cofferdam is adopted, along with 12 drilled-and-grouted piles with a diameter of 2.6m.

A novel technique was developed for the construction of the embedded rock in the deep foundation. A large-scale rotary drill machine was trial-produced and successfully operated for the first time during the construction of the drilled piles. The piers were constructed using a hydraulic press-based slip form method. In building the T-frame box girder, cable-stayed brackets and hanging baskets were utilized, marking the first adoption of the slip form method in box-girder construction. Additionally, an innovative self-developed cable-stayed bridge erection machine was employed to erect the suspended girder, which weighed approximately 1,200kN.

桥　　名： 重庆石板坡长江大桥
桥　　型： 预应力混凝土T形刚构桥
主跨跨径： 174m
桥　　址： 重庆市
建成时间： 1980年7月
设计单位： 上海市政工程设计研究院
施工单位： 重庆市桥梁工程总公司

**Name:** Chongqing Shibanpo Bridge over Yangtze River
**Type:** Prestressed Concrete T-shaped rigid frame bridge
**Main span:** 174m
**Location:** Chongqing City
**Completion:** July 1980
**Designer(s):** Shanghai Municipal Engineering Design Institute
**Contractor(s):** Chongqing Bridge Engineering Company

# 济南黄河大桥
## Jinan Bridge over Yellow River

济南黄河大桥位于山东省济南市，是市区南北向主干道二环东路跨越黄河的节点，全长 2.02km，设双向四车道。

主桥为双塔双索面预应力混凝土斜拉桥，总长 488m，宽 19.5m，跨径布置为 40m+94m+220m+94m+20m。主梁为单箱双室预应力混凝土箱梁，梁高 2.75m，采用挂篮悬浇施工。桥塔为 A 形门式空间框架结构，塔高 68.4m。桥塔与桥墩固结并与主梁分离，为全漂浮体系。索面采用扇形布置，索距 8m，每塔每侧 11 对索，拉索用铅制套管内压水泥浆进行防护。主墩基础由 24 根直径 1.5m 的钻孔灌注桩和承台组成。大桥基础施工采用水上平台及钢板桩围堰，桥塔施工采用独立式刚性万能拉杆支架，构成门式三层刚构。

济南黄河大桥是当时亚洲跨度最大的斜拉桥。

Jinan Bridge over Yellow River is located in Jinan City, Shandong Province. The bridge is a key crossing point for the north-south main artery of the city's Second Ring East Road over Yellow River. The total length of the bridge is 2.02km with four lanes in dual directions.

The main bridge is a double-tower double-cable-plane prestressed-concrete cable-stayed bridge. The bridge has a total length of 488m and a width of 19.5m. Its span arrangement is 40m+94m+220m+94m+20m. The main girder features a double-cell prestressed-concrete box section with a height of 2.75m. The construction of the main girder employed the cantilever casting method with hanging baskets. The bridge tower features an A-shaped portal space frame structure, standing at a height of 68.4m. This tower is rigidly fixed to the pier, while designed to be isolated from the main girder, thereby creating a fully floating system. The cables are configured in a fan-shaped arrangement, spaced 8m apart. Each side of the tower is equipped with 11 pairs of cables, each of which is protected by lead sleeves filled with cement paste inside. The foundation of the main pier comprises 24 1.5m-diameter drilled-and-grouted piles along with a pile cap. The foundation construction of the bridge was executed using platforms on the water, employing steel sheet pile cofferdams. Furthermore, the construction of the bridge tower involved the utilization of an independent rigid universal tie-rod scaffold, forming a portal three-layer rigid frame structure.

At the time of its completion, the bridge was the longest-span bridge in Asia.

桥　名：济南黄河大桥
桥　型：双塔双索面预应力混凝土斜拉桥
主跨跨径：220m
桥　址：山东省济南市
建成时间：1982年7月
设计单位：山东省交通规划设计院
施工单位：山东省交通工程公司

**Name:** Jinan Bridge over Yellow River
**Type:** Double-tower double-cable-plane prestressed-concrete cable-stayed bridge
**Main span:** 220m
**Location:** Jinan City, Shandong Province
**Completion:** July 1982
**Designer(s):** Shandong Provincial Communications Planning and Designing Institute
**Contractor(s):** Shandong Communication Construction Company

# 天津永和桥
## Tianjin Yonghe Bridge

  天津永和桥位于天津市东郊，跨越永定新河，是山广公路（山海关—广州）的重要通道，全长512.4m，设双向两车道。

  天津永和桥为双塔双索面预应力混凝土斜拉桥。主桥长512.4m，宽13.6m，跨径布置为26.15m+99.85m+260m+99.85m+26.55m。主梁由预制块件拼装而成，块件重约12000kN。桥塔基础采用直径18m的开口圆形沉井，深35m，桥台基础及中间墩基础为预应力混凝土打入桩。主梁施工采用临时栈桥运梁、悬臂拼装法架梁，节段间按"长线法"匹配浇筑。

  桥址处于8度地震烈度软土地区，且因濒临渤海，时有强风，故设计采用漂浮体系及流线型主梁断面，以满足抗震抗风的要求。建设期间，相关单位对该桥进行了抗风、抗震、内力分析、施工控制、制索及张拉工艺等方面的研究。

Tianjin Yonghe Bridge is located in the eastern suburb of Tianjin, crossing Yongding New River. The bridge holds a significant role as a vital segment of Shanhaiguan-Guangzhou Highway, The total length of the bridge is 512.4m with two lanes in dual directions.

Tianjin Yonghe bridge is a double-tower double-cable-plane prestressed-concrete cable-stayed bridge. The bridge has a length of 512.4m and a width of 13.6m. Its span arrangement is 26.15m+99.85m+260m+99.85m+26.55m. The main girder was assembled using prefabricated segments, each with a weight of 12,000kN. The foundation of the tower adopts a circular open caisson with a depth of 35m and a diameter of 18m, while the abutments and intermediate piers are supported by prestressed-concrete driven piles. The construction of the main girder involved the use of temporary trestles for transporting the girder segments. The cantilever assembly method was employed for girder erection, and the "long-line method" was utilized for match casting among the segments.

The bridge site is situated in an area characterized by soft soil and an 8-degree seismic intensity, occasionally exposed to strong winds from Bohai Sea. To meet the stringent requirements for both seismic and wind resistance, the bridge design incorporated a floating system and a streamlined girder cross-section. Throughout the construction period, relevant agencies conducted comprehensive research, including wind resistance, seismic resistance, internal force analysis, construction control, cable manufacturing, and tensioning technology.

桥　　名：天津永和桥
桥　　型：双塔双索面预应力混凝土斜拉桥
主跨跨径：260m
桥　　址：天津市
建成时间：1987年12月
设计单位：天津市市政工程勘测设计院
施工单位：铁道部大桥工程局

**Name:** Tianjin Yonghe Bridge
**Type:** Double-tower double-cable-plane prestressed-concrete cable-stayed bridge
**Main span:** 260m
**Location:** Tianjin City
**Completion:** December 1987
**Designer(s):** Tianjin Municipal Engineering Survey and Design Institute
**Contractor(s):** Bridge Engineering Bureau of Ministry of Railways

# 番禺洛溪桥

## Panyu Luoxi Bridge

番禺洛溪桥位于广东省广州市南郊，跨越珠江，是连接海珠区和番禺区的过江通道，全长1.92km，设双向四车道。

主桥为不对称四跨预应力混凝土连续刚构桥，全长480m，宽15.5m，跨径布置为65m+125m+180m+110m。主梁采用单箱单室截面，主墩支点梁高10m，跨中梁高3m。主梁除在各墩顶处设置横隔板外，其余截面均不设横隔板。腹板厚0.5~0.7m，底板厚0.32~1.2m，顶板厚0.28m。主梁施工采用悬臂浇筑法。主梁采用三向预应力体系，采用了大吨位纵向预应力VSL群锚锚固系统，预应力群锚的最大张拉力为4275kN，预应力钢丝束最大长度逾190m，钢束和锚固位置靠近腹板设置，同时腹板束一律采用S形平弯，以减小局部应力。主墩采用双壁式薄壁空心墩，双壁中心距离为7.8m，壁厚0.5m。墩外设人工岛以防船舶撞击，岛呈喇叭形，顶部直径28m，底部直径23m，高20m。

Panyu Luoxi Bridge is located in the southern suburb of Guangzhou City, Guangdong province crossing Zhujiang River. It serves as a vital river-crossing link connecting Haizhu District and Panyu District. The total length of the bridge is 1.92km with four lanes in dual directions.

The main bridge is an asymmetric four-span prestressed-concrete continuous-rigid-frame bridge, with a total length of 480m and a width of 15.5m. Its span arrangement is 65m+125m+180m+110m. The main girder features a single-cell box section, with a depth of 10m at the main pier top and 3m at the midpoint of the span. Diaphragms are set at the top of each pier, while other sections of the main girder remain devoid of diaphragms. The thicknesses of the web plate, the bottom plate and the top plate are 0.5~0.7m, 0.32~1.2m and 0.28m, respectively. The construction of the main girder employed the cantilever casting method. The main girder is equipped with a three-dimensional prestressing system, employing the large-tonnage longitudinal prestressing VSL anchor-group system. The maximum tension among the prestressing anchor groups reaches 4,275 kN, and the maximum length of prestressing steel tendons extends to over 190m. The steel tendons and anchorage positions are strategically positioned in proximity to the web plates, and all the web tendons adopt an S-shaped horizontal bending configuration to mitigate local stress concentrations. The main pier features a double thin-walled hollow section. The center distance of the double-wall is 7.8m, and the wall thickness is 0.5m. An artificial island outside the pier is set up to prevent ship collision. The island is flared, with a top diameter of 28m, a bottom diameter of 23m, and a height of 20m.

桥　　名：番禺洛溪桥
桥　　型：预应力混凝土连续刚构桥
主跨跨径：180m
桥　　址：广东省广州市
建成时间：1988年8月
设计单位：广东省公路勘察规划设计院，中交公路规划设计院
施工单位：广东省公路工程处

**Name:** Panyu Luoxi Bridge
**Type:** Prestressed concrete continuous rigid frame bridge
**Main span:** 180m
**Location:** Guangzhou City, Guangdong Province
**Completion:** August 1988
**Designer(s):** Guangdong Highway Investigation, Planning and Design Institute, CCCC Highway Planning & Design Institute
**Contractor(s):** Guangdong Highway Agency

# 上海南浦大桥
Shanghai Nanpu Bridge

桥　　名：上海南浦大桥
桥　　型：双塔双索面组合梁斜拉桥
主跨跨径：423m
桥　　址：上海市
建成时间：1991年12月
设计单位：上海市政工程设计院，同济大学建筑设计研究院
施工单位：上海市基础工程公司

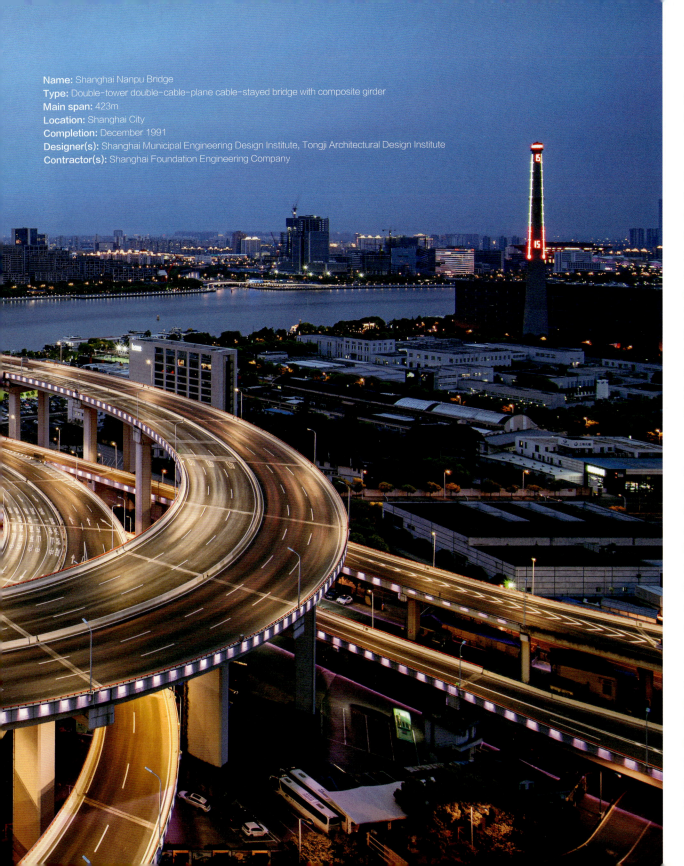

**Name:** Shanghai Nanpu Bridge
**Type:** Double-tower double-cable-plane cable-stayed bridge with composite girder
**Main span:** 423m
**Location:** Shanghai City
**Completion:** December 1991
**Designer(s):** Shanghai Municipal Engineering Design Institute, Tongji Architectural Design Institute
**Contractor(s):** Shanghai Foundation Engineering Company

| 追赶与自主 1980—1999

南浦大桥位于上海市，是连接黄浦区与浦东新区的跨越黄浦江通道，也是上海市内环线的重要组成部分，全长 8.35km，设双向六车道。南浦大桥是上海市区第一座跨黄浦江的大桥，开创了国人自主设计、施工大跨径桥梁的先河。

主桥为双塔双索面钢-混凝土组合梁斜拉桥，主桥长 846m，宽 30.35m，跨径布置为 40.5m+76.5m+94.5m+423m+94.5m+76.5m+40.5m，采用纵向漂浮体系。主梁采用工字形钢板梁与混凝土桥面结合的组合梁。桥塔高 150m，采用折线 H 形钢筋混凝土桥塔，桥塔基础为钢管桩群桩基础。主梁和主塔间无支座连接，仅有挡块限制主梁的横向摆动。斜拉索呈扇形布置，每个桥塔各设 22 对斜拉索，塔柱中央设置一对竖直索以代替竖向支承，拉索为塑包平行钢丝索。桥塔施工时采用"斜爬模"施工技术，解决了在高耸塔柱构筑物施工时作业面小、施工机具和施工材料堆放不便等困难。上部结构施工采用悬臂拼装法施工，桥面高程与索力双控，通过索力调整等方法，使梁、塔的内力和桥面高程处于最优状态。在易裂区域桥面板中分别施加纵、横向预应力，将锚箱从工字钢主梁移到工字梁腹板外侧，并通过横梁反拱调整内力等方法，有效控制了裂缝的产生。

1995 年，上海南浦大桥工程获得国家科技进步奖一等奖。

Nanpu Bridge, located in Shanghai City, serves as a vital link connecting Huangpu District and Pudong New District by spanning Huangpu River. It also constitutes an integral component of Shanghai City's Inner Ring Road. The total length of the bridge is 8.35km with six lanes in dual directions. Notably, Nanpu Bridge holds the distinction of being the first bridge to cross Huangpu River in Shanghai's urban area. It also marks the first instance of China's independent design and construction of a modern long-span bridge.

The main bridge is a double-tower double-cable-plane cable-stayed bridge with a composite girder. The bridge has a length of 846m and a width of 30.35m. Its span arrangement is 40.5m+76.5m+94.5m+423m+94.5m+76.5m+40.5m. The bridge employs a longitudinal floating system. The main girder features a composite section combining the I-shaped steel plate girder and concrete deck. The tower is designed as a polyline H-shaped reinforced concrete structure with a height of 150m. The foundation of the tower employs a group-pile foundation along with steel pipe piles. There is no support structure between the main girder and the tower, except for a stop-block designed to restrict the transverse movement of the main girder. The cables are arranged in a fan-shaped configuration, with each tower accommodating 22 pairs of cables and a pair of vertical cables at the tower serving as vertical supports. These cables are made of plastic-coated parallel steel wires. The construction of the bridge pylon employed the "inclined jump-form" construction technique, which successfully addressed several challenges associated with the construction of high-rise tower structures, such as the limited working space and the cumbersome arrangement of construction equipment and materials. The superstructure construction utilized the cantilever assembly method. The construction considered the dual control mechanisms governing deck elevation and cable forces. Optimization of both deck elevation and the internal force state has been achieved through the adjustment of cable forces and other associated parameters. Longitudinal and transverse prestressing were strategically applied in areas of the bridge deck plates prone to cracking. Additionally, the anchor box was relocated from the I-shaped girder to the exterior of the girder web, and internal force adjustments were implemented through measures such as the camber of crossbeams. These measures effectively contributed to the control of cracks.

In 1995, Shanghai Nanpu Bridge Project won the First Prize of National Science and Technology Progress Award.

CHASING AND INDEPENDENCE | 追赶与自主 1980—1999

# 九江长江大桥

## Jiujiang Bridge over Yangtze River

桥　名：九江长江大桥
桥　型：连续钢桁梁桥，连续钢桁梁拱组合体系桥
主跨跨径：216m
桥　址：江西省九江市
建成时间：1993年1月
设计单位：中铁大桥勘测设计院
施工单位：中铁大桥局集团有限公司

**Name:** Jiujiang Bridge over Yangtze River
**Type:** Continuous steel truss girder bridge, continuous steel-truss-girder-arch composite bridge
**Main span:** 216m
**Location:** Jiujiang City, Jiangxi Province
**Completion:** January 1993
**Designer(s):** China Railway Major Bridge Reconnaissance & Design Institute
**Contractor(s):** China Railway Major Bridge Engineering Group Co., Ltd.

　　九江长江大桥位于江西、湖北和安徽三省交界处，横跨长江水面，南接江西省九江市，北通湖北省黄冈市。大桥为双层公铁两用桥，公路桥梁全长4.460km，铁路桥梁全长7.675km。

　　九江长江大桥由1.806km主桥、2.654km公路引桥和5.870km铁路引桥组成。大桥上层公路四车道宽14m，两侧人行道各宽2m；下层承载双线铁路。主桥由三联钢桁连续梁桥和一联连续钢桁梁拱组合体系桥组成。钢桁梁拱组合体系桥跨径布置为180m+216m+180m，中跨矢跨比为1/6.75，两边跨矢跨比为1/7.5。主桁桁高16m，主桁中距12.5m；杆件以H形为主，仅受压斜杆和拱圈采用箱形截面，采用栓焊结构。主桥设有9个桥墩和2个桥台，基础采用多种形式，包括钢筋混凝土沉井、浮运钢沉井、双壁钢围堰及钢板桩围堰、管柱钻孔基础等。大桥上部结构架设主要采用悬臂拼装法，在最大跨的跨中合龙，并采用双层吊索塔架以减小安装应力。公路引桥采用40m预应力混凝土T形梁，每孔8片T梁；铁路引桥采用40m预应力混凝土箱形梁，每孔2片箱梁。

　　九江长江大桥是当时世界上最长的公铁两用钢桁梁桥，获国家科技进步奖一等奖。

Jiujiang Bridge over Yangtze River is located at the confluence of Jiangxi, Hubei and Anhui provinces. The bridge crosses the Yangtze River, connecting to Jiujiang City of Jiangxi Province in the south, and Huanggang City of Hubei Province in the north. Serving both highway and railway transits, the bridge features double layers and has total lengths of 4.460km and 7.675km for its highway and railway sections, respectively.

The bridge consists of three parts, i.e., main bridges with a total length of 1.806km, highway approach bridges with a total length of 2.654km and railway approach bridges with a total length of 5.870km. The upper layer of the bridge comprises four highway lanes with a total width of 14m, flanked by sidewalks of 2m width on each side, while the lower layer accommodates a two-track railroad. The main bridges are composed of three continuous steel-truss beam bridges and one continuous steel-truss bridge with a beam-arch combination system. The span arrangement for the beam-arch combination bridge is 180m+216m+180m; the rise-to-span ratio in the middle span is 1/6.75, and that in the two side spans is 1/7.5. The depth of the truss girder is 16m, with a horizontal spacing of 12.5m between two truss planes. Most truss members are designed as H-shaped sections, with only compression diagonals and arch members adopting box sections. Truss members were made in the factory by welding and connected in the field with bolts. Totally 9 piers and 2 abutments are set in the main bridge, and the foundations are designed as various forms, including reinforced-concrete caissons, floating steel caissons, double-wall steel cofferdams, steel sheet pile cofferdams, drilled-and-grouted pipe foundations, etc. The bridge superstructures were mostly constructed by the cantilever assembly method, and the closure point was set at the middle point of the longest span. A double-layer temporary tower with stay cables was additionally designed to reduce the stress during construction. The standard span of highway approach bridges is 40m long, adopting prestressed-concrete T-shaped girders with 8 pieces for each span. The standard span of railway approach bridges is also 40m long, adopting prestressed-concrete box-shaped girders with 2 pieces for each span.

At the time of completion, Jiujiang Bridge over Yangtze River was the longest highway-railway steel-truss bridge in the world, The bridge was rewarded with the First Prize of National Science and Technology Progress Award.

# 上海杨浦大桥

## Shanghai Yangpu Bridge

杨浦大桥位于上海市，是连接杨浦区与浦东新区的跨越黄浦江通道，也是上海市内环线重要组成部分，全长7.658km，设双向六车道及观光人行道。

主桥采用双塔双索面组合梁斜拉桥，桥长1172m，宽30.35m，跨径布置为40m+99m+144m+602m+144m+99m+44m。主跨一跨过江，通航净空48m。两侧边跨均设置辅助墩，桥塔与桥墩固结并与主梁分离，上部结构采用纵向漂浮体系，横向设置限位和抗震装置。主梁为矩形分离双钢箱组合梁，横隔梁为工字形钢梁。主桥桥塔高208m，桥塔采用倒Y钻石形钢筋混凝土结构。桥塔基础为钢管桩群桩基础。斜拉索呈空间扇形布置，每个桥塔各设32对斜拉索，全桥共256根斜拉索，其中最长拉索328m，重330kN。该桥采用空间索、双边钢箱-混凝土组合梁，增大了桥梁的整体抗风性能和抗扭刚度。

上海杨浦大桥主跨居当时世界同类型桥梁之首，该桥的建成使我国斜拉桥的设计和施工水平进入世界先进行列。

| | |
|---|---|
| 桥　　名： | 上海杨浦大桥 |
| 桥　　型： | 双塔双索面组合梁斜拉桥 |
| 主跨跨径： | 602m |
| 桥　　址： | 上海市 |
| 建成时间： | 1993年10月 |
| 设计单位： | 上海市政工程设计院，同济大学建筑设计研究院 |
| 施工单位： | 上海市基础工程公司 |

**Name:** Shanghai Yangpu Bridge
**Type:** Double-tower double-cable-plane cable-stayed bridge with composite girder
**Main span:** 602m
**Location:** Shanghai City
**Completion:** October 1993
**Designer(s):** Shanghai Municipal Engineering Design Institute, Tongji Architectural Design Institute
**Contractor(s):** Shanghai Foundation Engineering Company

Yangpu Bridge, located in Shanghai City, serves as a vital link connecting Yangpu District and Pudong New District by crossing Huangpu River. This bridge is also a significant component of Shanghai's Inner Ring Road. The total length of the bridge is 7.658km, with six lanes in dual directions and sightseeing sidewalks.

The main bridge is a double-tower double-cable-plane cable-stayed bridge with a composite girder. The bridge has a length of 1,172m and a width of 48m. Its span arrangement is 40m+99m+144m+602m+144m+99m+44m. The main bridge spans the river in a single span, offering a navigational clearance of 48m. Auxiliary piers are positioned in both side spans, and the tower is rigidly fixed with piers and separated from the main girder. The superstructure employs a longitudinal floating system, complemented by limiting and seismic-resistance devices in the transverse direction. The main girder features a rectangular separated double-steel-box composite section, complemented by I-shaped crossbeams. The tower of the main bridge stands at a height of 208m. Featuring a reinforced-concrete structure in the inverted-Y diamond shape, the bridge tower adopts the group-pile foundation with steel pipe piles. The cables are arranged in a fan-shaped configuration. The bridge is supported by 256 cables in total, and each pylon supports 32 pairs of cables. The longest cable measures 328m in length and 330kN in weight. The bridge design adopts spatial cables and bilateral steel-box steel-concrete-composite girder, which increase the overall wind-resistance and torsional stiffness of the structure.

The main span of Shanghai Yangpu Bridge ranked first among the same types of bridges in the world at its completion time. The completion of this bridge has brought the design and construction technologies of Chinese cable-stayed bridges into the advanced level around the world.

# 江界河大桥

## Jiangjie River Bridge

桥　　名：江界河大桥
桥　　型：预应力混凝土桁式拱桥
主跨跨径：330m
桥　　址：贵州省黔南布依族苗族自治州
建成时间：1995年6月
设计单位：贵州省交通厅大跨度桁式组合拱桥研究课题组
施工单位：贵州省桥梁工程总公司

**Name:** Jiangjie River Bridge
**Type:** Prestressed-concrete truss arch bridge
**Mian span:** 330m
**Location:** Qiannan Buyizu & Miaozu Autonomous Prefecture, Guizhou Province
**Completion:** June 1995
**Designer(s):** Design Group of Jiangjie River Bridge
**Contractor(s):** Guizhou Provincial Bridge Engineering Company

江界河大桥位于贵州省黔南布依族苗族自治州瓮安县江界河风景区，跨越乌江中游峡谷，全长461m，设双向四车道。

主桥为上承式预应力混凝土桁式组合拱桥，跨径布置为20m+25m+30m+330m+30m+20m，矢跨比为1/6，桥面宽13m。大桥桁式拱横向由两片结构组成，每片桁架的上、下弦杆均为单箱三室截面。中跨下弦杆的高度为2.7m、宽度10.56m，矢高55m，边跨利用山坡岩石地形桁架不设下弦杆。竖杆采用箱形截面，均按压杆构造布置，两片桁架间用剪刀撑连接；斜杆为箱形截面，均按拉杆构造布置，两片桁架间用横系梁连接。上弦杆配置 $\phi$ 32的高强冷拉预应力粗钢筋和轧丝锚具，斜腹杆采用24 $\phi$ 5的高强预应力钢丝束和弗氏锚具。大桥施工采用预制杆件悬臂拼装法，起重设备为钢制人字桅杆起重机，吊装重量达1200kN。

江界河大桥研发的桁式组合拱桥结构，利用山坡岩石地形替代边跨桁架下弦杆，斜杆预应力钢筋锚固于岩盘内。采用空心节点减轻自重，中跨上弦杆设置断缝改善受力，使结构设计得到了优化。

江界河大桥工程获得了国家科学技术进步奖二等奖。

Jiangjie River Bridge is located in Jiangjie River Scenic Area of Weng'an County, Qiannan Buyizu & Miaozu Autonomous Prefecture, Guizhou Province. Spanning over the valley in the midstream of Wujiang River, the bridge has a total length of 461m, with four traffic lanes in dual directions.

The main bridge is a deck-type prestressed-concrete truss composite arch bridge. Its span arrangement is 20m+25m+30m+330m+30m+20m with a rise-to-span ratio of 1/6. The bridge deck is 13m wide. The arch transversely consists of two planes of truss structures, each with upper and lower chords featuring a triple-cell box section. The depth of the lower chord in the middle span is 2.7m, with a width of 10.56m, and a rise of 55m. In the side spans, taking advantage of the mountainous rocky terrain, the trusses are designed without lower chords. The vertical chords are configured as compression members, adopting a box section and connected by shear bracing beams between the two trusses. The diagonal chords are configured as compression members, also adopting a box section, while connected by bracing beams between the two trusses. The upper chords are equipped with $\phi$ 32 high-strength cold-drawn prestressed steel bars and threaded anchors, while the diagonal web chords use 24 $\phi$ 5 high-strength prestressed Freyssinet anchorage. During the bridge construction process, the prefabricated chords were installed using the cantilever erection method. The lifting equipment employed for this purpose consisted of a steel herringbone mast crane with a lifting capacity of 1,200kN.

Jiangjie River Bridge adopts an innovative truss composite arch bridge structure. The rocks on the mountain slope have been utilized as the lower chord of side span trusses, and the diagonal prestressing tendons have been anchored into the rocks. The design has been further optimized through the incorporation of hollow joints to reduce the dead load and strategically placing the breaking joints along the upper chords in the mid-span to enhance stress distribution.

The project of Jiangjie River Bridge Won the Second Prize of National Science and Technology Progress Award.

# 汕头海湾大桥
## Shantou Bay Bridge

汕头海湾大桥位于广东省汕头市，南起南滨路，上跨礐石海及妈屿岛，北至泰星路，全长2.50km，设双向六车道。

主桥为双塔三跨吊预应力混凝土箱梁悬索桥，主跨跨径452m，在当时居世界同类桥型第一。跨径布置为154m+452m+154m，垂跨比为1/10。主缆由110束预制平行钢丝束组成，每束含91ϕ5.1钢丝。加劲梁采用薄壁鱼腹式单箱三室预应力混凝土箱梁，宽26.5m，高2.2m；顶板及腹板厚0.18m，底板厚0.14m；横向预应力沿底板配置，纵向预应力在顶板为体内束，在底板为置于板面的体外束。主塔塔高95.1m，为钢筋混凝土门式框架结构，设有上、中、下三道箱形截面横梁。主塔基础由一个承台连接两个上下游分离的沉井构成，每个沉井下设有6根直径2.2m的钻孔嵌岩群桩。两岸均采用嵌岩重力式锚碇。主缆采用预制平行束股制作架设，研发创新工艺以加快束股牵引速度。两端锚碇放置在主航道两岸的岩体上，锚碇结构在平面上呈U字形，环绕在天然岩体的后方，基坑开挖后，直接将锚体混凝土现浇到岩石之中。在锚碇的上方，依山体地形采用砌体挡土墙压重，回填成桥头观光平台。加劲梁分节段预制吊装就位后用湿接头浇筑而连接为整体。该桥抗震设防烈度为8度，为克服加劲梁自重的不利影响，在桥的纵横向设置了隔震、减震设施。

汕头海湾大桥桥址属台风频发区，是中国沿海干线公路（同江—三亚）上的重要工程，也是中国第一座大跨度现代悬索桥。

Shantou Bay Bridge, located in Shantou City, Guangdong Province, starts from Nanbin Road in the south, crosses Queshi Sea and Mayu Island, then ends at Taixing Road in the north. The total length of the bridge is 2.50km with six traffic lanes in dual directions.

The main bridge is a double-tower three-suspended-span suspension bridge with a prestressed-concrete-box girder. The main span of the bridge is 452m, a record-breaking achievement at the time of completion, surpassing all other suspension bridges of the same type around the world. The span arrangement cable is 154m+452m+154m, and the sag-to-span ratio is 1/10. The main cable was prefabricated with 110 steel wire bundles, and each includes 91ϕ5.1 steel wires. The stiffening girder features a thin-walled fish-belly-type triple-cell prestressed-concrete box section, with a width of 26.5m and a depth of 2.2m. Both the top plate and web are designed with a thickness of 0.18m, while the bottom plate has a thickness of 0.14m. The transversal l prestressing is applied along the bottom plates, and the longitudinal prestress is comprised of internal prestressed strands along the top plates and external prestressed strands along the bottom plates. The main tower is a portal frame reinforced-concrete structure, with a height of 95.1m and three box-shaped crossbeams for each tower. The foundation of the main tower comprises a cap and two separated caissons, each supported by 6 rock-embedded bored piles with a diameter of 2.2m. Rock-embedded gravity type anchorages are employed on both banks. The main cables were fabricated using prefabricated parallel wire strands. New techniques have been developed to accelerate the traction speed of bundles. The anchorages were strategically positioned on the rock formations on both banks of the main channel. These anchorage structures take on a U-shaped configuration on a flat surface, enveloping the rear of the natural rock bodies. The anchor concrete was cast into the rock after the foundation excavation. Additionally, above the anchorage, a masonry retaining wall was constructed to accommodate the mountainous terrain, providing additional weight. This structure was subsequently backfilled to create a viewing deck. The stiffening girder segments were prefabricated and precisely positioned, followed by their connection to adjacent segments using wet joints. Given that the bridge is situated in a region with a seismic intensity of 8 degree, longitudinal and transverse seismic isolation devices, along with shock-absorbing devices, were systematically installed to mitigate the potential adverse effects incurred by the weight of the stiffening girder.

Located in a region prone to typhoons, this bridge holds a pivotal position as a key project along the national Tongjiang-Sanya coastal highway. It stands as the first long-span modern suspension bridge in China.

桥　名：汕头海湾大桥
桥　型：双塔三跨吊预应力混凝土箱梁悬索桥
主跨跨径：452m
桥　址：广东省汕头市
建成时间：1995年12月
设计单位：中铁大桥勘测设计院
施工单位：中铁大桥局集团有限公司

**Name:** Shantou Bay Bridge
**Type:** Double-tower three-suspended-span suspension bridge with prestressed-concrete-box girder
**Main span:** 452m
**Location:** Shantou City, Guangdong Province
**Completion:** December 1995
**Designer(s):** China Railway Major Bridge Reconnaissance & Design Institute
**Contractor(s):** China Railway Major Bridge Engineering Group Co., Ltd.

| 桥　名： | 香港青马大桥 | **Name:** Hong Kong Tsing Ma Bridge |
|---|---|---|
| 桥　型： | 双塔两跨吊钢桁梁悬索桥 | **Type:** Double-tower double-suspended-span suspension bridge with steel truss girder |
| 主跨跨径： | 1377m | **Mian span:** 1,377m |
| 桥　址： | 香港特别行政区 | **Location:** Hong Kong Special Administrative Region |
| 建成时间： | 1997年5月 | **Completion:** May 1997 |
| 设计单位： | 万隆顾问香港有限公司 | **Designer(s):** Mott Connell Ltd., Hong Kong |
| 施工单位： | 英高日建筑联营所 | **Contractor(s):** Anglo Japanese Construction Joint Venture |

中国桥梁 1949—2024　　　　　　　　　　　　　　　　　　　　　　　　　　　　　BRIDGES IN CHINA

青马大桥位于香港特别行政区，是连接葵青区青衣岛与荃湾区马湾岛的主要通道，大桥东起青衣岛，上跨马湾海峡，西至马湾岛。青马大桥为公铁两用双层桥面悬索桥。全长2.16km，上层为双向六车道城市快速路，设计速度100km/h，下层为双线铁路，设计速度135km/h。

主桥为双塔两跨吊公铁两用钢桁梁悬索桥，主跨跨径1377m。主缆跨径布置为455m+1377m+300m，垂跨比约1/10.8。钢桁加劲梁桥面宽41m，梁高约7.6m。主缆采用Ø5.38镀锌钢丝，空中纺丝法施工，直径达1.1m。吊索采用钢丝绳吊索，每个吊点设2根吊索，钢丝绳吊索公称直径为76mm，吊索间距18m。桥塔采用门式钢筋混凝土结构，塔高206m。青衣塔基础为支承于基岩上的扩大基础，马湾塔采用沉井基础，并筑人工岛以防船舶撞击。两岸均采用重力式锚碇，青衣锚碇挖土深度达到50m，马湾锚碇大部分被埋置。

加劲梁采用流线型中央开孔钢桁架结构，流线型加上独特的中央通风隙设计，有效地降低了加劲梁底面风致压差，大大提高了气动稳定性。施工中采用安装在主缆上的钢绞线起重机，吊装重达10000kN的加劲梁组件，大大提高了吊装能力，缩减了吊装工时。大桥内安装了桥梁结构健康监测系统，可以实时监测桥梁健康变化和进行结构评估。

Tsing Ma Bridge, located in Hong Kong Special Administrative Region, is the primary link connecting Tsing-Yi Island in Kwai-Tsing District with Ma-Wan Island in Tsuen-Wan District. The bridge starts from Tsing-Yi Island in the east, crosses Ma-Wan Strait, then ends at Ma-Wan Island in the west. Tsing Ma Bridge is a highway and railway double-deck bridge. The bridge is 2.16km in length, and has six highway lanes in dual directions on the upper deck, designed for a speed of 100km/h, as well as a double-track railway on the lower deck, designed for a speed of 135km/h.

The main bridge is a double-tower double-suspended-span highway-railway suspension bridge with a steel-truss girder. The main span of the bridge is 1,377m, with the span arrangement of the main cable 455m+1377m+300m. The sag-to-span ratio is approximately 1/10.8. The steel-truss stiffening girder has a width of 41m and a depth of around

7.6m. The main cables were formed by the aerial spinning technique with $\phi$ 5.38 galvanized steel wires, and have an overall diameter of approximately 1.1 m. The hangers consist of steel wire rope hangers, and two rope hangers for each hanging point. The steel wire rope hangers have a nominal diameter of 76mm, and the spacing between hangers is set as 18m. The tower is a portal frame reinforced concrete structure with a height of 206m. Tsing-Yi tower is anchored by a spread foundation resting upon bedrock, while the tower on Ma-Wan side employs a caisson foundation, complemented by an artificial island to provide resistance against ship collisions. Gravity anchorages are utilized on both banks of the bridge. The anchorage on Tsing-Yi side involves an excavation depth of up to 50m, and the majority of the anchorage on Ma-Wan side is buried.

The stiffening girder adopts a streamlined steel-truss structure with a central air-gap. The aerodynamic design, i.e., the streamlined shape and provision of an air gap at the center, has effectively reduced wind-induced pressure differences on the underside of the main deck, significantly enhancing its aerodynamic stability. The cable crane installed on the main cable was used to hoist stiffening girder segments, which weighed up to 10,000kN, thus greatly enhancing the hoisting capacity and reducing the hoisting time. A bridge structural health monitoring system was installed, enabling real-time monitoring of the bridge state change and structural assessment.

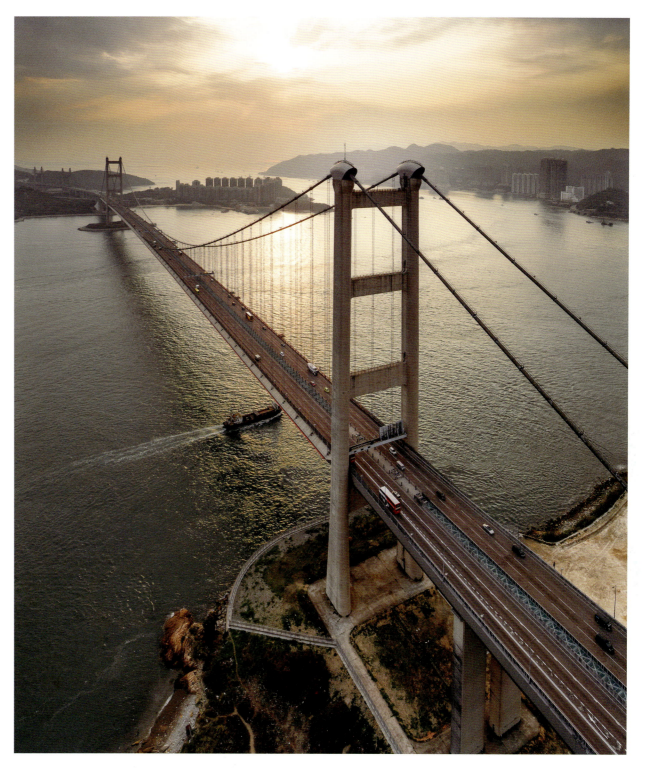

# 虎门珠江大桥
## Humen Bridge over Pearl River

虎门珠江大桥位于广东省珠江出海口，横跨狮子洋水域，东接东莞市虎门镇，西接番禺市南沙镇，全长4.6km，设双向六车道。

主桥为双塔单跨钢箱梁悬索桥，主跨跨径888m。主缆跨径布置为302m+888m+348.5m，垂跨比为1/10.5。加劲梁采用流线型扁平钢箱梁，宽35.6m，高4m。主缆采用127∅5.2高强镀锌钢丝索股，每根主缆110股，标准强度1600MPa。主缆间距为33m，吊索标准间距12m。桥塔采用钢筋混凝土门式框架结构，塔高147.55m，东塔基础为钻孔灌注桩，西塔基础上游部分为扩大基础，下游部分为钻孔灌注桩。两岸均采用重力式锚碇。

加劲梁采用扁平钢箱梁节段间全焊接的结构形式，解决了在箱梁吊装情况下的焊缝间隙调整工艺和焊接问题。通过气弹性风洞试验，对施工期间与成桥后的抗风性能进行了分析，提出了钢箱梁拼装过程中的抗风技术措施，保证了大桥的抗风稳定性。本桥为国内首次在钢箱梁和锚室内采用自动除湿系统。

追赶与自主 1980—1999

Humen Bridge over Pearl River, located in the Pearl River estuary of Guangdong Province, serves as a vital connection, linking Humen Town of Dongguan City in the east with Nansha Town of Panyu City in the west by crossing the waters of Shiziyang Ocean. The total length of the bridge is 4.6km with 6 traffic lanes in dual directions.

The main bridge is a double-tower single-suspended-span suspension bridge with a steel-box girder. The main span of the bridge is 888m, with the span arrangement of main cable 302m+888m+348.5m. The sag-to-span ratio is 1/10.5. The stiffening girder employs a streamlined flat steel box section with a 35.6m width and a 4m depth. Both main cables adopt 110 parallel wire bundles, and each bundle includes 127$\phi$5.2 galvanized steel wires with standard strength of 1,600MPa. The horizontal spacing between two main cables is set as 33m, and the longitudinal standard spacing between hangers is set as 12m. The tower is a portal frame reinforced concrete structure with a height of 147.55m. The eastern tower is supported by drilled-and-grouted piles. The spread foundation is adopted for the upstream part of the western tower, and the drilled-and-grouted piles are used for the downstream part. Gravity type anchorages are adopted on both banks.

The stiffening girder employs a fully welded design between the segments, addressing the issues of weld gap adjustment and welding techniques during girder hoisting. Based on the wind tunnel tests, the wind resistance performance under construction and operation has been analyzed, and technical measures were proposed to improve the wind resistance during the assembly of steel box girders. An automated air dehumidification system inside the steel box girders and anchor chambers was used for the first time in China.

桥　　名：虎门珠江大桥
桥　　型：双塔单跨吊钢箱梁悬索桥
主跨径：888m
桥　　址：广东省东莞市
建成时间：1997年6月
设计单位：中交公路规划设计院
施工单位：广东省公路工程总公司

Name: Humen Bridge over Pearl River
Type: Double-tower single-suspended-span suspension bridge with steel-box girder
Main span: 888m
Location: Dongguan City, Guangdong Province
Completion: June 1997
Designer(s): CCCC Highway Planning & Design Institute
Contractor(s): Guangdong Provincial Highway Engineering Company

# 万州长江大桥
## Wanzhou Bridge over Yangtze River

| | |
|---|---|
| 桥　　名：万州长江大桥 | **Name:** Wanzhou Bridge over Yangtze River |
| 桥　　型：钢筋混凝土拱桥 | **Type:** Reinforced-concrete arch bridge |
| 主跨跨径：420m | **Main span:** 420m |
| 桥　　址：重庆市 | **Location:** Chongqing City |
| 建成时间：1997年6月 | **Completion:** June 1997 |
| 设计单位：四川省公路规划勘测设计研究院 | **Designer(s):** Sichuan Highway Planning, Survey, Design and Research Institute |
| 施工单位：四川省公路桥梁建设集团总公司 | **Constructor(s):** Sichuan Highway and Bridge Construction Group Co., Ltd. |

万州长江大桥，原名万县长江大桥，位于重庆市万州区，是连接318国道线的一座特大型公路桥梁，主跨跨径420m，建成时为世界上跨度最大的钢筋混凝土拱桥，设双向四车道。

主桥为上承式钢筋混凝土拱桥，全长814m，桥面宽度24m，矢跨比1/5。大桥主拱圈采用悬链线轴线，为单箱三室截面。拱箱的高度7m、宽度16m，采用钢管混凝土桁架拱为劲性骨架，外包C60混凝土；桁架拱横向由5片组成，其上下弦杆采用直径400mm、壁厚16mm的钢管并内灌混凝土，腹杆与横联采用4根75mm×75mm×10mm的角钢和4根直径20mm的钢筋。拱上建筑为全空腹式结构，采用双立柱加盖梁和14跨预应力混凝土简支T梁结构，各跨桥面铺装纵向连续。大桥采用缆索吊装、斜拉扣索法先形成两铰钢管桁架拱，钢管内灌注混凝土后以钢管混凝土桁架拱为劲性骨架，分层分段浇筑箱拱，最后形成组合截面拱圈。

lower chords of the truss arch adopt the steel tubular with a diameter of 400mm and a thickness of 16mm, filled with concrete. The web and transverse braces adopt four angle-steel members of 75mm×75mm×10mm and four rebars with a diameter of 20mm. The arch spandrel is open, with two columns, along with cap beams and 14-span prestressed concrete simply-supported T-beam structures. The pavement layer of each span is longitudinally continuous. The bridge adopted the cable hoisting with stayed buckle cables to form a two-hinged steel tubular truss arch first; the concrete-filled steel tubular truss arch was then used as the stiff skeleton after being filled with concrete; the box arch rib was sequentially poured in multi-layers and multi-segments, finally forming the composite arch.

The design of this bridge has paid more attention to the impact of the sequential construction of the arch structure on the bridge's conditions, particularly regarding shrinkage and creep effects. Computational methods were developed to account for issues including shrinkage, creep, as well as geometric and material nonlinearities.

The Project of Wanzhou Bridge over Yangtze River won the First Prize of National Science and Technology Progress Award.

万州长江大桥设计中，解决了拱圈截面逐次形成时混凝土收缩、徐变对结构受力影响的难题，提出了劲性骨架拱桥的混凝土收缩、徐变、几何与材料非线性等因素的分析方法。

万州长江大桥工程获得了国家科技进步奖一等奖。

Wanzhou Bridge over Yangtze River, originally named as Wanxian Bridge over Yangtze River, located in Wanzhou District of Chongqing City, is a grand highway bridge connecting the 318 National Highway. The total length of the bridge is 814m, with four traffic lanes in dual directions.

The main bridge is a deck-type reinforced-concrete arch bridge, with a main span of 420m, a deck width of 24m and a rise-to-span ratio of 1/5. The arch axis is designed as a catenary curve, and the arch structure features a triple-cell box section. The derth of the arch box is 7m and the width is 16m. The concrete-filled steel tubular truss arch is used as the stiff skeleton, with C60 concrete encasement. This truss arch is transversely composed of five pieces. The upper and

# 江阴长江大桥

## Jiangyin Bridge over Yangtze River

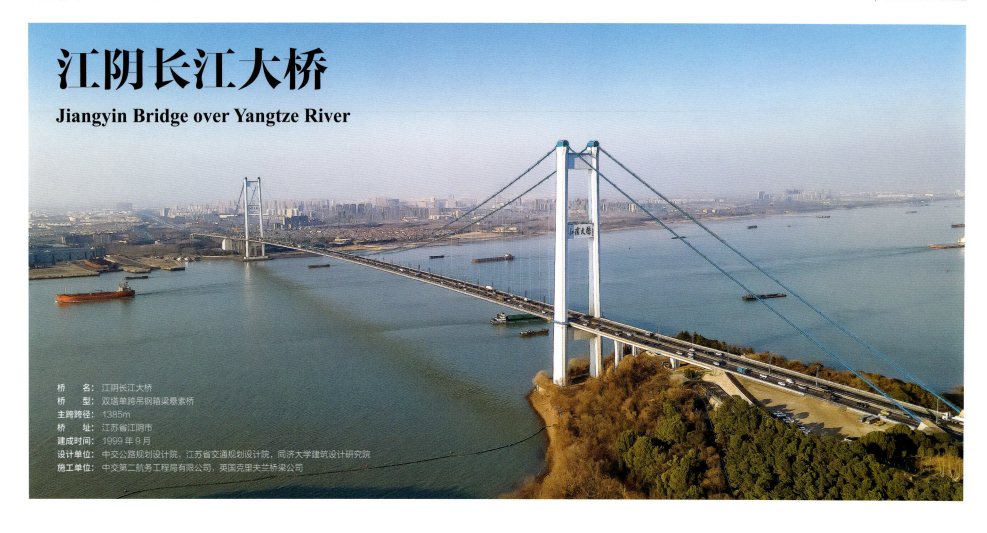

桥　　名：江阴长江大桥
桥　　型：双塔单跨吊钢箱梁悬索桥
主跨跨径：1385m
桥　　址：江苏省江阴市
建成时间：1999年9月
设计单位：中交公路规划设计院，江苏省交通规划设计院，同济大学建筑设计研究院
施工单位：中交第二航务工程局有限公司，英国克里夫兰桥梁公司

江阴长江大桥位于江苏省江阴市，北起靖江南互通，南至江阴北互通，全长3km，设双向六车道。

主桥为双塔单跨吊钢箱梁悬索桥，主跨跨径1385m。主缆跨径布置为336.5m+1385m+309.34m，垂跨比1/10.5。加劲梁采用流线型扁平钢箱梁，宽36.9m，高3.0m。主缆采用127Φ5.35镀锌平行钢丝索股，边、中跨主缆分别为177股、169股，标准强度1600MPa。吊索间距16m，每个吊点设2根吊索，由预制平行镀锌钢丝束股组成，短吊索则采用钢丝绳以增加其柔性。桥塔采用双室箱形塔柱、三道预应力混凝土双室箱形横梁组成的框架式结构，塔高190m。南塔采用24根直径2.8m的嵌岩钻孔桩基础，北塔采用96根直径2.0m的支承桩基础。南锚为嵌岩重力式锚碇，北锚为重力式锚碇，采用深埋沉井基础。

该桥边跨主缆和中跨主缆采用不同索股数量，提高了全桥刚度，节省了主缆用钢量。采用特大型整体沉井基础作为大跨悬索桥的锚碇基础，首节沉井采用钢壳混凝土，利用土模支承，以利沉井下沉。主缆锚固系统采用了预应力钢绞线，充分利用预应力束受力和布置灵活的特点，采用了非放射型布置，最大限度地减小了后锚面的尺寸和锚碇基础的规模和难度，加快了施工进度。

Jiangyin Bridge over Yangtze River, located in Jiangyin City of Jiangsu Province, starts from Jingjiang South Interchange in the north, and ends at Jiangyin North Interchange in the south. The total length of the bridge is 3km with six traffic lanes in dual directions.

The main bridge is a double-tower single-suspended-span suspension bridge with a steel-box girder. The main span of the bridge is 1,385m, and the span arrangement of the main cable is 336.5m+1,385m+309.34m. The sag-to-span ratio is 1/10.5. The stiffening girder features a streamlined flat steel

**Name:** Jiangyin Bridge over Yangtze River
**Type:** Double-tower single-suspended-span suspension bridge with steel-box girder
**Main span:** 1,385m
**Location:** Jiangyin City, Jiangsu Province
**Completion:** September 1999
**Designer(s):** CCCC Highway Planning & Design Institute, Jiangsu Provincial Communications Planning and Design Institute, Tongji Architectural Design Institute.
**Contractor(s):** CCCC Second Harbor Engineering Company Ltd., CHEC, Cleveland Bridge Co., Ltd.

box section with a 36.9m width and a 3.0m depth. The main cables in the middle span and those in the side span adopt 177 and 169 parallel wire bundles, respectively, and each bundle includes 127$\phi$5.4 galvanized steel wires with standard strength of 1,600MPa. The longitudinal spacing between hangers is 16m. Two hangers, made of prefabricated parallel galvanized wire strands, are set at each hanging point, while steel wire rope slings are used for short hangers to increase their flexibility. The tower, 190m in height, features a frame structure, composed of double-cell box-shaped columns and three-dimensional-prestressed double-cell concrete box crossbeams. The southern tower is supported by 24$\phi$2.8m rock-socketed drilled-and-grouted piles, and the northern tower is supported by 96$\phi$2.0m point-bearing piles. The southern anchorage is designed as a gravity type embedded in rock, and the northern anchorage is designed as a gravity type supported by a deeply-buried caisson foundation.

The main cables in the main span and that in the side spans are designed with different number of bundles in order to enhance the bridge stiffness and save the steel cost. The super-large caisson foundation has been employed as the anchorage foundation. The first segment of the caisson adopts concrete-filled steel-shell, supported by the soil mold, therefore facilitating the caisson sinking. The main cable anchoring system uses prestressed steel strands, fully utilizing the characteristics of prestressed bundles in terms of force application and flexible arrangement. A non-radial layout has been adopted to minimize the size of the rear anchoring surface, and to reduce the scale and difficulty of the anchorage foundation, thereby accelerating the construction progress.

BRIDGES IN CHINA

中 国 桥 梁

# 发展与图强
DEVELOPMENT AND STRENGTHENING

2000

2009

# 引 言

随着改革开放的不断深入，中国国民经济持续大幅增长，催生了各地区、各部门对交通发展和桥梁建设的迫切需求。一方面经济发展需要建设更多的桥梁等交通基础设施，另一方面经济增长提供了更多的桥梁建设资金和政策环境，全国掀起了桥梁建设的高潮。

中国现代桥梁技术在20世纪最后20年通过自主建设取得了令世人惊叹的进步和成就，与发达国家一起跨入了面向21世纪更加宏伟的跨江跨海大桥工程建设高潮中。在21世纪最初10年，不仅继续拓展大江、大河上大跨度桥梁建设，而且走向海洋跨入了长大跨海桥梁建设的新时代，通过设计和施工技术创新，实现了跨越式发展，大大提升了中国桥梁的国际知名度和竞争力。

在跨大江、大河的大跨度铁路桥梁建设方面，建成了跨越长江的公铁两用斜拉桥——芜湖长江大桥和天兴洲长江大桥；在大跨度公路拱桥建设方面，先后建成了世界最大跨径的石拱桥——丹河大桥、世界最大跨径的拱桥——上海卢浦大桥和重庆朝天门长江大桥等，卢浦大桥第一次获得了国际桥梁与结构协会杰出结构奖；在大跨度斜拉桥建设方面，相继建成了南京大胜关长江大桥、苏通长江公路大桥和香港昂船洲大桥，其中苏通长江公路大桥再次创造了斜拉桥跨径的世界纪录；在大跨度梁桥建设方面，建成了创造并保持世界跨径纪录的重庆石板坡长江大桥复线桥；在大跨度悬索桥建设方面，建成了润扬长江公路大桥和西堠门大桥，后者是世界上第一座分体钢箱梁悬索桥，建成时也是世界上跨径最大的钢箱梁悬索桥；在跨海大桥建设方面，先后建成了世界最长的跨海桥梁——东海大桥和杭州湾跨海大桥等。

21世纪最初10年，中国建成大跨度公路和铁路桥梁，梁桥、拱桥、斜拉桥和悬索桥建设全面开花，长大跨海桥梁不断涌现。本章选取了中国大跨度铁路或公铁两用桥梁3座，大跨度拱桥3座、斜拉桥3座、悬索桥3座，长大跨海桥梁2座和大跨度梁桥1座。多座拱桥、梁桥、斜拉桥和跨海大桥的跨径或长度都创造了新的世界纪录，标志着中国已经成为了名副其实的大跨度桥梁建设大国。

# INTRODUCTION

As the Reform and Opening-up deepened in China, the national economy experienced sustained and substantial growth, which in turn spurred an urgent demand for the development of transportation infrastructure and bridge construction across various regions and sectors. On the one hand, economic development necessitated the construction of more bridges and other transportation infrastructure. On the other hand, economic growth provided increased funding and a favorable policy environment for bridge construction, leading to a nationwide surge in bridge building activity.

In the last two decades of the 20th century, China's modern bridge technology made astonishing progress and and achieved extraordinary results through independent construction. This placed China alongside developed countries at the beginning of a grand era of building monumental cross-river and cross-sea bridges in the 21st century. In the first decade of the 21st century, China not only continued to expand the construction of long-span bridges over major rivers but also ventured into the new era of constructing long-span bridges across seas. Through innovations in design and construction techniques, China made great strides in the development in bridge engineering, significantly enhancing the international recognition and competitiveness of Chinese bridges. This period marked a transformative phase of bridge engineering in China, showcasing its capabilities in tackling complex and large-scale bridge projects.

In the realm of long-span railway bridge construction over major rivers, several notable bridges were completed, including the Wuhu Bridge over the Yangtze River and the Tianxingzhou Bridge over the Yangtze River, both of which are road-rail cable-stayed bridges. In this period, the world's longest span stone arch bridge, the Danhe Bridge, was built, along with the Shanghai Lupu Bridge and the Chongqing Chaotianmen Bridge over the Yangtze River, which both held the record for the world's longest span arch bridge of any type. Notably, the Lupu Bridge was the first Chinese bridge to receive the Outstanding Structure Award by the International Association for Bridge and Structural Engineering. For long-span cable-stayed bridge construction, notable achievements include the completion of the Nanjing Dashengguan Bridge over the Yangtze River, the Sutong Highway Bridge over the Yangtze River, and the Hong Kong Stonecutters Bridge. The Sutong Highway Bridge over the Yangtze River set a new world record for the span of cable-stayed bridges. In the realm of long-span girder bridge construction, the Chongqing Shibanpo Parallel Bridge over the Yangtze River set and still maintains the world record for span length. In the construction of long-span suspension bridges, the Runyang Highway Bridge over the Yangtze River and the Xihoumen Bridge were completed, with the latter being the first steel twin-box girder suspension bridge in the world and the longest span steel box girder suspension bridge at the time of its completion. Regarding sea-crossing bridge construction, the longest sea-crossing bridges in the world, the Donghai Bridge and the Hangzhou Bay Sea-crossing Bridge, were built. Both bridges represent remarkable achievements in China's bridge construction history.

In the first decade of the 21st century, China witnessed the completion of a significant number of long-span bridges for both highways and railways. The construction of girder bridges, arch bridges, cable-stayed bridges, suspension bridges, and extensive sea-crossing bridges flourished during this period. This chapter highlights a selection of these engineering marvels: three long-span railway or road-rail bridges, four long-span arch bridges, three cable-stayed bridges, three suspension bridges, two long sea-crossing bridges, and one long-span girder bridge. Several of these arch bridges, girder bridges, cable-stayed bridges, and sea-crossing bridges set new world records in terms of span length or total length. These achievements underscore China's status as a true powerhouse in the construction of long-span bridges and reflect China's significant advancements and leadership in bridge engineering and construction on a global scale.

# 丹河大桥

## Dan River Bridge

| | |
|---|---|
| 桥　名： | 丹河大桥 |
| 桥　型： | 上承式石板拱桥 |
| 主跨跨径： | 146m |
| 桥　址： | 山西省晋城市 |
| 建成时间： | 2000年7月 |
| 设计单位： | 中交第一公路勘察设计研究院 |
| 施工单位： | 中铁第十七工程局第四工程处和晋城公路分局二处 |

丹河大桥位于太行山脉南端，山西省晋城市泽州县珏山脚下，是晋焦高速公路上的一座特大型桥梁。大桥主跨146m，是世界上跨径最大的石拱桥。大桥全长413.17m，主桥结构高度为81.6m，桥面宽度24.8m，按双向四车道高速公路布置。

丹河大桥为上承式石板拱桥，跨径布置为2×30m+146m+5×30m，矢跨比1/4.5。主拱圈采用悬链线轴线，矢高为32.44m，变厚度石砌板形截面，拱顶厚度2.5m、拱脚厚度3.5m，拱脚与拱座固结；拱上建筑采用全空腹式构造，拱式腹孔，边腹孔设三铰拱，腹孔墩为横向分离双柱式构造；拱上桥面系轻质蒸压粉煤灰加气混凝土。主跨设置单向推力墩，桥台采用石砌重力式明挖扩大基础。丹河大桥主拱圈施工采用了钢构架与木拱盔组合拱架，高度约为80m，钢构架下设置组合楔块卸架装置。拱架上主拱圈的拱石采用小石子混凝土分环分段砌筑施工。

作为世界最大跨径石拱桥，丹河大桥建设克服了许多关键技术问题。丹河大桥被列入吉尼斯世界纪录。

Dan River Bridge is located at the south end of the Taihang Mountains, at the foot of Jueshan in Zezhou County, Jincheng City, Shanxi Province. It connects Jincheng-Jiaozuo Expressway with a main span of 146m and is the world's longest stone arch bridge. The total length of the bridge is 413.17m, with a main structure height of 81.6m and a bridge deck width of 24.8m, configured for a double-deck, four-lane highway.

Dan River Bridge is a stone slab deck-arch bridge with a span arrangement of 2×30m+146m+5×30m and a rise-to-span ratio of 1/4.5. The main arch adopts a catenary arch axis, with a rise height of 32.44m. This stone masonry arch has a plate section with variable thickness, 2.5m at the arch crown and 3.5m at both arch feet. Both arch feet are firmly set to the abutment. The spandrel structure utilizes a fully hollow structure with an open spandrel arch, and the side spandrels are three-hinge arches. The piers for the spandrel arches are laterally separated double-column structures. The lightweight steam-pressured fly ash aerated concrete was used as filler for the spandrel bridge deck. The main span incorporates a mono-direction thrust resistance pier, and the abutments adopt stone masonry gravity-type open-cut foundations. The construction of the main arch ribs of Dan River Bridge utilized a combination of steel frames and wooden arch helmets with a height of approximately 80m, and a disassembling equipment with combined wedges was installed beneath the steel frame. The arch blocks for the main arch ring were constructed in segments using small stone aggregate concrete.

As the world's longest-span stone arch bridge, its construction technologies overcame numerous critical challenges. Dan River Bridge has been included in the Guinness World Records.

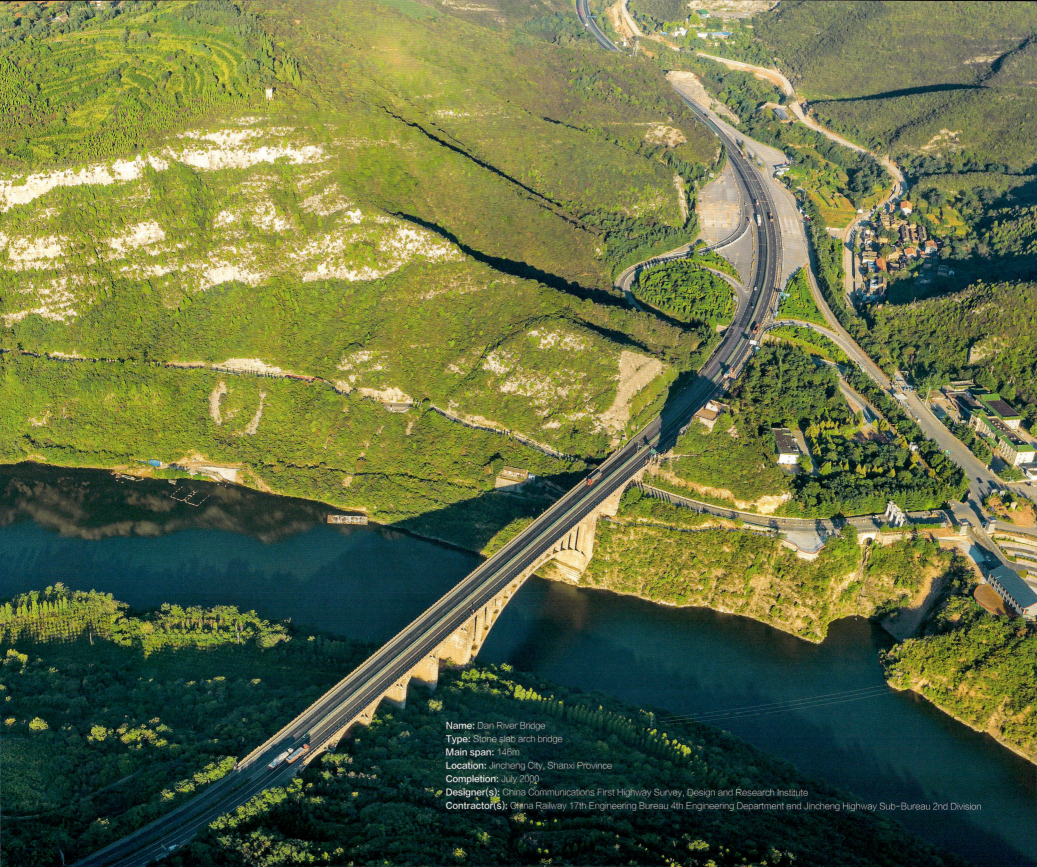

**Name:** Dan River Bridge
**Type:** Stone slab arch bridge
**Main span:** 146m
**Location:** Jincheng City, Shanxi Province
**Completion:** July 2000
**Designer(s):** China Communications First Highway Survey, Design and Research Institute
**Contractor(s):** China Railway 17th Engineering Bureau 4th Engineering Department and Jincheng Highway Sub-Bureau 2nd Division

# 芜湖长江大桥
## Wuhu Bridge over Yangtze River

| | | |
|---|---|---|
| 桥　名： | 芜湖长江大桥 | **Name:** Wuhu Bridge over Yangtze River |
| 桥　型： | 低塔钢桁梁斜拉桥 | **Type:** Low tower steel truss girder cable-stayed bridge |
| 主跨跨径： | 312m | **Main span:** 312m |
| 桥　址： | 安徽省芜湖市和巢湖市 | **Location:** Wuhu City and Chaohu City, Anhui Province |
| 建成时间： | 2000年9月 | **Completion:** September 2000 |
| 设计单位： | 中铁大桥勘测设计院 | **Designer(s):** China Railway Major Bridge Reconnaissance & Design Institute |
| 施工单位： | 中铁大桥局集团有限公司 | **Constructor(s):** China Railway Major Bridge Engineering Group Co., Ltd. |

　　芜湖长江大桥位于安徽省芜湖市和巢湖市之间，为双层公铁两用桥，上层为线路长度5.681km的四车道公路桥，下层为线路长度10.521km的双线铁路桥。

　　芜湖长江大桥主桥为主跨312m的双塔双索面钢桁梁低塔斜拉桥。主桥公路桥面采用与钢桁梁上弦杆结合的钢筋混凝土板，桥塔采用钢筋混凝土结构，承台顶面以上塔高分别为112m和100m，其中公路桥面以上两塔塔高均为33m。芜湖长江大桥建成时主跨钢桁梁跨径达到同类公铁两用桥梁世界最大跨度，在净空受限制的情况下，以低塔结构设计解决了大跨度桥梁的受力问题。首次采用14MnNbq厚板焊接整体节点，主桥钢桁梁采用双向对称悬臂架设，并运用了当时新型的钢筋混凝土桥面板与钢桁梁结合技术。中跨主梁施工采用双铰合龙技术，使钢桁梁跨中迅速、精确合龙。

　　芜湖长江大桥大跨度低塔斜拉桥板桁组合结构建造技术获得了国家科技进步奖一等奖。

Wuhu Bridge over Yangtze River is a double deck highway and railway bridge situated between Wuhu City and Chaohu City in Anhui Province. The upper deck is a 5.681km-long, 4-lane in dual directions highway bridge, while the lower deck is a 10.521km-long double-track railway bridge.

The main bridge is a dual-tower, double cable plane, steel truss girder cable-stayed bridge with low towers with a main span of 312m. The bridge towers are reinforced concrete structures, with the heights above the pile cap of 112m and 100m for the east and west towers, respectively. Both towers above the road deck are 33m in height. The upper deck is reinforced concrete deck combined with the top chords of the steel truss girder. The main span truss girder of the bridge held the world record among highway and railway bridges at the time of its completion. Under the constrained clearance conditions, low towers successfully solved the structural challenges for such a long-span bridge. The welded monolithic joints for 14MnNbq steel thick plate were adopted first time in China. The novel technology was employed for connecting the steel truss with the reinforced concrete road deck. The main truss girder was erected using a two-way symmetrical cantilever construction method. A double-hinge joint technology was applied to enable rapid and precise alignment of the steel truss girder of center span.

The Construction Technology for Wuhu Bridge over Yangtze River won the First Prize of National Science and Technology Progress Award.

DEVELOPMENT AND STRENGTHENING | 发展与图强 2000—2009

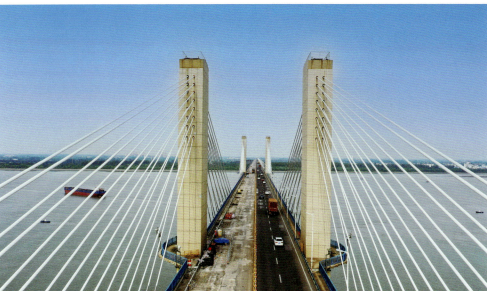

# 上海卢浦大桥
## Shanghai Lupu Bridge

| | |
|---|---|
| 桥　名： | 上海卢浦大桥 |
| 桥　型： | 中承式钢箱拱肋拱桥 |
| 主跨跨径： | 550m |
| 桥　址： | 上海市 |
| 建成时间： | 2003年6月 |
| 设计单位： | 上海市政工程设计研究院，上海市城市建设设计研究院 |
| 施工单位： | 上海建工集团股份有限公司 |

**Name:** Shanghai Lupu Bridge
**Type:** Steel box rib arch bridge
**Main span:** 550m
**Location:** Shanghai City
**Completion:** June 2003
**Designer(s):** Shanghai Municipal Engineering Design Institute, Shanghai Urban Construction Design and Research Institute
**Constructor(s):** Shanghai Construction Group Co., Ltd.

| 发展与图强 2000—2009

  卢浦大桥是一座横跨上海黄浦江的大跨度拱桥，西岸与南北高架相连，东岸与外环线相通，主跨550m，建成时是世界上最大跨径的拱桥。大桥桥面采用双向六车道城市快速路布置，桥面使用宽度为29.8m，桥下通航净空46m×340m。

  卢浦大桥主桥为中承式钢箱系杆拱桥，跨径布置为100m+550m+100m，矢跨比为1/5.5。大桥采用双钢箱拱肋构造，拱平面向内倾斜度为1:5，拱的矢高为100m，拱箱的宽度为5m、高度从跨中的6m 增加到拱脚的9m，采用陀螺形截面。桥面以上双拱肋横向由25根一字形风撑连接，桥面以下设置8个K形横向连接。主梁采用正交异性桥面板钢箱梁，主跨为分离双边箱构造，边跨为单箱多室构造。恒载水平推力由设置在钢箱梁两侧顶面的32根水平拉索承担，拉索锚固于边跨尾端。全桥共采用每组4根、28组吊杆，拱上立柱8对，钢箱梁通过吊杆或立柱支承在拱肋上。大桥除拱肋合龙段采用一端栓接、一端焊接外，其余拱肋、立柱和加劲梁均采用焊接。卢浦大桥主桥的边跨拱肋、加劲梁及主跨桥面以下的拱肋，均在支架上拼装，两侧形成锚孔后，采用临时塔架悬臂吊装桥面以上的拱肋，拱肋合龙后张拉临时水平拉索，利用吊杆拼装主跨箱梁节段，主梁合龙后将临时水平拉索转换为永久拉索，形成系杆拱结构。

  上海卢浦大桥设计与施工关键技术研究获得了国家科技进步奖二等奖，并且是中国第一个获得国际桥梁与结构工程协会杰出结构奖的桥梁。

Lupu Bridge is a long-span arch bridge spanning the Huangpu River in Shanghai with the main span of 550m. It connects the North-South Elevated Road on the west bank to the Outer Ring Road on the east bank. At the time of completion, it held the span record for the world's longest arch bridge. The bridge is an urban expressway with six lanes in dual directions, the deck width is 29.8m, and the navigational clearance beneath the bridge is 46m × 340m.

The main span of Lupu Bridge is a half-through steel box arch bridge with a span arrangement of 100m+550m+100m and a rise-to-span ratio of 1/5.5. The bridge employs double steel box arch ribs, inclined inward in transversal direction at a ratio of 1:5, with an arch rise of 100m. Each arch box has a gyroscopic-shaped cross-section with a width of 5m, and the box depth rises from 6m at the crown to 9m at both feet. The double arch ribs above the bridge deck are connected by 25 straight wind bracings, and other 8 K-shaped transverse connections are installed below the bridge deck. The main steel girder has an orthotropic deck panel, with a separated double-side box structure for the main span and a single-box multi-cell structure for the side spans. The horizontal thrust from dead load is balanced by 32 horizontal steel tendons located on the top side surfaces of the steel box girder, anchored at the ends of both side spans. The entire girder is supported on the arch ribs by 28 sets of suspenders and 8 pairs of columns. During the construction, the regular arch rib sections were welded to each other except for the closure sections which were bolted. The construction of the side span arch ribs and stiffening beams, as well as the main span arch ribs below the deck employed the full scaffold method. Once forming anchor holes on both sides, temporary tower cranes were used to hoist the arch ribs above the bridge deck. After the closure of the main arch ribs, temporary horizontal tendons were tensioned and the main span box girder segments were lifted by utilizing the suspenders. Then the temporary horizontal tendons were replaced by the permanent ones after the main girder closed.

The Design and Construction Key Technology of Shanghai Lupu Bridge was awarded with the Second Prize of National Science and Technology Progress Award. Lupu Bridge also won the Outstanding Structure Award of International Association for Bridge and Structural Engineering as the first bridge in China.

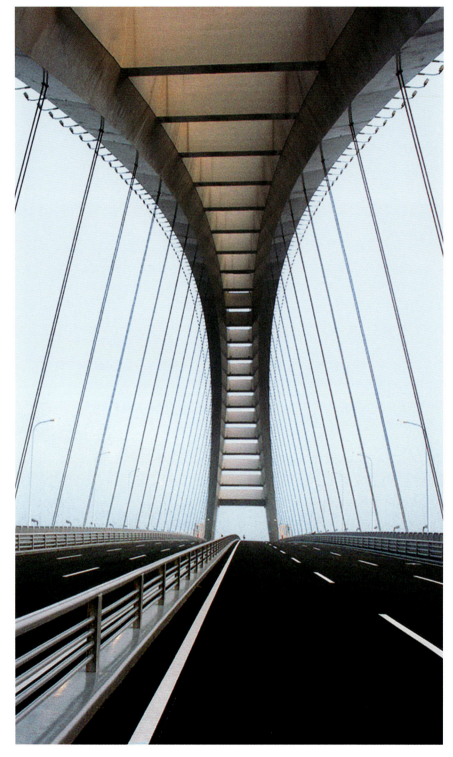

# 润扬长江公路大桥
## Runyang Highway Bridge over Yangtze River

润扬长江公路大桥位于长江江苏段，北起扬州市，南接镇江市，全长 35.66km，设双向六车道。

南汊桥主桥为双塔单跨吊钢箱梁悬索桥，主跨跨径 1490m，桥面净宽 32.5m。钢箱梁总宽 38.7m，梁中心高 3.0m。主缆跨径布置为 470m+1490m+470m，主跨垂跨比 1/10，采用 127ϕ5.3 预制平行钢丝索股，每根主缆 184 股；吊索纵向间距为 16.1m，采用平行钢丝束索股。桥塔采用钢筋混凝土式门式框架结构，塔高 210m，采用钻孔灌注桩基础。南、北锚碇均为重力式锚碇、预应力锚固系统。

润扬长江公路大桥主缆采用刚性中央扣，以改善结构性能并减轻短吊索弯折，用中央稳定板提高大桥的抗风稳定性，施工猫道不设抗风索，采用干空气除湿防护来提高主缆的耐久性。润扬长江公路大桥两岸均是开阔的软土地基，因此锚碇施工非常困难。经过专家反复论证，确定采用矩形地下连续墙施工方案。南锚碇基坑施工采用大型排桩冻结围护技术，同时在冻土侧浇筑 140 根钻孔灌注桩，以承受挡土压力。排桩冻结施工法实现了排桩和冻结两大施工工艺的首次结合，成为世界建桥技术史上的突破。北锚碇采用矩形地下连续墙支护结构。

Runyang Highway Bridge over Yangtze River, having a total length of 35.66km and featuring six lanes in dual directions, is located in Jiangsu Province connecting Yangzhou City in the north bank and Zhenjiang City in the south bank.

The main bridge crossing the southern branch of the Yangtze River is a double-tower single-suspended-span suspension bridge with a main span of 1,490m and a deck width of 32.5m. The bridge girder is a 38.7m wide and 3.0m deep steel box. The sag-to-span ratio of the main cables is 1/10. Each main cable consists of 184 parallel wire bundles, and each bundle includes 127ϕ5.3 steel wires. The hangers are made with parallel wire bundles. The towers supported by bored piles are portal frame shape structures with a height of 210m. Both the northern and southern anchor blocks are gravity anchorages with prestressing anchorage systems.

The main features of the bridge are the rigid central clamps applied on the main cable to improve the structural performance and to reduce the bending moment of short hanger rods, the central stabilizer plates to improve the wind-resistant stability, the construction catwalks without wind-resistant cables, and the development of a cable dehumidification system to improve the durability of main cables. Both banks of the bridge are expansive soft soil foundations, making anchorage construction challenging. After expert analysis, a rectangular continuous underground wall construction plan was chosen. For the south anchorage pit construction, a large-scale sheet pile freezing protection technique was adopted. Simultaneously, 140 bored piles were cast on the frozen soil side to withstand earth pressure. This method, for the first time, realized the combination of sheet piles and freezing construction, and achieved a breakthrough in the history of world bridge construction technology. The north anchorage adopts a rectangular continuous underground wall support structure.

| | |
|---|---|
| 桥　名： | 润扬长江公路大桥 |
| 桥　型： | 双塔单跨吊钢箱梁悬索桥 |
| 主跨跨径： | 1490m |
| 桥　址： | 江苏省镇江市和扬州市 |
| 建成时间： | 2005年4月 |
| 设计单位： | 江苏省交通规划设计院股份有限公司 |
| 施工单位： | 中交第二公路工程局有限公司，中交第二航务工程局有限公司，中交第三航务工程局有限公司 |

**Name:** Runyang Highway Bridge over Yangtze River
**Type:** Double-tower single-suspended-span suspension bridge with steel box girder
**Main span:** 1,490m
**Location:** Zhenjiang City and Yangzhou City, Jiangsu Province
**Completion:** April 2005
**Designer(s):** Jiangsu Provincial Communication Planning and Design Institute Co., Ltd.
**Contractor(s):** CCCC Second Highway Engineering Co., Ltd., CCCC Second Harbor Engineering Company Ltd., CCCC Third Harbor Engineering Co., Ltd.

# 东海大桥
## East Sea Bridge

东海大桥起于上海南汇区芦潮港，跨越杭州湾东北部海域，连接洋山岛，是上海国际航运中心洋山深水港区唯一陆路集疏运通道，大桥全长32.5km，包括陆上段3.7km，海上段25.3km，港桥连接段3.5km。其中，海上段平面线形设计主要考虑桥轴线与海流的夹角、航道位置和走向、路线最短和投资最小等因素。东海大桥桥面标准宽度为31.5m，分上、下行双幅桥面，设双向六车道加紧急停车带。

主通航孔桥采用双塔单索面组合梁斜拉桥，跨径布置为73m+132m+420m+132m+73m，混凝土桥面板与单箱三室钢梁结合，斜拉索采用扇形密索布置，主塔为150m高的钻石形钢筋混凝土结构，主塔和边墩分别采用钻孔桩和钢管桩基础。颗珠山桥采用双塔双索面组合梁斜拉桥，跨径布置为50m+139m+332m+139m+50m，混凝土桥面板与两个分离钢箱结合，主塔为96m高的门式钢筋混凝土结构。三个辅通航孔桥统一采用四跨一联预应力混凝土连续箱梁，主跨分别为120m、140m和160m，下部结构统一采用预制式钢筋混凝土空心墩。全桥非通航孔桥统一采用多跨一联等高度预应力混凝土连续箱梁，跨径有30m、50m、60m和70m等。

东海大桥是中国第一座真正意义上的跨外海桥梁，创造了跨海桥梁长度的世界纪录。通过全方位结构耐久性设计研究，研发并实施了保证100年设计基准期的防腐蚀综合技术，采用大规模桥墩和主梁构件预制吊装，最大整孔吊装跨径70m，促进了我国大型预制构件施工技术的发展，全桥八个节段安装了结构健康监测系统，从而极大地提升了中国跨海大桥的建设和养护技术，获得了国家科技进步奖一等奖。

桥　　名：东海大桥
桥　　型：组合梁斜拉桥两座，预应力混凝土连续梁桥多座
桥梁长度：全长32.5km，主跨跨径420m
桥　　址：上海市
建成时间：2005年5月
设计单位：上海市政工程设计研究总院，中铁大桥勘测设计院有限公司，中交第三航务工程勘察设计院
施工单位：中铁大桥局集团有限公司，上海建工集团股份有限公司，中国交通建设集团有限公司，上海城建（集团）公司

East Sea Bridge starts at Luchao Harbor in Nanhui District of Shanghai, and connects to Yangshan Island after crossing the northeastern sea area of Hangzhou Bay. It is the sole landway link for gathering and distributing transportation of Yangshan Deep-Water Port of Shanghai International Shipping Center. The bridge is 32.5km in total, including a 3.7km-long land part, a 25.3km-long sea-crossing part and a 3.5km-long link park to the port zone. The major factors considered in the alignment design of the sea-crossing part include the inclination angle between the route and the ocean current, the location and direction of the navigation channel, the shortest distance and the lowest investment, etc. The bridge has six traffic lanes plus two emergency lanes in dual directions. The bridge width is 31.5m, including the dual deck parts.

The bridge over the main navigation channel is a two-tower composite-girder cable-stayed bridge with the span arrangement of 73m+132m+420m+132m+73m, and a single fan-shaped cable-plane. Its main girder is composed of reinforced concrete deck plate and a single-box three-cells steel girder. The diamond-shaped reinforced concrete tower is 150m in height. The bridge towers and piers are supported by the bored pile foundations and the steel-pipe foundations, respectively. The Kezhushan Bridge is also a double-tower composite-girder cable-stayed bridge, with five spans of 50m+139m+332m+139m+50m, and double parallel fan-shaped cable-planes. Its main girder is composed of reinforced concrete deck plate and two separate steel box girders. Its two 96m high towers are of portal-shaped reinforced concrete structure. The structures of four-span prestressed concrete continuous box girder are used for all the bridges over three auxiliary navigation channels with the main spans of 120m, 140m and 160m respectively. Their substructures are of precast reinforced concrete hollow piers. The structures of multi-span prestressed concrete continuous box girder with constant girder depths are employed for all the non-navigation spans with the various span lengths of 30m, 50m, 60m and 70m, etc.

Donghai bridge is the first sea-crossing project in China, setting a world record for the length of sea-crossing bridges. Through comprehensive research and design of structural durability, an integrated anticorrosive technique was developed and implemented to ensure the 100-year design service life. The extensive hoisting of precast pier and girder components was carried out in the bridge construction, with the longest span length of the entire-span hoisting reaching 70m. The structural health monitoring system was installed in 8 sections of the whole bridge. The construction and maintenance techniques of large precast components and sea-crossing bridges of our country were thus promoted greatly. The bridge project was awarded with the First Prize of National Science and Technology Progress Award.

**Name:** East Sea Bridge
**Type:** Two cable-stayed bridges with composite girder, several prestressed concrete continuous box girder bridges
**Length:** Total length 32.5km, main span 420m
**Location:** Shanghai City
**Completion:** May 2005
**Designer(s):** Shanghai Municipal Engineering Design Institute, China Railway Major Bridge Reconnaissance & Design Institute Co., Ltd., CCCC Third Harbor Consultants Institute
**Contractor(s):** China Railway Major Bridge Engineering Group Co., Ltd., Shanghai Construction Group Co., Ltd., China Communications Construction Group Co., Ltd., Shanghai Urban Construction (Group) Corporation

# 南京大胜关长江大桥

## Nanjing Dashengguan Bridge over Yangtze River

南京大胜关长江大桥，原称南京长江第三大桥，是上海至成都国道于南京跨越长江的快速过江通道上的重要节点。大桥及连接线全长约15.6km，其中跨江大桥长4744m，南引桥长680m，北引桥长2780m。全线采用双向六车道高速公路标准。

主桥为双塔双索面钢箱梁斜拉桥，主跨648m，两边跨各设一个辅助墩，跨径布置为63m+257m+648m+257m+63m，半漂浮结构体系，纵向采用非线性约束装置，用于限制活载及强风作用下主梁的纵向漂移及抗震消能。索塔为人字形曲线钢塔，主塔高215m，设4道横梁，其中下塔柱及下横梁为钢筋混凝土结构，其余部分为钢结构。大桥建设的两大技术难点是高桩承台群桩基础和人字形钢索塔施工，其中，承台群桩基础施工水深流急，常水位下水深45m，水流速度为2.9m/s，水文条件复杂，采用了钢套箱和钢护筒有机结合形成稳定的刚构平台进行深水基础

| | |
|---|---|
| 桥　　名： | 南京大胜关长江大桥 |
| 桥　　型： | 双塔双索面钢箱梁斜拉桥 |
| 主跨跨径： | 648m |
| 桥　　址： | 江苏省南京市 |
| 建成时间： | 2005年10月 |
| 设计单位： | 中交公路规划设计院有限公司 |
| 施工单位： | 湖南路桥建设集团公司，中交第二航务工程局有限公司 |

**Name:** Nanjing Dashengguan Bridge over Yangtze River
**Type:** Double-tower double-cable-plane steel box girder cable-stayed bridge
**Main span:** 648m
**Location:** Nanjing City, Jiangsu Province
**Completion:** October 2005
**Designer(s):** CCCC Highway Consultants Co., Ltd.
**Contractor(s):** Hunan Highway and Bridge Construction Group Corporation, CCCC Second Harbor Engineering Company Ltd.

施工，将施工临时结构与永久结构合二为一，形成先浮运钢套箱，后插打钢护筒的深水基础施工创新技术；人字形钢索塔下横梁以下部分为混凝土，以上部分为钢，属国内首次采用，主塔上下塔柱连接处钢-混凝土结合段采用PBL剪力键作为传递荷载的主要构件，即在钢塔柱板件上开孔，与穿过的钢筋和混凝土形成PBL剪力键的构造设计，结合弧线形钢塔设计施工，形成了中国钢塔设计、制造及架设工艺等新技术。

南京大胜关长江大桥是中国第一座采用钢塔的大跨度斜拉桥，也是世界上第一座弧线形钢塔斜拉桥，采用了高度252m的世界第一高的塔式起重机，创造了长江水下基础施工水位最深、工期最短的新纪录。

Nanjing Dashengguan Bridge over Yangtze River, originally named Third Nanjing Bridge over Yangtze River, is a crucial node on the fast-crossing Yangtze River route from Shanghai to Chengdu. The total length of the bridge including approaches is 15.6km. The main bridge, the southern and the northern approaching bridges are 4,744m, 680m and 2,780m in length, respectively. The entire route adheres to the dual-way six-lane highway standard.

The main bridge is a double-tower double-cable-plane steel box girder cable-stayed bridge, with a main span of 648m. Each side span features one auxiliary pier, resulting in a span arrangement of 63m+257m+648m+257m+63m. It features a semi-floating structural system with a nonlinear restraint device employed longitudinally to limit the longitudinal drift and seismic energy dissipation under live loads and strong winds. The towers are reversed Y-shaped curved steel towers, with the main tower reaching a height of 215m and having four crossbeams. The lower tower column and lower crossbeam are made of reinforced concrete, while the upper part is constructed of steel. The two main challenges in the construction of the bridge are the high-rise cap group foundation and the reversed Y-shaped steel towers. In order to overcome the complex hydrological conditions due to deep water, strong currents, and the common water depth of 45m below the normal water level with a flow velocity of 2.9m/s, a creative approach combining the construction temporary structures and permanent structures was proposed. The approach provided an innovative construction sequence which involved floating the steel boxed cofferdam into position first and then piling the steel casing. The main tower was designed in a reversed Y-shaped steel structure, which consisted of two segments. The upper part was steel and the lower one was concrete, which was also adopted for the first time in China. The connection between the two segments adopted PBL shear connector as the main mechanical components. Along with the design and construction of the curved steel tower, an integrated technology innovation in the design, construction and erection technique of steel bridge tower was developed.

The bridge is the first long-span cable-stayed bridge in China with steel towers, and it is the world's first cable-stayed bridge with arc-shaped steel towers. It introduced the world's tallest tower crane with a height of 252m, setting dual new records for the deepest underwater construction level and the shortest construction period in the Yangtze River.

# 重庆石板坡长江大桥复线桥

## Chongqing Shibanpo Parallel Bridge over Yangtze River

重庆石板坡长江大桥复线桥位于原桥上游，是一座城市主干道特大桥。桥梁全长1.104km，宽19m，单向四车道；桥下通航净空为18m×290m。复线桥结构为钢-混凝土混合连续刚构，由北向南跨径布置为87.75m+4×138m+330m+133.75m，是世界跨径最大的梁桥。

大桥的主梁采用单箱单室构造，为预应力混凝土结构和钢结构的混合结构，主跨中段108m采用钢箱梁，主跨还设置了后期补充体外预应力钢束的构造。为降低混凝土收缩徐变效应，对材料提出了具体性能指标与工艺要求。设计方案为解决混凝土连续刚构桥自重大、跨越能力有限的难题，克服该类桥梁跨中下挠等病害进行了有益实践。该桥的钢与混凝土箱梁接头采用了PBL剪力板、预应力钢筋和普通钢筋并在钢-混凝土结合段内填充了混凝土，还通过大比例模型试验检验了其受力的可靠性。利用混凝土箱梁悬臂端设置的体外定位劲性骨架，有效控制了与钢箱梁连接接头的各向位移及转角偏差，保证了主跨钢箱梁的合龙精度。

基于周密的施工组织，完成了长103m，重14000kN预制钢箱梁的整体浮运、转向及定位，克服了钢箱梁底面出水瞬间强大的吸附力。计算机控制液压千斤顶吊装系统和横向偏移调整技术，确保了钢箱梁连续平稳提升和精确合龙。

| 桥　　名： | 重庆石板坡长江大桥复线桥 | **Name:** Chongqing Shibanpo Parallel Bridge over Yangtze River |
| --- | --- | --- |
| 桥　　型： | 钢-混凝土混合连续刚构桥 | **Type:** Steel-concrete hybrid continuous rigid frame bridge |
| 主跨跨径： | 330m | **Main span:** 330m |
| 桥　　址： | 重庆市 | **Location:** Chongqing City |
| 建成时间： | 2006年9月 | **Completion:** September 2006 |
| 设计单位： | 林同棪国际工程咨询（中国）有限公司 | **Designer(s):** T.Y. Lin International Engineering Consulting (China) Co., Ltd. |
| 施工单位： | 重庆城建控股（集团）有限责任公司 | **Contractor(s):** Chongqing Urban Construction Holding (Group) Co., Ltd. |

Chongqing Shinbanpo Parallel Bridge over Yangtze River is located in the upstream of the existing Chongqing Shibanpo Bridge over Yangtze River. It is a one-way four-lane bridge with a total length of 1.104km and a deck width of 19m. The navigation clearance is 18m×290m. The bridge is a steel-concrete hybrid continuous bridge with integral piers, which has the span arrangement of 87.75m+4×138m+330m+133.75m from the north to the south. It is the longest span girder bridge in the world.

A steel box girder of 108m long is adopted for the middle part of the main span, while the prestressed concrete girder is adopted for other parts of the bridge. It has been considered that the external tendons can be added to the main span during the service stage. Specific criteria and technology of the materials used are adopted to reduce the creep and shrinkage of concrete. These measures mentioned above not only improve the spanning capability of heavy concrete bridges with integral piers, but also provide practical example for the deflection control at midspan of this kind of bridge. Several connection devices such as PBL shear-plate, prestressing tendons, steel reinforcement and filling concrete in the vicinity of steel girders, etc., have been used to ensure good connections between the prestressed girders and steel girder at midspan. The reliability of these measures was verified by large scale model testing. With positioning stiffening frame installed at the cantilever ends of the concrete box girder, the displacement and angle deviation of the joint section were effectively controlled. The closure accuracy of the steel girder in the midspan was ensured.

The 103m long, 14,000kN weighing steel box section were floated to the site with full length. To reduce the huge water absorption force when the girder is lifted up out of the water, the following hoisting process was adopted. Firstly, the steel box section was rotated until one end of the section was lifted out of water. Secondly, two ends of the steel section were lifted simultaneously until the whole girder getting out of the water. Finally, the steel box section was adjusted to be horizontal. To ensure the steel box section being lifted continuously and smoothly and the closure accuracy of the girders, computer controlled hydraulic jack lifting system and lateral deviation adjustment method were adopted during the construction.

# 菜园坝长江大桥

## Caiyuanba Bridge over Yangtze River

菜园坝长江大桥位于重庆市主城区中心地带，是连接渝中区与南岸区的过江通道，大桥线路全长 7km。主桥采用双层桥面布置，上层设双向六车道加双侧人行道，桥面净宽 30.5m；下层设双线城市轻轨，桥面净宽 8.6m。

菜园坝长江大桥主桥是刚构、钢桁梁、提篮式钢箱系杆拱组合结构体系的拱式桥梁，跨径布置为 88m+102m+420m+102m+88m，横桥向双拱肋内倾后呈提篮形。主跨矢高为 56.44m，主拱肋内倾角为 10.67°。主拱为宽 2.4m，高 4m 的钢箱结构，拱肋之间设 6 道钢横撑。钢桁梁采用正交异性桥面板与桁架的组合结构。桁梁高 11.2m，顶宽 39.8m，底宽 13m。桥面以下的中跨拱腿、边跨斜撑及桥墩组成 Y 形的刚构，采用变截面钢筋混凝土空心薄壁结构，Y 形刚构两伸臂的截面外形尺寸分别为 10m×6m 到 5.2m×3.6m 和 10m×6m 到 4m×3.6m，两伸臂的上端设为实心段，墩身采用 14m×9m 到 12m×6.2m 的变截面钢筋混凝土空心薄壁结构，Y 形刚构的横桥向由主横梁、次横梁及系杆拉索锚固构造等组成。大桥的钢箱拱采用缆索吊装、斜拉扣索悬臂拼装施工方法，钢桁梁采用大节段吊杆辅助吊装。

菜园坝长江大桥采用了正交异性桥面板与钢桁梁节段整体安装技术，中跨系杆与边跨系杆分开设置、独立锚固，可在施工过程中及成桥后对大桥进行内力与线形进行调整。

桥　　名：菜园坝长江大桥
桥　　型：中承式钢桁梁钢箱系杆拱桥
主跨跨径：420m
桥　　址：重庆市
建成时间：2007 年 10 月
设计单位：招商局重庆交通科研设计院有限公司，
　　　　　林同棪国际工程咨询（中国）有限公司
施工单位：中铁大桥局集团有限公司，中铁山桥集团有限公司

Caiyuanba Bridge over Yangtze River is located in the downtown of Chongqing, serving as a river-crossing passage connecting Yuzhong District and Nan'an District. The total length of the bridge route is 7km. The main bridge features a double-deck design, with the upper deck accommodating dual six-lane carriageways and dual pedestrian sidewalks, providing a net width of 30.5m. The lower deck is designed for a double-track urban light rail, offering a net width of 8.6m.

The main bridge is the combination of rigid frame, steel truss and steel tied arch bridge, with a span arrangement of 88m+102m+420m+102m+88m. The transverse bridge exhibits an inward tilt with a basket-handle shape. The main span arch is rising 56.44m. The arch ribs incline towards each other with an angle in relation to vertical line of 10.67°. The width of the arch rib is 2.4m and the depth is 4m. Six steel transverse braces with box sections are installed. The main girder is composed of orthotropic decks and a truss girder. The truss girder is 11.2m deep and 39.8m wide at the top and 13m wide at the bottom. The mid-span arch legs, inclined struts for side spans, and piers below the bridge form a Y-shaped rigid structure, utilizing variable-section reinforced concrete hollow thin-walled structures. The cross-sectional dimensions of the two extending arms of the Y-shaped rigid structure are 10m×6m to 5.2m×3.6m and 10m×6m to

4m×3.6m, with the upper ends of the two arms being solid sections. The piers use variable-section reinforced concrete hollow thin-walled structures with dimensions of 14m×9m to 12m×6.2m. The Y-shaped rigid structure in the transverse direction is composed of main beams, secondary beams, tie rods and anchorages for cable stay structures. The steel box arch of the bridge is constructed using cable-stayed lifting and cantilever assembly with diagonal cable stay and post-tensioning assembly for the steel truss girder.

Caiyuanba Bridge over Yangtze River incorporates the technology of integral installation of orthotropic bridge deck panels and steel truss girder segments. The mid-span tie rods and side-span tie rods are independently anchored, allowing for adjustments to internal forces and alignment during and after construction.

**Name:** Caiyuanba Bridge over Yangtze River
**Type:** Half through steel truss girder and steel box tie-rod arch bridge
**Main span:** 420m
**Location:** Chongqing City
**Completion:** October 2007
**Designer(s):** China Merchants Chongqing Communications Technology Research & Design Institute Co., Ltd., T.Y.Lin International Engineering Consulting (China) Co., Ltd.
**Contractor(s):** China Railway Major Bridge Engineering Group Co., Ltd., China Railway Shanhaiguan Bridge Group Co., Ltd.

# 杭州湾跨海大桥
## Hangzhou Bay Sea-crossing Bridge

| | |
|---|---|
| 桥　　名: | 杭州湾跨海大桥 |
| 桥　　型: | 钢箱梁斜拉桥两座，等高度预应力混凝土连续梁桥多联 |
| 桥梁长度: | 全长35.7km，主跨跨径448m |
| 桥　　址: | 浙江省嘉兴市至慈溪市 |
| 建成时间: | 2008年5月 |
| 设计单位: | 中交公路规划设计院有限公司，中铁大桥勘测设计院有限公司，中交第三航务工程勘察设计院有限公司 |
| 施工单位: | 中交第二航务工程局有限公司，中铁大桥局集团有限公司，广东省长大公路工程有限公司等 |

**Name:** Hangzhou Bay Sea-crossing Bridge
**Type:** Cable-stayed bridges with steel box girder, prestressed concrete continuous girder bridges
**Length:** Total length 36km, main span 448m
**Location:** Jiaxing City to Cixi City, Zhejiang Province
**Completion:** May 2008
**Designer(s):** CCCC Highway Consultants Co., Ltd., China Railway Major Bridge Reconnaissance & Design Institute Co., Ltd., CCCC Third Harbor Consultants Co., Ltd.
**Contractor(s):** CCCC Second Harbor Engineering Company Ltd., China Railway Major Bridge Engineering Group Co., Ltd., Guangdong Provincial ChangDa Highway Engineering Co., Ltd., etc.

杭州湾跨海大桥北起浙江省嘉兴市海盐县，横跨杭州湾，南止宁波市慈溪市。大桥包括北引桥、北航道桥、北高墩区引桥、中引桥、南航道桥、南高墩区引桥、南深水区引桥、南滩涂区引桥、南陆地区引桥九大部分，全长36km。大桥桥面宽度为33m，设双向六车道加紧急停车带。

北航道桥采用双塔双索面钢箱梁斜拉桥，跨径布置为70m+160m+448m+160m+70m，斜拉索采用扇形密索布置，主塔为钻石形钢筋混凝土结构、钻孔桩基础。南航道桥采用独塔双索面钢箱梁斜拉桥，跨径布置为80m+160m+318m，主塔为A字形钢筋混凝土结构。南、北航道桥相邻的高墩区引桥、中引桥和南深水区引桥均采用70m跨径等高度预应力混凝土连续箱梁，南滩涂区引桥为50m跨径等高度预应力混凝土连续箱梁，北引桥和南陆地区引桥采用30~80m跨径等高度预应力混凝土连续箱梁，引桥基础分别采用钢管桩和钻孔桩。

杭州湾跨海大桥刷新了跨海桥梁长度世界纪录。建设者们立足于工厂化、大型化和机械化设计和施工理念，研制了吊重25000kN和吊重30000kN两条中心起吊运架一体吊船，克服了强涌潮激流中基础施工和主梁运架的极端困难条件。杭州湾跨海大桥获得了国家科技进步奖二等奖。

Located in Zhejiang Province, Hangzhou Bay Sea-crossing Bridge starts in Haiyan County, Jiaxing City in the north, and ends in Cixi County, Ningbo City in the south after crossing the Hangzhou bay. The total length of the bridge is 36km including the following nine parts: the northern approach bridge, the northern sea-route bridge, the northern high-pier zone approach bridge, the middle approach, the southern sea-route bridge, the southern high-pier zone approach bridge, the southern deep-water zone approach bridge, the southern intertidal zone approach bridge and the southern land approach bridge. The deck width of the bridge is 33m, containing six traffic lanes plus two emergency lanes in dual directions.

The northern sea-route bridge is a double-tower steel box girder cable-stayed bridge with a span arrangement of 70m+160m+448m+160m+70m, and two inclined cable-planes. The cables are arranged densely with fan-shaped. Its diamond-shaped reinforced concrete towers are supported by bored piles. The southern sea-route bridge is a single-tower steel box girder cable-stayed bridge with a span arrangement of 80m+160m+318m, and two inclined cable-planes. Its tower is of A-shaped reinforced concrete structure. The prestressed concrete continuous box beams with constant girder depth are adopted for the approach bridges. The span length is 70m for the high-pier zone and middle approach bridges adjacent to the northern and southern sea-route bridges, and the southern deep-water zone approach bridge. The span length is 50m for the southern intertidal zone approach bridge. The span lengths of the northern and southern land approach bridges are between 30m and 80m. The steel-pipe pile and bored pile foundations are adopted for the piers of the approach bridges.

Hangzhou Bay Sea-crossing Bridge once again sets a new world record for the length of sea-crossing bridges. Based on the principles of industrialization, large-scale construction and mechanization, the builders developed two central lifting and hoisting systems integrated with a lifting barge, capable of lifting weights of 25,000kN and 30,000kN. They successfully overcame the extreme challenges of foundation construction and main girder erection in the strong tidal currents, earning the project the Second Prize of National Science and Technology Progress Award.

# 苏通长江公路大桥
## Sutong Highway Bridge over Yangtze River

苏通长江公路大桥位于江苏省东南部长江南通河段，连接苏州、南通两市，是沈海高速公路跨越长江的重要枢纽。大桥全长8.146km，由主桥、辅桥和引桥组成，全线采用双向六车道高速公路标准。

主桥为双塔双索面钢箱梁斜拉桥，跨径布置为100m+100m+300m+1088m+300m+100m+100m，桥面宽度为36.5m。主梁采用纵向黏滞阻尼约束、横向主从约束的体系，以减小强风和地震作用下的结构响应、提高结构抗灾能力。主塔为倒Y形钢筋混凝土结构，塔高300.4m，在斜拉索锚固段，采用在混凝土塔壁内侧设置钢锚箱的锚固构造，形成钢锚箱和混凝土塔壁组成的组合结构。斜拉索采用平行钢丝索，最长拉索长达577m，安装有MR、黏滞型及高阻尼橡胶减振装置以抑制拉索风雨振和高阶涡振。主塔墩基础采用大型群桩基础，由131根长约120m、直径2.5～2.8m的钻孔灌注桩组成，建立在40m水深以下厚达300m的软土地基上。

苏通长江公路大桥是世界首座主跨超过千米的斜拉桥，建成时主塔基础规模、塔高、索长均为世界之最，获得了国家科技进步奖一等奖。

Sutong Highway Bridge over Yangtze River is located in the Nantong River section of the Yangtze River in the southeast of Jiangsu Province, connecting Suzhou City and Nantong City, and is an important hub of the Shenyang-Haikou Expressway across the Yangtze River. The total length of the bridge is 8.146km, consisting of the main bridge, auxiliary bridges and approach bridges, and the whole line adopts the standard of dual six-lane highway.

The main bridge is a double-tower double cable plane steel box girder cable-stayed bridge with a span arrangement of 100m+100m+300m+1088m+300m+100m+100m and a deck width of 36.5m. The main girder adopts the system of viscous damping restraint in the longitudinal direction and master-slave restraint in the transverse direction, in order to reduce the structural response and improve the structural resistance under the action of strong wind and earthquake. The main tower is an inverted Y-shaped reinforced concrete structure with a tower height of 300.4m. In the anchor section of the tension cable, the anchor structure of steel anchor box is set on the inner side of the concrete tower wall, forming a combined structure composed of steel anchor box and concrete tower wall. The longest cable is 577m long, and MR, viscous type and high damping rubber vibration damping devices are installed to suppress wind and rain induced vibration and high order vortex induced vibration of cables. The foundation of the main tower pier adopts a large group pile foundation, which consists of 131 drilled piles with a length of about 120m and a diameter of 2.5~2.8m, and is built on a soft ground with a thickness of 300m below 40m water depth.

Sutong Highway Bridge over Yangtze River is the world's first cable-stayed bridge with a main span of more than 1,000 meters. It created the records of the scale of the main tower foundation, height of the tower and length of the cable at the time of completion, and won the First Prize of National Science and Technology Progress Award.

| 桥　　名： | 苏通长江公路大桥
| 桥　　型： | 双塔双索面钢箱梁斜拉桥
| 主跨跨径： | 1088m
| 桥　　址： | 江苏省苏州市和南通市
| 建成时间： | 2008年6月
| 设计单位： | 中交公路规划设计院有限公司，江苏省交通规划设计院股份有限公司，同济大学建筑设计院（集团）有限公司
| 施工单位： | 中交第二航务工程局有限公司，中交第二公路工程有限公司

**Name:** Sutong Highway Bridge over Yangtze River
**Type:** Double-tower double-cable-plane steel box girder cable-stayed bridge
**Main span:** 1,088m
**Location:** Suzhou City and Nantong City, Jiangsu Province
**Completion:** June 2008
**Designer(s):** CCCC Highway Consultants Co., Ltd., Jiangsu Provincial Communications Planning and Design Institute Co., Ltd., Tongji Architecture Design Group Co., Ltd.
**Contractor(s):** CCCC Second Harbor Engineering Company Ltd., CCCC Second Highway Engineering Co., Ltd.

# 香港昂船洲大桥
## Hong Kong Stonecutters Bridge

桥　　名：香港昂船洲大桥
桥　　型：双塔双索面混合梁斜拉桥
主跨跨径：1018m
桥　　址：香港特别行政区
建成时间：2008年6月
设计单位：奥雅纳工程顾问公司（香港）
施工单位：Media-Hitachi-Yokogawa-HsinChong JV（前田-日立-横河-新昌联合体）

**Name:** Hong Kong Stonecutters Bridge
**Type:** Double-tower double-cable-plane hybrid girder cable-stayed bridge
**Main span:** 1,018m
**Location:** Hong Kong Special Administrative Region
**Completion:** June 2008
**Designer(s):** Ove Arup & Partners Hong Kong Ltd.
**Contractor(s):** Media-Hitachi-Yokogawa-HsinChong JV

昂船洲大桥位于香港，跨越蓝巴勒海峡，连接青衣与昂船洲两地，是8号干线疏缓工程青衣至长沙湾段中的主要工程。大桥采用六车道高速公路标准，设计速度为100km/h，桥面宽度53.3m，通航净高73.5m、净宽900m。

　　主桥为双塔双索面混合梁斜拉桥，跨径布置为69.25m+2×70m+79.75m+1018m+79.75m+2×70m+69.25m。大桥主跨为1018m，桥宽49.75m，主梁为流线型分体式钢箱梁，其余边跨部分为双箱预应力混凝土梁。桥塔为独柱式，圆锥形断面，塔高298m，从塔底至塔高175m段为混凝土结构，175~293m段为钢-混凝土组合结构，外层表面采用不锈钢材料；再向上5m至塔顶为外装玻璃的通透钢结构，用作建筑照明标志。斜拉索为半扇形布置，主跨梁上索距18m，边跨梁上索距10m，索梁锚固采用钢锚箱的形式。桥塔基础采用钻孔桩，承台尺寸为47.4m×36.4m×8m。

　　香港昂船洲大桥的主梁采用分离式钢箱梁，有效提升了结构抗风性能，独柱式桥塔造型特点突出，上半部混凝土塔壁采用不锈钢包裹，既解决了耐久性问题，同时保持了金属质感，结合独特的照明设计，使全桥更富现代感。在桥塔与主梁之间加装竖直支座承托和纵向液压缓冲器，形成了独特的超大跨径斜拉桥结构体系。

Stonecutters Bridge is the major project in Tsing-Cheung Sha Wan section of the Route 8 Expressway, connecting Tsing Yi and Stonecutters Island in Hong Kong. The bridge was designed for six traffic lanes and the design vehicle speed is 100km/h. The width of the bridge is 53.3m. The height and width of the navigation clearance are 73.5m and 900m, respectively.

The main bridge is a double-tower, double-cable-plane hybrid girder cable-stayed bridge, with a span arrangement of 69.25m+2×70m+79.75m+1018m+79.75m+2×70m+69.25m. The main span is 1,018m and the bridge width is 49.75m. A streamlined separated steel box girder and a prestressed concrete twin box girder were adopted for the main spans and back spans, respectively. The bridge towers are single-column in a conical shape, with a tower height of 298m. The lower section from the tower base to 175m is made of concrete, the 175~293m section is a steel-concrete composite structure with an outer surface using stainless steel material. The upper 5m to the tower top is a transparent steel structure with exterior glass, serving as architectural lighting signage. The stay cables are arranged in a semi-fan shape, with a stay distance of 18m on the main span and 10m on the side spans. The cable anchorage adopts steel anchor boxes. The tower foundation is constructed using bored piles, with a pier cap size of 47.4m×36.4m×8m.

The main girder of Hong Kong Stonecutters Bridge, featuring a separated steel box girder, effectively enhances its wind resistance. The design is distinctive. The modern flavor of single-column tower is expressed perfectly by the combination of the unique illumination design on the top and the middle part with metal texture brought by the stainless steel skin which additionally provides a durable skin. The vertical support bearing and longitudinal hydraulic buffer installed between the main tower and girder create a special structure form of mega cable-stayed bridge.

# 朝天门长江大桥
## Chaotianmen Bridge over Yangtze River

朝天门长江大桥位于重庆市朝天门下游，是连接江北区与南岸区的公轨两用拱桥，主跨跨径552m，建成时为世界上跨径最大的拱桥。大桥全长4.888km，主桥采用双层桥面布置，上层为双向六车道和两侧人行道，下层中间为双线轻轨，两侧为双向两车道。

朝天门长江大桥的主桥为中承式钢桁梁系杆拱桥，跨径布置为190m+552m+190m，中跨钢桁拱的矢跨比为1/4.3。主桥两个边跨为变高度桁梁，桁梁宽度为36.5m。中跨下层系杆内配置了体外预应力束。桁架杆件采用Q420qD、Q370qD和Q345qD三种强度的钢材混合设计，以优化截面、降低造价。中墩顶的主支承节点采用整体式节点，以减小节点板的厚度。大桥北岸侧主墩采用固定支座，其余桥墩处均设纵向滑动支座，中墩支座反力达到145000kN，采用铸钢球形铰抗震支座，其设计寿命为100年。主桥基础采用钻孔灌注桩。

钢桁梁从边墩开始利用临时墩拼装，到达主墩后，再悬臂拼装主跨拱圈，最后在跨中合龙，为保证成桥后的内力与线形达到一次落架状态，边墩高度、主墩支座位置在架设过程中均可调。

Chaotianmen Bridge over Yangtze River is situated at the downstream of Chaotianmen in Chongqing, serving as a dual-purpose arch bridge with the main span of 552m for both road and rail connectivity between Jiangbei District and Nan'an District. Upon the completion, it was the world's longest arch bridge in terms of span. The bridge spans a total length of 4.888km and features a double-deck configuration. The upper deck comprises dual six-lane carriageways with pedestrian walkways on both sides, while the lower deck accommodates a double-track light rail in the center, flanked by dual two-lane roadways.

The main span of the bridge is a half-through steel truss girder tied arch bridge, with a span arrangement of 190m+552m+190m. The rise-to-span ratio of the central arch is 1/4.3. The side spans of the main bridge consist of variable-depth truss girders with a width of 36.5m. External prestressed cables are arranged in the lower chords of the deck truss in the middle span. The truss members are constructed from a combination of three steel grades (Q420qD, Q370qD and Q345qD) to optimize sections and reduce costs. The main support joint at the top of the central pier employs a monolithic joint to minimize the thickness of the joint plate. The north bank abutment utilizes fixed bearings, while the other piers employ longitudinal sliding bearings. The bearing reaction at the central pier reaches 145,000 kN, using steel cast ball and socket supports for seismic resistance, with a design life of 100 years. The main bridge foundation employs bored piles.

The truss girders in the side spans are erected by the cantilever method with auxiliary piers. The arch in the main span is assembled with the aids of temporary towers and stay cables. The level and longitudinal location of every bearing are adjustable during the erection process to control the internal force and deflection of the truss.

桥　名：朝天门长江大桥
桥　型：中承式钢桁梁系杆拱桥
主跨跨径：552m
桥　址：重庆市
建成时间：2009年5月
设计单位：中铁大桥勘测设计院有限公司，招商局重庆交通科研设计院有限公司
施工单位：中交第二航务工程局有限公司

**Name:** Chaotianmen Bridge over Yangtze River
**Type:** Half through steel truss girder tied arch bridge
**Main span:** 552m
**Location:** Chongqing City
**Completion:** May 2009
**Designer(s):** China Railway Major Bridge Reconnaissance & Design Institute Co., Ltd., China Merchants Chongqing Communications Research & Design Institute Co., Ltd.
**Contractor(s):** CCCC Second Harbor Engineering Company Ltd.

# 天兴洲长江大桥
## Tianxingzhou Bridge over Yangtze River

桥　名：天兴洲长江大桥
桥　型：双塔三索面钢桁梁斜拉桥
主跨跨径：504m
桥　址：湖北省武汉市
建成时间：2009年9月
设计单位：中铁大桥勘测设计院有限公司
施工单位：中铁大桥局集团有限公司，中铁十二局集团有限公司，
　　　　　中交第二航务工程局有限公司

天兴洲长江大桥位于湖北省武汉市，是京广高速铁路、漯武铁路、武汉三环快速路的共用过江通道，是中国首座跨越长江的高速铁路桥梁，也是世界首座按照四线铁路、六线公路标准建设的公铁两用斜拉桥。上层公路部分按照城市快速路标准设计，双向六车道；下层铁路部分按照双线客运专线和双线I级干线共四线设计，旅客列车设计行车速度为200km/h。

主桥为双塔三索面钢桁梁斜拉桥，跨径布置为98m+196m+504m+196m+98m，桥面宽27m。主桥采用半漂浮体系，主梁采用板桁结合钢桁梁、三片主桁、N形桁架，外侧桁中心宽度为30m，桁高15.2m，节间长度14m。斜拉索三个索面分别锚于三片主桁的上弦杆上。上层公路桥面在梁端168m范围内采用混凝土板，其余部分为钢正交异性板，钢桁梁与桥面板结合共同受力。主塔结构设计为倒Y形钢筋混凝土结构，塔高190m。斜拉索采用镀锌高强度平行钢丝束，最长索长度为271m，单根索索力最大约为12500kN。主塔墩基础均采用ø3.4m钻孔灌注桩。

主桥具有跨度大、活载重、列车速度高等特点，采用了三索面三主桁斜拉桥新结构体系，钢桥面板、混凝土桥面板与主桁结合的组合结构，以及黏滞阻尼器与磁流变阻尼器约束体系等一系列新技术。建设过程中，全面开展了大跨公铁两用斜拉桥的关键技术研究，为中国铁路建设的发展积累了宝贵经验。

**Name:** Tianxingzhou Bridge over Yangtze River
**Type:** Double-tower three-cable-plane steel truss girder cable-stayed bridge
**Main span:** 504m
**Location:** Wuhan City, Hubei Province
**Completion:** September 2009
**Designer(s):** China Railway Major Bridge Reconnaissance & Design Institute Co., Ltd.
**Contractor(s):** China Major Bridge Engineering Group Co., Ltd., China Railway 12th Bureau Group Co., Ltd., CCCC Second Harbor Engineering Company Ltd.

Tianxingzhou Bridge over Yangtze River, serving as the common river-crossing passageway of Beijing-Guangzhou High-speed Railway, Shekou-Wuchang Railway and Wuhan Third Ring Urban Expressway, is the first bridge for high-speed railway over the Yangtze River in China. It is the first highway-railway bridge constructed in the standard of four railway lanes and six highway lanes in the world. The upper highway part is designed according to the standard of urban expressway, with a six-lane dual carriageway; the lower railroad part is designed according to the four-lane design of two-lane passenger line and two-lane Class I trunk line, and the design speed of passenger train is 200km/h.

The main bridge is a double-tower three cable plane steel truss girder double-deck cable-stayed bridge for both railway and highway transports, with the span arrangement of 98m+196m+504m+196m+98m, and the deck width of 27m. Semi-floating system was adopted for connecting the main tower and girder. The main plate-truss composite girder consists of three main N-shaped trusses. The transverse dimension of the truss girder is 30m in the width and 15.2m in the depth. The stay cables in the three planes were anchored at the top chord of the three main trusses, respectively. The highway deck was a combination of concrete slabs and steel orthotropic plates, so the load effect was shared by both steel trusses and the deck. The main reinforced concrete towers were designed in reversed Y shape and is 190m tall. Zinc coated high strength steel wire bunches were adopted as stay cables. The length of the longest cable is 271m and the maximum cable force is about 12,500kN. The bored piles with a diameter of 3.4m were employed for the foundation of main towers.

To overcome the technical problems brought up by long span, heavy loads and high speed of trains, the new technologies such as composite structure combing steel and concrete deck with main trusses, viscous and MR dampers were introduced. During construction, the research on these key technologies of long-span cable-stayed bridges have accumulated valuable experience for the development of China's rail-road Bridges construction.

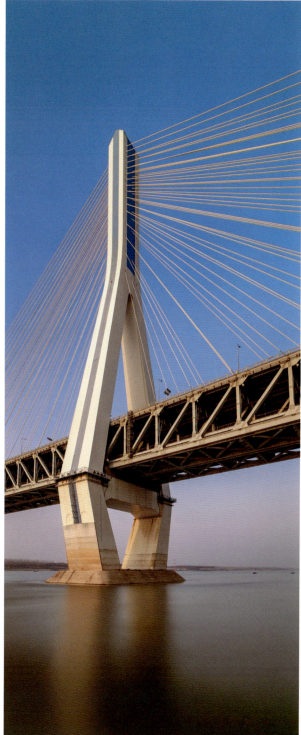

# 西堠门大桥
## Xihoumen Bridge

西堠门大桥位于浙江省舟山市，是长达 50km 的舟山连岛工程中的跨海特大桥之一，连接舟山群岛的册子岛与金塘岛，工程全长 2.588km，为双向四车道。

主桥为双塔两跨吊分体式钢箱梁悬索桥，主跨 1650m。分体式钢箱梁横向净距 6m，全宽 37.4m，梁高 3.5m。主缆跨径布置为 578m+1650m+485m，主跨主缆垂跨比 1/10，采用 127$\phi$5.25 预制平行钢丝索股，每根主缆 169 股，南边跨（金塘岛侧）增加 2 股，北边跨（册子岛侧）增加 6 股。吊索采用钢丝绳索股，纵向间距为 18m。索塔采用钢筋混凝土门式框架结构，塔高 211.3m。主塔基础采用钻孔灌注桩，北锚碇为扩大基础重力式锚碇，南锚碇为重力式嵌岩锚。

西堠门大桥首次采用了分体式钢箱梁，以中央开槽方式解决了大跨径小宽跨比悬索桥颤振稳定问题。大桥主缆采用国产 1770MPa 索股，减轻了主缆自重。运用水平成圈放索技术，解决了索股架设中的"呼啦圈"现象，节省索盘，减轻运输重量。

| 桥　　名： | 西堠门大桥 |
|---|---|
| 桥　　型： | 双塔两跨吊分体式钢箱梁悬索桥 |
| 主跨跨径： | 1650m |
| 桥　　址： | 浙江省舟山市 |
| 建成时间： | 2009 年 12 月 |
| 设计单位： | 中交公路规划设计院有限公司 |
| 施工单位： | 中交第二公路工程局有限公司，四川路桥建设集团股份有限公司 |

**Name:** Xihoumen Bridge
**Type:** Double-tower two-suspended-span suspension bridge with twin steel box girder
**Main span:** 1,650m
**Location:** Zhoushan City, Zhejiang Province
**Completion:** December 2009
**Designer(s):** CCCC Highway Consultants Co., Ltd.
**Contractor(s):** CCCC Second Highway Engineering Co., Ltd., Sichuan Road & Bridge Group Co., Ltd.

DEVELOPMENT AND STRENGTHENING | 发展与图强 2000—2009

Xihoumen Bridge, located in Zhoushan City, Zhejiang Province, is one of the sea-crossing bridges in the 50km-long Zhoushan Islands Conjunction Project, connecting Cezi Island and Jintang Island, with a total length of 2.588km, and a 4-lane dual carriageway.

The main bridge is a Double-tower two-suspended-span suspension bridge with a main span of 1,650m. The bridge girder is a 37.4m wide and 3.5m deep twin separated box girder with a central slot. The width of the central slot is 6.0m. The sag-to-span ratio of the main cables is 1/10. Each main cable consists of 169 parallel wire bundles and each bundle includes 127 $\phi$ 5.25 steel wires, and the south side of the span (on the side of Jintang Island) is increased by 2 strands, and the north side of the span (on the side of Cezi Island) is increased by 6 strands. The hangers placed along the bridge at each 18m are made with wire ropes. The towers supported by bored piles are reinforced concrete portal frame shape structures with a height of 211.3m. The northern and southern anchor blocks are both gravity anchorages.

The twin steel box girder with a central slot was firstly applied to improve flutter stability of long-span suspension bridge with small width-to-span ratio. The weight of main cables was reduced by the use of wire bundles of 1,770MPa tensile strength made in China. The new technique of horizontal unreeling cables is developed to solve the "hoop" problem during the cable erection, to save the quality of the cable, and to reduce the shipping weight.

# 坝陵河大桥
## Baling River Bridge

| | |
|---|---|
| 桥　名： | 坝陵河大桥 |
| 桥　型： | 双塔单跨吊钢桁梁悬索桥 |
| 主跨跨径： | 1088m |
| 桥　址： | 贵州省安顺市 |
| 建成时间： | 2009年12月 |
| 设计单位： | 中交公路规划设计院有限公司 |
| 施工单位： | 贵州桥梁建设集团有限责任公司，中交第二航务工程局有限公司 |

**Name:** Baling River Bridge
**Type:** Double-tower single-suspended-span suspension bridge with steel truss girder
**Main span:** 1,088m
**Location:** Anshun City, Guizhou Province
**Completion:** December 2009
**Designer(s):** CCCC Highway Consultants Co., Ltd.
**Contractor(s):** Guizhou Bridge Construction Group Co., Ltd., CCCC Second Harbor Engineering Company Ltd.

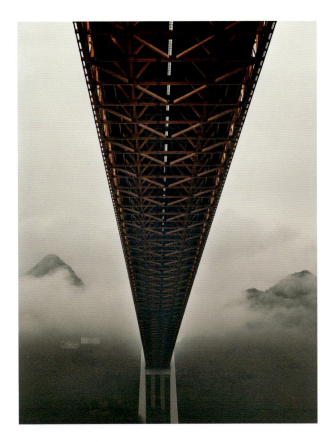

坝陵河大桥位于贵州省安顺市内G60高速公路上，上跨坝陵河水道，工程全长2.237km，设双向四车道。

主桥为双塔单跨吊钢桁梁悬索桥，主跨为1088m，桥面宽24.5m，钢桁梁高10.0m。主跨主缆垂跨比为1/10.3，采用91ϕ15.2预制平行钢丝索股，每根主缆208股，边跨增加8股。吊索纵向间距为10.8m，采用钢丝绳，上端为骑跨索夹，下端为销铰式连接。索塔采用门式框架结构，东西塔分别高185.788m和201.316m，采用人工挖孔群桩基础。东锚碇采用重力式框架锚，西锚碇采用隧道式锚碇。

坝陵河大桥是国内首座超千米的钢桁梁悬索桥，中跨主缆、主梁间设置柔性中央扣作为纵向约束系统。在钢桁梁下检修道位置设置气动翼板来提高桥梁颤振稳定性。

Baling River Bridge is located on G60 Expressway in Anshun City, Guizhou Province, spanning the Baling River watercourse. The total length of the project is 2.237km, featuring a dual 4-lane carriageway.

The main bridge is a double-tower single-suspended-span steel truss girder suspension bridge with a main span of 1,088m. The bridge deck is 24.5m wide. The steel truss main girder has a depth of 10.0m. The sag-to-span ratio of the main cables is 1/10.3. Each main cable consists of 208 parallel wire bundles and each bundle includes 91 ϕ 5.2 steel wires. The hangers placed along the bridge at each 10.8m are made with wire ropes. The towers supported by artificial group piles are portal frame shape structures with different height: 185.788m in the east and 201.316m in the west. The eastern and western anchor blocks are a gravity frame anchorage and a rock tunnel anchorage, respectively.

The steel truss stiffening girder with the span over 1,000m is applied in suspension bridges in China for the first time. The flexible central clamp is installed on the cable at the mid-span to restrain the longitudinal movement of the bridge. The aerodynamic wings are mounted at both sides of the steel truss girder to improve flutter stability.

BRIDGES IN CHINA

中国桥梁

# 创新与提高
INNOVATION AND IMPROVEMENT

2010
2019

# 引　言

中国国民经济和社会发展"十二五"规划提出以科学发展为主题，以加快转变经济发展方式为主线，深化改革开放，保障和改善民生，为全面建成小康社会打下具有决定性意义的基础。"十三五"规划进一步明确要扩大有效供给，满足有效需求，确保如期全面建成小康社会。扩大和满足内需、保障和改善民生等政策，赋予了桥梁和交通基础设施新一轮建设的动力。

到2010年，中国已经建成的公路和铁路桥梁的数量和里程进入了世界前列，仅次于美国，在建的大跨度桥梁数量更是达到了全世界总量的一半。为了加快转变桥梁建设发展方式，在继续兴建长大或跨海桥梁以及大跨度桥梁的同时，不断提升桥梁连续跨越能力，开拓多主跨桥梁建设，提升技术水平和品质，争取与国际先进水平并跑，甚至部分领跑。

在长大或跨海桥梁建设方面，建成了以港珠澳大桥为代表的跨海大桥，再次刷新了跨海桥梁长度世界纪录，并获得了国际桥梁与结构工程协会杰出结构奖，建成了全世界最长的桥梁——165km的丹昆特大桥；为提升桥梁连续跨越能力，先后建成了两座创造世界跨径纪录的双主跨悬索桥——泰州长江大桥（获得了国际桥梁与结构工程协会杰出结构奖）和马鞍山长江大桥，创造世界跨径纪录的双主跨斜拉桥——武汉二七长江大桥，多主跨拱桥——杭州九堡大桥等；在其他大跨度桥梁建设方面，相继建成了南沙大桥等悬索桥、东水门长江大桥等斜拉桥、波司登长江大桥和沪昆高铁北盘江特大桥等拱桥（后者刷新了混凝土拱桥跨径的世界纪录）、水盘高速北盘江特大桥等梁桥。

21世纪第二个10年，中国建成了一大批长大或跨海桥梁，多主跨桥梁和大跨度悬索桥、斜拉桥、拱桥和梁桥。本章选取了中国长大或跨海桥梁3座，多主跨桥梁6座，大跨度悬索桥3座、斜拉桥3座、拱桥3座和梁桥1座。这一时期，长大或跨海桥梁的长度、双主跨悬索桥和斜拉桥的跨径以及混凝土拱桥的跨径都创造了世界纪录，标志着中国已经从桥梁建设大国开始走向桥梁强国。

# INTRODUCTION

During China's "Twelfth Five-Year Plan" period, the national economic and social development strategy emphasized scientific development as its core theme, focusing on accelerating the transformation of the economic development model. This strategy involved the deepening of Reform and Opening-up, ensuring and improving people's livelihoods, and comprehensively building a more prosperous society. The "Thirteenth Five-Year Plan" further clarified the goals of expanding supply to meet demand and ensuring the timely achievement of a prosperous society. Policies aimed at expanding and satisfying domestic demand, as well as ensuring and improving the welfare of the populace, provided new momentum for the construction of transportation infrastructure and bridges.

By 2010, China had become second only to the United States in terms of the number and total mileage of highway and railway bridges. Remarkably, the number of long-span bridges under construction in China accounted for half of the global total. In the attempt to accelerate the development and transformation of bridge construction, China not only continued to build long bridges, sea-crossing bridges, and long-span bridges, but also focused on enhancing the continuous spanning capabilities of bridges. This effort involved pioneering the construction of multi-span bridges, improving technical standards and quality, and striving to match or even surpass the most advanced international level in bridge engineering.

In the construction of long or sea-crossing bridges, the Hong Kong-Zhuhai-Macao Bridge, a representative sea-crossing bridge, was completed, breaking the world record for the length of sea-crossing bridges once again and receiving the Outstanding Structure Award by International Association for Bridge and Structural Engineering (IABSE). The longest bridge in the world, the 165km Danyang-Kunshan Grand Bridge, was built. To enhance the continuous spanning capability of bridges, several world-record-breaking double-main-span bridges were constructed, including the Taizhou Bridge over the Yangtze River (which received the Outstanding Structure Award by IABSE) and the Ma'anshan Bridge over the Yangtze River, as well as the double-main-span cable-stayed Wuhan Erqi Bridge over the Yangtze River and the multi-main-span arch Jiubao Bridge. Notable long-span bridges of this period included the Nansha Bridge and other suspension bridges, and the Dongshuimen Bridge over the Yangtze River and other cable-stayed bridges. Notable arch bridges included the Bosideng Bridge over the Yangtze River and the Shanghai-Kunming High-speed Railway Bridge over the Beipan River. The latter bridge set a new world record for the span of concrete arch bridges. Significant girder bridges included the Liupanshui-Panxian Expressway Bridge over the Beipan River.

In the second decade of the 21st century, China completed a large number of bridges of all types, including long bridges, sea-crossing bridges, multi-span bridges, long-span suspension bridges, cable-stayed bridges, arch bridges, and girder bridges. This chapter presents three long or sea-crossing bridges, six multi-span bridges, three long-span suspension bridges, three cable-stayed bridges, three arch bridges, and one girder bridge. The length of the long or sea-crossing bridges, the span of the double-main-span suspension and cable-stayed bridges, and the span of the concrete arch bridges all set new world records. These achievements confirm China's transition from a major bridge-building country to a leading power in bridge construction.

# 京沪高铁南京大胜关长江大桥
## Beijing-Shanghai High-speed Railway Nanjing Dashengguan Bridge over Yangtze River

京沪高铁南京大胜关长江大桥位于江苏省南京市,是京沪高速铁路跨越长江的关键控制性工程,也是沪汉蓉快速客运专线和南京地铁S3号线的过江通道,建成时为世界首座六线铁路桥和跨度最大、设计荷载最大的高速铁路桥。大桥设计活载为六线铁路,包括两线高速铁路,两线快速客运专线,两线轻轨交通。

京沪高铁南京大胜关长江大桥的主桥为六跨连续钢桁梁拱组合桥,跨径布置为108m+192m+336m+336m+192m+108m,桥梁宽度为40.4m,其中两个336m的主跨为中承式钢桁梁拱结构。大桥横桥向为三片平面主桁结构,主桁间距2×15m。高速铁路、客运专线分别位于三片主桁组成的两个空间之中,轻轨则布置在两侧桁架外挑悬臂上。主跨桁拱拱顶处拱圈桁高12m,拱脚处拱圈桁高47.9m,桁拱矢跨比为1/4。行车桥面采用由闭口纵肋加劲的正交异性钢桥面板,钢桥面板与主桁下弦杆焊接形成板桁组合结构体系,桥面板顶面现浇厚度150mm混凝土砟道槽。主墩基础采用钻孔桩,桩长102~112m。

京沪高铁南京大胜关长江大桥的主桥采用的拱梁组合结构体系,具有适合高速、大跨及满足多线荷载作用的特点。

桥　名：京沪高铁南京大胜关长江大桥
桥　型：连续钢桁梁拱组合桥
主跨跨径：2×336m
桥　址：江苏省南京市
建成日期：2011年1月
设计单位：中铁大桥勘测设计院有限公司
施工单位：中铁大桥局集团有限公司，中铁山桥集团有限公司，
　　　　　中铁宝桥集团有限公司

**Name:** Beijing-Shanghai High-speed Railway Nanjing Dashengguan Bridge over Yangtze River
**Type:** Continuous steel-truss-girder-arch composite bridge
**Main span:** 2×336m
**Location:** Nanjing City, Jiangsu Province
**Completion:** January 2011
**Designer(s):** China Railway Major Bridge Reconnaissance & Design Institute Co., Ltd.
**Contractor(s):** China Railway Major Bridge Engineering Group Co., Ltd., China Railway Shanhaiguan Bridge Group Co., Ltd., China Railway Baoji Bridge Group Co., Ltd.

Beijing-Shanghai High-speed Railway Nanjing Dashengguan Bridge over Yangtze River is located in Nanjing City, Jiangsu Province, serving as a crucial control project for the Beijing-Shanghai High-speed Railway crossing the Yangtze River. It also serves as a crossing for the Shanghai-Wuhan-Chengdu Rapid Passenger Passage and Nanjing Metro Line S3. Upon completion, it became the world's first six-track railway bridge with the longest span and highest design load for high-speed railways. The bridge is designed to accommodate six railway tracks, including two high-speed railway lines, two express passenger lines, and two light rail lines.

The main span of Beijing-Shanghai High-speed Railway Nanjing Dashengguan Bridge over Yangtze River consists of a continuous steel truss-girder-arch composite bridge with six spans, arranged as follows: 108m+192m+336m+336m+192m+108m. The bridge has a width of 40.4m, with the two 336m main spans adopting a half-through steel truss-girder-arch composite structure. The bridge is composed of three main trusses, and the distance between two trusses is 15m. The high-speed railway lines and the passenger railway lines are located in the spaces between the trusses, while the light-rail lines are situated on the cantilever connected to the trusses.

The arch cross section is 12m deep at the crown and 47.9m at the springing. The rise-to-span ratio of the arch is 1/4. The roadway uses an orthogonal steel bridge deck with closed-section longitudinal ribs. The steel bridge deck is welded to the lower chord of the main trusses to form a composite structure, and the top surface of the bridge deck is cast with a 150mm thick concrete ballast trough. The main pier foundation uses bored piles with a length ranging from 102m to 112m.

The bridge adopts a truss-girder-arch composite structure system, characterized by its suitability for high speed, long spans, and the ability to withstand multiple line loads.

# 胶州湾大桥
## Jiaozhou Bay Bridge

| | |
|---|---|
| 桥　名： | 胶州湾大桥 |
| 桥　型： | 单塔钢箱梁自锚式悬索桥，双塔双索面钢箱梁斜拉桥，单塔双索面钢箱梁斜拉桥，预应力混凝土连续箱梁 |
| 桥梁长度： | 全长31.63km，最大跨径260m |
| 桥　址： | 山东省青岛市 |
| 建成时间： | 2011年6月和2020年3月 |
| 建设单位： | 山东高速集团有限公司 |
| 设计单位： | 中交公路规划设计院有限公司，山东省交通规划设计院，江苏省交通规划设计院有限公司 |
| 施工单位： | 山东省路桥集团有限公司，路桥集团国际建设股份有限公司，中交第三公路工程局有限公司 |

**Name:** Jiaozhou Bay Bridge
**Type:** Self-anchored suspension bridge with single pylon and slotted steel box girder; Double-pylon cable-stayed bridges with steel box girder; Single-pylon cable-stayed bridges with steel box girder; Prestressed concrete continuous box girder bridges.
**Length:** Total length 31.63km, main span 260m
**Location:** Qingdao City, Shandong Province
**Completion:** June 2011 (1st Stage) and March 2020 (2nd Stage)
**Owner(s):** Shandong Hi-Speed Group Co.,Ltd.
**Designer(s):** CCCC Highway Consultants Co., Ltd., Shandong Provincial Communications Planning and Design Institute Group Co.,Ltd., Jiangsu Provincial Communications Planning and Design Institute Co., Ltd.
**Contractor(s):** Shandong Luqiao Group Co., Ltd., Road & Bridge International Co., Ltd., CCCC Third Highway Engineering Co., Ltd.

胶州湾大桥是跨越胶州湾东、西岸的重要通道，连接青岛、黄岛和红岛，桥梁全长31.63km，包括先建成的主线桥梁26.707km和后建成的胶州连接段桥梁4.923km，桥面按双向六车道城市快速路兼高速公路布置。

胶州湾大桥的主线桥梁包括大沽河航道桥、沧口航道桥、红岛航道桥、水上非通航孔桥、陆域引桥、水中区引桥、红岛连接线、西岸滩涂区引桥、李村河互通立交和红岛互通立交等。大沽河航道桥为单塔钢箱梁自锚式悬索桥，跨径布置为80m+260m+190m+80m，主梁采用中央开槽式钢箱结构，其中箱梁全宽47m，高3.6m，槽宽11.4m，两根主缆空间布置；沧口航道桥为双幅双塔双索面钢箱梁斜拉桥，跨径布置为80m+90m+260m+90m+80m，两幅桥中心距30.5m，采用半漂浮结构体系；红岛航道桥为双幅单塔双索面钢箱梁斜拉桥，跨径布置为2×120m，两幅桥中心距为20.5m，采用半漂浮结构体系。水中区引桥总长15.9km，采用整跨预制吊装，先简支后连续的60m跨径预应力混凝土连续箱梁；西岸滩涂区引桥总长5km，采用移动模架浇筑的4至5跨一联50m跨径连续梁；李村河互通立交采用变梁高预应力混凝土连续箱梁；红岛互通立交主线长1.98km，为50m跨径预应力混凝土连续箱梁。

胶州湾大桥结构新颖、造型独特、美观大气，三座航道桥与蜿蜒的非通航孔桥、海上互通立交等共同谱写了一部气势磅礴的桥梁组曲，既与青岛市的城市及建筑风格相呼应，又富有现代的气息，是屈指可数的现代化桥梁集群工程。

Jiaozhou Bay Bridge is an important passage across the east and west coasts of Jiaozhou Bay in Shandong Province, connecting Qingdao, Huangdao and Hongdao. Its total length is 31.63km, including 26.707km of the mainline bridge and 4.923km of the Jiaozhou connecting section built later. The bridge deck is laid out as a six-lane urban expressway and highway in dual directions.

The mainline bridges of Jiaozhou Bay Bridge include Daguhe Channel Bridge, Cangkou Channel Bridge, Hongdao Channel Bridge, non-navigation channel bridges over water, land approach bridges, Hongdao Connection Bridge, Licunhe Interchange and Hongdao Interchange. Daguhe anchored suspension bridge, with a span arrangement of 80m+260m+190m+80m. The deck adopts a central-slotted steel box girder, with a total width of 47m, a depth of 3.6m, a slot width of 11.4m, and two main cables are spatially arranged. Cangkou Channel Bridge is comprised of separated twin parallel bridges. Each of them is a double pylon, double-cable-plane steel box girder cable-stayed bridge adopting semi-floating structural system, with a span arrangement of 80m+90m+260m+90m+80m. The central distance between the two decks is 30.5m. Hongdao Channel Bridge is also comprised of separated twin parallel bridges. Each of them is a single pylon, double-cable-plane steel box girder cable-stayed bridge adopting semi-floating structural system, with a span arrangement of 2×120m. The central distance between the two decks is 20.5m. The total length of the approach bridge in the water area is 15.9km, and it adopts 60m spanned prestressed concrete continuous box girder. It was constructed through a whole span lifting method in conjunction with a system transformation from the simply-supported beam to continuous beam. The total length of the approach bridge in the west coast beach area is 5km, and it is comprised of a series of 50m span continuous bridges with 4~5 spans for each, and was cast on movable formworks. Licunhe Interchange Bridge adopts prestressed concrete continuous box girders with variable girder depth. The length of Hongdao Interchange Bridge is 1.98km, and it is a 50m spanned prestressed concrete continuous box girder bridge.

Jiaozhou Bay Bridge is novel in structure, unique in shape, beautiful and majestic. The three channel bridges together with the meandering non-navigation channel bridges and interchange overpasses over the sea compose a magnificent bridge suite, which not only echoes the urban and architectural style of Qingdao City, but also rich in modern flavor. It is one of the few modern bridge group projects.

# 丹昆特大桥

## Danyang-Kunshan Grand Bridge

丹昆特大桥是京沪高速铁路南京至上海段的特大桥梁。桥梁西起丹阳，途经常州、无锡、苏州，东至昆山，先后跨越150多条河流和180余条道路，并在桥上设置4个高架车站。大桥全长164.851km，是世界第一长桥，主线桥面按双线高速铁路布置。

丹昆特大桥上部结构主要采用32m和24m标准跨径整跨预制架设的预应力混凝土简支箱梁。特殊结构桥梁合计139座，包括位于主线的预应力混凝土连续梁桥88座、位于道岔的预应力混凝土连续梁桥41座、单跨下承式预应力混凝土梁拱组合桥9座和三跨下承式预应力混凝土连续梁拱组合桥1座。其中，单跨梁拱组合桥的最大跨径为128m，三跨连续梁拱组合桥跨径布置为70m+136m+70m。大桥下部结构主要采用钢筋混凝土单柱、双柱墩，截面类型为矩形、圆形或圆端形实心和空心截面，桥台主要为矩形空心台及框架台等，基础采用钢筋混凝土桩。

丹昆特大桥采用了铁路客运专线的大多数桥型及施工方法，其中阳澄湖区桥梁基础采用了"双排桩筑坝围堰"的施工方法，很好满足了湖区绿色施工要求。

Danyang-Kunshan Grand Bridge is a super-long bridge in Nanjing-Shanghai section of Beijing-Shanghai High-Speed Railway. It starts from Danyang in the west, passing through Changzhou, Wuxi and Suzhou, and ends at Kunshan in the east. It has successively crossed more than 150 rivers and more than 180 roads, with four elevated stations on the bridge. The total length of the bridge is 164.851km, which is the longest bridge in the world. The deck of the mainline bridge is arranged according to the two-lane high-speed railway.

Danyang-Kunshan Grand Bridge is composed mainly of prestressed concrete simply-supported box girders with the standard span length of 32m and 24m, which were prefabricated and erected on site. There are also 139 bridges with different bridge types in the whole line, including 88 prestressed concrete continuous girder bridges in the main line, 41 prestressed concrete continuous girder bridges in the switch sections, 9 single-span through arch bridges combined with prestressed concrete continuous girder deck and a three-span through arch bridges combined with prestressed concrete continuous girder deck. The maximum span length of the single-span through arch bridges is 128m, and the span layout of the three-span through arch bridge is 70m+136m+70m. The substructures mainly adopt reinforced concrete single-column and double-column piers, with rectangular, circular or round-end solid and hollow sections. The abutments are mainly rectangular hollow abutments and frame abutments, etc., and the foundation adopts reinforced concrete piles.

Danyang-Kunshan Grand Bridge covers most bridge types and construction methods for passenger dedicated lines. The construction method of "double row pile cofferdam construction technology" was used for the foundations of the bridge in Yangcheng Lake area, which meets the requirement for green construction in lake areas.

# INNOVATION AND IMPROVEMENT

**Name:** Danyang-Kunshan Grand Bridge
**Type:** Beam-arch composite bridge, continuous girder bridge and simply-supported girder bridge, etc.
**Length:** Total length 164.851km, main span 136m
**Location:** Danyang City, Changzhou City, Wuxi City, Suzhou City, Kunshan City, Jiangsu Province
**Completion:** June 2011
**Owner(s):** Beijing-Shanghai High Speed Railway Co., Ltd.
**Designer(s):** China Railway Siyuan Survey and Design Group Co., Ltd.
**Contractor(s):** China Communications Construction Company Limited, China Railway No.3 Engineering Group Co., Ltd., China Railway No.5 Engineering Group Co., Ltd., etc.

桥　　名：丹昆特大桥
桥　　型：梁拱组合桥，连续梁桥，简支梁桥等
桥梁长度：全长 164.851km，主跨跨径 136m
桥　　址：江苏省丹阳市、常州市、无锡市、苏州市和昆山市
建成时间：2011 年 6 月
建设单位：京沪高速铁路股份有限公司
设计单位：中铁第四勘察设计院集团有限公司
施工单位：中国交通建设股份有限公司，中铁三局集团有限公司，中铁五局集团有限公司等

# 新疆果子沟大桥

## Xinjiang Guozigou Bridge

| | |
|---|---|
| 桥　　名： | 新疆果子沟大桥 |
| 桥　　型： | 双塔双索面钢桁梁斜拉桥 |
| 主跨跨径： | 330m |
| 桥　　址： | 新疆维吾尔自治区伊宁市 |
| 建成时间： | 2011年11月 |
| 建设单位： | 新疆维吾尔自治区交通建设管理局 |
| 设计单位： | 中国公路工程咨询集团有限公司 |
| 施工单位： | 中交第二航务工程局有限公司 |

**Name:** Xinjiang Guozigou Bridge
**Type:** Double-pylon double-cable-plane steel truss girder cable-stayed bridge
**Main span:** 330m
**Location:** Yining City, Xinjiang Uygur Autonomous Region
**Completion:** November 2011
**Owner(s):** Xinjiang Uygur Autonomous Region Transportation Construction Bureau
**Designer(s):** China Highway Engineering Consulting Corporation
**Contractor(s):** CCCC Second Harbor Engineering Company Ltd.

新疆果子沟大桥位于新疆维吾尔自治区伊宁市连云港—霍尔果斯高速公路（G30）赛里木湖至果子沟口段，跨越果子沟与将军沟交汇处山谷，桥面距谷底约180m。大桥全长700m，桥面宽度26.93m，按双向四车道高速公路布置。

新疆果子沟大桥主桥为双塔双索面钢桁梁斜拉桥，跨径布置为170m+330m+170m。主梁采用钢桁梁、预制混凝土桥面板结构，钢桁梁上、下弦杆与塔柱间设四个横向抗风支座，纵向采用液压阻尼器装置。主塔为三阶梯形钢筋混凝土框架结构，单箱单室截面，两塔的高度分别为209m和215.5m。斜拉索采用镀锌平行钢丝束拉索，高密度聚乙烯（HDPE）外护套表面设防风雨振螺旋线，端部内置橡胶减振块，并设体外减振器。梁上索距为12m，塔上索距为2.1m。主墩基础承台平面采用哑铃形构造，基础采用钻孔桩基础。

新疆果子沟大桥是新疆维吾尔自治区首座大跨度斜拉桥，为高寒、强震、高海拔及复杂风环境下的山区桥梁建设提供了新思路。

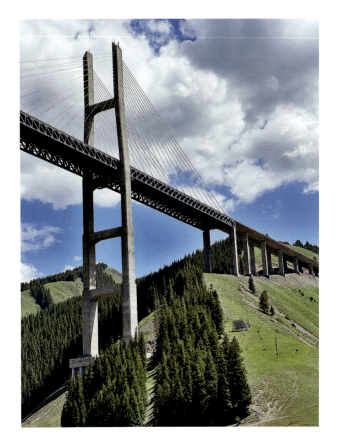

Xinjiang Guozigou Bridge is located on the section from Sayram Lake to Guozigou Mouth of Lianyungang-Khorgos Expressway (G30) in Yining City, Xinjiang Uygur Autonomous Region of China. It spans the Valley at the intersection of Guozigou and Jiangjungou, with the bridge deck about 180m from the valley bottom. The bridge is 700m long, with the bridge deck width of 26.93m, and is arranged as a dual-way four-lane highway.

The main bridge is a double-pylon double cable plane steel truss girder cable-stayed bridge, with the span arrangement of 170m+330m+170m. The main girder adopts steel truss and precast concrete deck, with four transverse wind bearings between the upper and lower chords of the steel truss girder and the pylon columns, and hydraulic damper devices in the longitudinal direction. The pylon is a three-step trapezoidal reinforced concrete frame structure with single box and single cell cross-section, and the heights of the two pylons are 209m and 215.5m respectively. The cables are galvanized parallel steel wire cables, with anti-wind and rain vibration spirals on the surface of the high-density polyethylene (HDPE) outer sheaths and internal rubber vibration-damping blocks at the ends, as well as external dampers. The spacing of the cables on the girders is 12m, and the spacing of the cables on the towers is 2.1m. The foundation bearing plane of the main piers adopts the dumbbell-shaped structure, and the foundation of the piers is made by drilled piles.

Xinjiang Guozigou Bridge is the first long-span cable-stayed bridge in Xinjiang Uygur Autonomous Region, which provides a new idea for the construction of bridges in mountain areas under extremely cold, strong earthquake, high altitude and complex wind environment.

# 武汉二七长江大桥
## Wuhan Erqi Bridge over Yangtze River

武汉二七长江大桥是湖北省武汉市的跨越长江通道，为武汉二环线组成部分。主桥全长1.732km，桥面净宽度30.5m，按双向八车道城市快速路布置。

武汉二七长江大桥的主桥为三塔双索面组合梁斜拉桥，跨径布置为90m+160m+2×616m+160m+90m，是当时世界上最大跨度的双主跨斜拉桥。大桥采用半漂浮结构体系，在中塔横梁顶面设置竖向支座及纵向限位挡块，边塔横梁顶面设双向活动支座，边塔横梁两侧设四套纵向阻尼装置。主梁为钢梁-混凝土桥面板的组合梁结构，宽度32.3m、高度3.5m，两根I形钢梁的横向中心距离为30.5m，混凝土桥面板厚度为260mm。桥塔为花瓶形钢筋混凝土结构，塔高均为209m。斜拉索采用平行镀锌钢绞线、高密度聚乙烯（HDPE）外护套拉索，最多由79根钢绞线组成，最大索力8000kN。拉索在主梁上的纵向间距为13.5m，采用锚拉板式锚固结构。基础采用高桩承台钻孔灌注桩。

武汉二七长江大桥的钢绞线拉索可以单根穿索、单根张拉、单根检测及单根更换，索力可按单根钢绞线调整。

Wuhan Erqi Bridge over Yangtze River is a passageway across the Yangtze River in Wuhan City, Hubei Province, and is part of the Wuhan Second Ring Road. The total length of the main bridge is 1.732km, the net width of the bridge deck is 30.5m, and it is arranged as a dual-way eight-lane urban expressway.

The main bridge of Wuhan Erqi Bridge over Yangtze River is a cable-stayed bridge with three pylons, double cable planes and steel-concrete composite girders, with the span arrangement of 90m+160m+2×616m+160m+90m. It adopts a semi-floating system, and was the longest twin-main-span cable-stayed bridge in the world at that time. There are vertical bearings and longitudinal restriction blocks on the top surface of the cross beam in the middle pylon, two-way movable bearings on the top surface of that in the side pylon, and four sets of longitudinal damping devices on both

桥　　名：武汉二七长江大桥
桥　　型：三塔双索面组合梁斜拉桥
主跨跨径：2×616m
桥　　址：湖北省武汉市
建成时间：2011年12月
建设单位：武汉市城市建设投资开发集团有限公司
设计单位：中铁大桥勘测设计院集团有限公司
施工单位：中铁大桥局集团有限公司　中交第二航务工程局有限公司

**Name:** Wuhan Erqi Bridge over Yangtze River
**Type:** Three-tower double-cable-plane steel-concrete composite girder cable-stayed bridge
**Main span:** 2×616m
**Location:** Wuhan City, Hubei Province
**Completion:** December 2011
**Owner(s):** Wuhan Urban Construction Investment Development Co., Ltd.
**Designer(s):** China Railway Major Bridge Reconnaissance & Design Institute Co., Ltd.
**Contractor(s):** China Railway Major Bridge Engineering Group Co., Ltd. CCCC Second Harbor Engineering Company Ltd.

sides of the cross beam in the side pylon. The main girder is a composite structure with steel beam and concrete deck, with a width of 32.3m and a depth of 3.5m, the transverse center distance of the two I-shaped steel beams is 30.5m, and the thickness of the concrete deck slab is 260mm. The pylon is a vase shaped reinforced concrete structure, with a height of 209m. The cables are made of parallel galvanized strands with high-density polyethylene (HDPE) outer sheaths, and are made up of 79 strands at most, with a maximum cable force of 8,000kN. The cables are connected to girders with steel tensile anchorage plates with 13.5m longitudinal spacing. The foundations are rise pile cap with drilled pile foundation.

The strand cables of Wuhan Erqi Bridge over Yangtze River can be singly threaded, singly tensioned, singly tested and singly replaced, and the cable force can be adjusted for each single strand.

# 矮寨大桥

## Aizhai Bridge

| | |
|---|---|
| 桥　名： | 矮寨大桥 |
| 桥　型： | 双塔单跨吊钢桁梁悬索桥 |
| 主跨跨径： | 1176m |
| 桥　址： | 湖南省湘西土家族苗族自治州 |
| 建成时间： | 2012年3月 |
| 建设单位： | 湖南省高速公路建设开发总公司 |
| 设计单位： | 湖南省交通规划勘察设计院有限公司 |
| 施工单位： | 湖南路桥建设集团有限责任公司 |

　　矮寨大桥是湖南省湘西土家族苗族自治州包头—茂名高速公路（G65）上吉首至茶洞段上跨越德夯大峡谷的特大桥梁。大桥两端直接与隧道相连，桥面距离峡谷底部垂直高度达355m。大桥全长1.414km，桥面宽度24.5m，按双向四车道高速公路布置。

　　矮寨大桥为双塔单跨钢桁梁悬索桥，主跨跨径1176m。钢桁梁长1000.5m、宽27m、高7.5m，采用纵向工字梁与混凝土桥面板组合的桥面结构。主缆跨径布置为242m+1176m+116m，主跨垂跨比为1/9.6；主缆由169股、每股为127根 $\phi$5.25 的预制平行钢丝索股组成，吉首侧边跨增加6个索股，跨中设三组柔性中央扣。吊索纵向间距14.5m，采用钢丝绳索股。桥塔采用门式框架结构，吉首和茶洞侧塔高分别为129.316m和61.924m，采用扩大基础。吉首侧采用重力式锚碇，茶洞侧采用隧道式锚碇。

　　矮寨大桥结合桥址的地形和地质条件，采用塔梁分离式悬索桥结构，缩短了梁长、降低了塔高、减少了山体开挖；在主缆无吊索区设竖向碳纤维锚索，研发"CFRP-RPC"高性能岩锚体系，解决了主缆刚度突变引起的结构受力问题；针对山区钢桁梁运输和架设的难题，结合节段预制研发了柔性轨索滑移法节段架设的新工艺。

Aizhai Bridge is a long bridge across the Dehang Grand Canyon on the Jishou-Chadong section of Baotou-Maoming Expressway（G65）in Xiangxi Tujiazu & Miaozu Autonomous Prefecture, Hunan Province. The two ends of the bridge are directly connected to the tunnel, and the vertical height of the bridge deck from the bottom of the canyon reaches 355m. The bridge has a total length of 1.414km, a deck width of 24.5m, and is arranged as a dual-way four-lane expressway.

Aizhai Bridge is a double-pylon, single span steel truss girder suspension bridge with a main span of 1,176m. The steel truss girder is 1,000.5m long, 27m wide and 7.5m high, and it adopts a composite bridge deck structure with longitudinal I-beams and concrete deck slabs. The main cable span arrangement is 242m+1,176m+116m, with sag span ratio of 1/9.6. The main cable consists of 169 bundles and each bundle includes 127 prefabricated parallel steel wires of $\phi$5.25. The cable of the Jishou side span increases 6 bundles, and there are three sets of flexible central buckles in the main span. The longitudinal spacing of the hangers that use steel wire bundles is 14.5m. The pylon adopts portal frame structure, and the heights of the pylons in Jishou and Chadong sides are 129.316m and 61.924m respectively, and the expanded foundation is adopted. The anchor blocks in Jishou and Chadong side are a gravity anchorage and a rock tunnel anchorage, respectively.

Considering the topography and geological conditions of the bridge site, the suspension structure system of separated pylon and main girder is adopted for Aizhai Bridge, which shortens the girder length, lowers the tower height and reduces the excavation of the mountain. The application of vertical carbon fibre anchor cables installed in the region without hangers increases the local structural stiffness, which solves the structural stress problem caused by the sudden change of the stiffness of the main cables, and CFRP-RPC high-performance rock anchorages are developed. Aiming at the difficulties of transportation and erection of steel truss girders in mountainous areas, a new technology of section erection by flexible rail cable sliding method was developed in combination with section prefabrication.

**Name:** Aizhai Bridge
**Type:** Double-tower single-suspended-span suspension bridge with steel truss girder
**Main span:** 1,176m
**Location:** Xiangxi Tujiazu & Miaozu Autonomous Prefecture, Hunan Province
**Completion:** March 2012
**Owner(s):** Hunan Provincial Highway Construction and Development Corporation
**Designer(s):** Hunan Province Communication Planning, Survey & Design Institute Co., Ltd.
**Contractor(s):** Hunan Road & Bridge Construction Group Corporation

# 杭州九堡大桥
## Hangzhou Jiubao Bridge

桥　　名：杭州九堡大桥
桥　　型：连续组合梁钢箱拱组合桥
主跨跨径：3×210m
桥　　址：浙江省杭州市
建成时间：2012年7月
建设单位：杭州市城市建设投资集团有限公司，杭州市城市基础设施开发总公司
设计单位：上海市政工程设计研究总院（集团）有限公司
施工单位：中交第二航务工程有限公司，路桥集团国际建设股份有限公司

**Name:** Hangzhou Jiubao Bridge
**Type:** Steel box arch bridge combined with continuous steel-concrete composite girder
**Main span:** 3×210m
**Location:** Hangzhou City, Zhejiang Province
**Completion:** July 2012
**Owner(s):** Hangzhou Urban Construction Investment Group Co., Ltd., Hangzhou Urban Infrastructure Development Corporation.
**Designer(s):** Shanghai Municipal Engineering Design Institute (Group) Co., Ltd.
**Contractor(s):** CCCC Second Harbor Engineering Company Ltd., CRBC International Co., Ltd.

inclination and curved shape are connected by transverse bracing to form a spacial structure. The longitudinal girder is a steel-concrete composite structure with a girder depth of 4.5m. In transverse direction, two narrow steel box sections with a center distance of 27.6m between the two boxes are used, and an I-shape steel transverse beam is arranged every 4.25m in the longitudinal direction. The reinforced concrete deck slab is installed on the steel beams. The bridge substructure adopts double V-shaped thin-walled piers in transverse direction and the curve of the pier follows the arch axis above the deck. The bearing platforms of each pier are dumbbell-shaped, with drilled pile foundation.

Hangzhou Jiubao Bridge is located in a region with strong surge, which is the first to adopt the long-span arch bridge combined with continuous girder structure. All of the three-span steel structure of the main bridge adopted the incremental launching construction method. Temporary bracings are installed between the arch ribs and the steel beams and one temporary pier is built in the middle of each span.

　　九堡大桥位于浙江省杭州市，跨越钱塘江，是连接萧山区和上城区的过江通道。桥梁全长 1.855km，由主桥和南北引桥组成。主桥桥面宽度为 37.7m，按双向六车道城市快速路布置。

　　杭州九堡大桥的主桥为连续组合梁钢箱拱组合桥，跨径布置为 3×210m。拱肋采用箱钢结构，由主副拱肋组成，主副拱肋的立面矢高分别为 43.784m 和 33m。外倾 12°的主拱肋与内倾曲线形的副拱肋由横撑连接成空间结构。纵梁为钢-混凝土组合梁结构，梁高为 4.5m，横向两侧采用窄形钢箱梁，两箱中心距为 27.6m，纵向每 4.25m 设一道工字形钢横梁，上设钢筋混凝土桥面板。大桥下部采用横桥向双 V 形薄壁墩结构，墩身线形顺接梁上拱轴线，各墩承台平面均为哑铃形，基础为钻孔灌注桩。

　　杭州九堡大桥位于强涌潮河段，首创连续大跨径梁拱组合结构。主桥三跨钢结构采用整体顶推施工法，拱肋与钢纵梁间设置临时加强杆件，每跨间设 1 个临时墩。

Jiubao Bridge, over the Qiantang River, is located in Hangzhou City, Zhejiang Province, as a river crossing passage connecting Xiaoshan District and Shangcheng District. The total length of the bridge is 1.855km, consisting of the main bridge and the north and south approach bridges. The deck of the main bridge is 37.7m wide and is arranged as a dual-way six-lane urban expressway.

The main bridge of Hangzhou Jiubao Bridge is a steel box arch bridge combined with continuous composite girder with a span arrangement of 3×210m. The ribs of the arches have a section of steel box, and are composed of main arch ribs and secondary arch ribs, the elevations of which are 43.784m and 33m respectively. The main arch rib with 12° outward inclination and the secondary arch rib with inward

# 泰州长江大桥

## Taizhou Bridge over Yangtze River

泰州长江大桥位于江苏省内长江中段，北接泰州市，南连镇江市扬中市，全长62.088km，跨越长江与夹江。桥面宽度为33.0m，按双向六车道高速公路布置。

泰州长江大桥的主桥为三塔两跨连续钢箱梁悬索桥，主跨跨径2×1080m，是世界上最大跨度的双主跨悬索桥。钢箱梁宽度为39.1m、高度为3.5m。主缆跨径布置为390m+2×1080m+390m，主跨垂跨比为1/9，采用91根ø5.2预制平行钢丝索股，每根主缆169股。吊索纵向间距16m，采用平行钢丝索股。边塔采用钢筋混凝土门式框架结构，塔高171.7m，采用钻孔灌注桩基础。中塔采用钢结构，横桥向为门式框架结构、纵桥向呈人字形，塔高191.5m，采用沉井基础。锚碇为重力式沉井基础。

泰州长江大桥是首座大跨度三塔两跨悬索桥体系，通过中塔采用刚度适中的人字形钢桥塔等措施，既解决了中塔塔顶主缆与鞍座的抗滑移问题，又兼顾了结构刚度。中塔的基础采用浮式沉井基础，确保了工程质量，简化了施工，节约了材料。

泰州长江大桥获得了国际桥梁与结构工程协会杰出结构奖。

Taizhou Bridge over Yangtze River is located in the middle part of Yangtze River in Jiangsu Province, connecting Taizhou City in the north and Yangzhong County, Zhenjiang City in the south. The bridge has a total length of 62.088km and a deck width of 33.0m, crossing the Yangtze River and the Jiajiang River respectively, which is arranged as a dual-way six-lane expressway.

The main bridge of Taizhou Bridge over Yangtze River is a three-tower double-suspended-span suspension bridge with central spans of 2×1,080m, as the longest twin-main-span suspension bridge. The bridge deck is a 39.1m wide and 3.5m deep two-span continuous steel box. The sag span ratio of the main cables is 1/9. Each main cable consists of 169 parallel bundles, and each bundle includes 91$\phi$5.2 steel wires. The hangers placed along the bridge at 16m spacing are made with parallel wire bundles. The side towers supported by bored piles are portal frame shape reinforced concrete structures with the height of 171.7m. The middle tower supported by a floating caisson foundation is a steel structure with a portal frame in the lateral direction and with a herringbone shape in the longitudinal direction with the height of 191.5m. Both the northern and southern anchorage blocks are gravity anchorages rest on caissons.

Taizhou Bridge over Yangtze River has adopted three towers and two main spans in suspension bridges for the first time. A herringbone shaped steel structure with moderate stiffness is adopted in the middle tower of the bridge to solve the anti-slipping problem between the main cable and the cable saddle at the top of the middle tower and the structural stiffness has been taken into account. The floating caisson is adopted as the foundation of the middle tower to ensure the engineering quality, simplify the construction procedure and save materials.

The Project of Taizhou Bridge over Yangtze River has won the Outstanding Structure Award International Association for Bridge and Structural Engineering.

| | |
|---|---|
| 桥　名： | 泰州长江大桥 |
| 桥　型： | 三塔两跨吊连续钢箱梁悬索桥 |
| 主跨跨径： | 2×1080m |
| 桥　址： | 江苏省泰州市和镇江市 |
| 建成时间： | 2012年11月 |
| 建设单位： | 江苏省长江公路大桥建设指挥部 |
| 设计单位： | 江苏省交通规划设计院股份有限公司，中铁大桥勘测设计院集团有限公司，同济大学建筑设计研究院（集团）有限公司 |
| 施工单位： | 中交第二公路工程局有限公司，中交第二航务工程局有限公司，中铁大桥局集团有限公司 |

**Name:** Taizhou Bridge over Yangtze River
**Type:** Three-tower double-suspended-span suspension bridge with continuous steel box girder
**Main span:** 2×1,080m
**Location:** Taizhou City and zhenjiang City, Jiangsu Province
**Completion:** November 2012
**Owner(s):** Jiangsu Yangtze River Highway Bridge Construction Command Headquarter
**Designer(s):** Jiangsu Provincial Communications Planning and Design Institute Co., Ltd., China Railway Major Bridge Reconnaissance & Design Institute Co., Ltd., Tongji Architectural Design (Group) Co., Ltd.
**Contractor(s):** CCCC Second Highway Engineering Co., Ltd., CCCC Second Harbor Engineering Company Ltd., China Railway Major Bridge Engineering Group Co., Ltd.

# 波司登长江大桥

## Bosideng Bridge over Yangtze River

波司登长江大桥位于四川省泸州市合江县，是国家高速公路网成渝地区环线上的一座特大桥，为世界上首座跨度突破500m的钢管混凝土拱桥。大桥全长840.9m，桥面宽度30.6m，按双向四车道高速公路布置。

波司登长江大桥的主桥为中承式钢管混凝土拱桥，主跨跨径为530m，矢跨比为1/4.5。桥梁横向采用双拱肋结构，拱肋中心间距为28.6m，双拱肋之间设置钢管和钢管混凝土桁架式风撑。拱肋宽度为4m，高度由拱顶8m变化到拱脚16m。4根直径1.32m的钢管组成上下弦，通过横联、竖向钢管构成桁架式结构。上下弦杆钢管内填充C60混凝土，拱脚与拱座固结。桥面结构采用钢梁-混凝土桥面板组合梁，由两道主纵梁、三道次纵梁及横梁形成的钢格构与混凝土桥面板组合，纵、横梁均采用工字形截面。吊杆采用整体挤压锚固的钢绞线拉索，吊杆和拱上立柱间距14.3m。双拱肋的拱座采用分离式结构，基础埋置于弱风化岩层内。

波司登长江大桥的拱肋采用缆索吊运、斜拉扣索悬臂拼装施工。首创的真空辅助压力连续灌注管内混凝土工法大大提高了混凝土灌注质量，研发的索鞍横移、摇臂抱杆安装扣塔技术与装备节省了安装费用。

波司登长江大桥获得国家科技进步奖二等奖。

Bosideng Bridge over Yangtze River, located in Hejiang County, Luzhou City, Sichuan Province, is a super long bridge on the loop line of Chengdu-Chongqing area in the national highway network. It is the first concrete-filled steel tube arch bridge with a span breaking 500m in the world. This bridge is 840.9m long and 30.6m wide. It is arranged as a dual-way four-lane highway.

The main bridge of Bosideng Bridge over Yangtze River is a concrete-filled steel tube half through arch bridge, which has a main span of 530m and the rise span ratio of the arch is 1/4.5. The bridge adopts double arch ribs structure in transverse direction, with the arch ribs spaced 28.6m apart. Steel tube and concrete-filled steel tube truss wind bracings are incorporated between two arch ribs. Arch ribs are 4m wide, while the depth is 8m at the crown and 16m at the springing, consisting of 4 steel tubes with a diameter of 1.32m as the upper and lower chords. Arch ribs constitute a truss structure through transverse and vertical steel tubes, the upper and lower chords of the trusses are filled with C60 concrete, and the arch foot is fixed to the arch base. The bridge deck adopts steel beam-concrete deck composite structure, formed by the steel grillage including two main longitudinal beams, three secondary longitudinal beams and transverse beams with the concrete deck. I-shaped sections are used for longitudinal and transverse beams. The hangers adopt steel strands with integral extrusion anchorage, and the spacing between the hangers and the columns on the arch is 14.3m. The arch bases of the two arch ribs are seperated structures with the foundation buried in a weakly weathered rock layer.

The arch ribs of Bosideng Bridge over Yangtze River were constructed by cantilever erection method supported by temporary stays and temporary suspension cables were used to transport and erect the segments. The technology of vacuum-assisted pressure continuous filling of concrete in tubes was created that greatly improves the quality of concrete filling. The development of technology and equipment of the saddle traverse, temporary tower installation with holding pole with rotating arm, saves the installation costs greatly.

The Project of Bosideng Bridge over Yangtze River has won the Second Prize of National Science and Technology Progress Award.

桥　　名：波司登长江大桥
桥　　型：中承式钢管混凝土拱桥
主跨跨径：530m
桥　　址：四川省泸州市
建成时间：2013年6月
建设单位：泸州东南高速公路发展有限公司
设计单位：四川省交通运输厅公路规划勘察设计研究院
施工单位：广西壮族自治区公路桥梁工程总公司

**Name:** Bosideng Bridge over Yangtze River
**Type:** Half through concrete-filled steel tube arch bridge
**Main span:** 530m
**Location:** Luzhou City, Sichuan Province
**Completion:** June 2013
**Owner(s):** Luzhou Southeast Expressway Development Co., Ltd.
**Designer(s):** Sichuan Provincial Transport Department Highway Planning, Survey, Design and Research Institute.
**Contractor(s):** Guangxi Road & Bridge Engineering Corporation.

# 嘉绍大桥

## Jiashao Bridge

| | |
|---|---|
| 桥　名： | 嘉绍大桥 |
| 桥　型： | 六塔四索面钢箱梁斜拉桥 |
| 主跨跨径： | 5×428m |
| 桥　址： | 浙江省绍兴市 |
| 建成时间： | 2013年7月 |
| 建设单位： | 浙江嘉绍跨江大桥投资发展有限公司 |
| 设计单位： | 中交公路规划设计院有限公司 |
| 施工单位： | 中交第二航务工程局有限公司，广东省长大公路工程有限公司 |

嘉绍大桥位于浙江省杭州湾海域内，是嘉兴至绍兴跨越钱塘江河口段的一座特大型桥梁，全长 10.137km。跨江段设有主航道桥和副航道桥。桥梁总宽度为 55.6m，按双向八车道高速公路布置。

嘉绍大桥主航道桥为六塔四索面钢箱梁斜拉桥，跨径布置为 70m+200m+5×428m+200m+70m，采用单柱塔、四索面、分幅式结构，半漂浮结构体系。每幅主梁采用栓焊流线型扁平钢箱梁，梁高 4.0m、梁宽 24m，两幅箱梁之间设置长度 9.8m 的横梁；主梁跨中设置刚性铰构造的伸缩缝。桥塔采用独柱形构造，塔下钢箱梁的支承横梁为 X 形空间托架结构，塔梁之间纵向设置双排支座。副航道桥为预应力混凝土变截面连续刚构桥。大桥基础均采用大直径钻孔灌注桩。

嘉绍大桥独柱形塔采用的 X 形空间托架式横梁及相应的纵向双支承体系，提升了小体量塔柱多塔斜拉桥主梁的竖向刚度；在多塔斜拉桥跨中设置释放轴向变形的"刚性铰"构造，解决了多塔斜拉桥超长主梁的温度变形问题。

Jiashao Bridge is located in Hangzhou Bay, Zhejiang Province. It is a super long bridge from Jiaxing to Shaoxing across the estuary of Qiantang River, with a total length of 10.137km. A main navigation channel bridge and a secondary navigation channel bridge are arranged in the river-crossing section. The total width of the bridge is 55.6m, which is a dual-way eight-lane expressway.

The main navigation channel bridge of Jiashao Bridge is a steel box girder cable-stayed bridge with six towers and four cable planes. The span arrangement is 70m+200m+5×428m+200m+70m. It adopts single-column towers, four cable planes, separated parallel girders and semi-floating structural system. Each girder is a bolt-welded streamlined flat steel box structure with the depth of 4.0m and the width of 24m. A transverse beam with a length of 9.8m are set between the two box girders. An expansion joint with rigid hinge is set in the midspan of each main girder. The tower is a single-column structure. The supporting beam of the steel box girder under the tower is an X-shaped bracing structure, and double-row longitudinal supports are set between towers and girders. The secondary navigation channel bridge is a prestressed concrete continuous rigid-frame bridge with various cross-section. The foundations of the bridge are all large-diameter bored piles.

The X-shaped spatial transverse bracings and the longitudinal double-row support system for the single-column tower improve the vertical girder stiffness for cable-stayed bridge with small size multi-towers. The rigid hinges set in the mid-span of the multi-tower cable-stayed bridge releases the axial deformation, which solved the problem of the deformation due to temperature for extra-long girders.

**Name:** Jiashao Bridge
**Type:** Six-tower four-cable-plane steel box girder cable-stayed bridge
**Main span:** 5×428m
**Location:** Shaoxing City, Zhejiang Province
**Completion:** July 2013
**Owner(s):** Zhejiang Jiashao Cross-river Bridge Investment Development Co., Ltd.
**Designer(s):** CCCC Highway Consultants Co., Ltd.
**Contractor(s):** CCCC Second Harbor Engineering Company Ltd., Guangdong Provincial Changda Highway Engineering Co., Ltd.

# 水盘高速北盘江特大桥

## Liupanshui-Panxian Expressway Bridge over Beipan River

水盘高速北盘江特大桥位于贵州省西部的六盘水市水城县发耳乡和营盘乡交会处，跨越北盘江大峡谷。桥梁全长 1.261km，最大墩高 170m，单幅桥宽 10.5m，按双向四车道高速公路布置。

水盘高速北盘江特大桥的主桥为空腹式预应力混凝土连续刚构桥，跨径布置为 82.5m+220m+290m+220m+82.5m，为世界首座该类结构的桥梁。主梁采用直腹板单箱单室截面，箱梁底宽 6.5m。290m 跨径段结构为带空腹段的 T 形刚构，墩顶结构高度为 35m，跨中梁高为 4.5m；空腹段的下弦采用高度 7.5m 的等截面箱形结构，上弦为单箱单室截面，高度由 5m 过渡到 7m，下弦与上弦相交区段采用单箱双室截面。两个边墩上的主梁为双悬臂 75m 的箱形截面 T 形刚构，墩顶梁高 10m，跨中（端部）梁高 4.5m。上部结构采用三向预应力、全预应力混凝土结构设计。纵向预应力钢束采用交错锚固方式，以减少超长钢束的预应力损失。大桥空腹段的下弦采用斜爬挂篮结合临时扣挂系统分段悬臂浇筑、上弦通过下弦上的支架结合移动模架分段浇筑的工法，上弦节段浇筑滞后下弦，为上、下弦异步平行施工。

水盘高速北盘江特大桥刚度大、自重轻。其采用的空腹段结构具有梁拱组合结构的力学特征，不仅跨越能力大、抗变形能力强，而且为山区桥梁设计提供了新的可选形式。

Liupanshui-Panxian Expressway Bridge over Beipan River is located at the junction of Fa'er Town and Yingpan Town of Shuicheng County, Liupanshui City, west of Guizhou Province. The bridge has a total length of 1.261km and maximum pier height of 170m. It is arranged as a dual-way four-lane expressway with two parallel bridges of 10.5m wide each.

The main bridge of the Liupanshui-Panxian Expressway Bridge over Beipan River is the open spandrel prestressed concrete rigid frame bridge with the span arrangement of

82.5m+220m+290m+220m+82.5m, which is the first bridge of this kind in the world. The straight web single cell box section is adopted for the deck, and the bottom width of the box section is 6.5m. The structure of 290m span is T-shaped rigid frame with open spandrel. The structure depth of the superstructure on the pier top is 35m, and the depth of girder at the mid-span is 4.5m. Constant box section is adopted for the lower chord of the open spandrel, the depth of which is 7.5m. The upper chord adopts single cell box section, and the depth of girder varies from 5m to 7m. At the intersection of the lower and upper chord, a double cell single box section is adopted. The superstructure on both side piers is T-shaped rigid frame with box section, which is 75m symmetrical balanced cantilevers. The depth of the girder on the pier top is 10m, while the depth of the girder at mid-span (cantilever end) is 4.5m. The superstructure is designed as a fully prestressed concrete girder bridge with three-dimensional prestressing. The longitudinal prestressing steel tendons adopt cross anchoring method, which reduces the prestress loss of the super long prestressing tendons. The balanced cantilever construction method using inclined climbing hanging basket combined with temporary cable system was adopted for the lower chord of the open spandrel, while the scaffolding on the lower chord combined with mobile formwork was used for the segmental casting of the upper chord. The construction of the upper chord is one segment behind the construction of the lower chord, forming the asynchronous parallel construction process.

The Liupanshui-Panxian Expressway Bridge over Beipan River has large stiffness and light deadweight. Its structure of the open spandrel has combined the mechanical characteristics of girder bridge and arch bridge, and has strong spanning ability and deformation resistance, which provides a new optional design form of long-span girder bridge in mountainous areas.

**Name:** Liupanshui-Panxian Expressway Bridge over Beipan River
**Type:** Open spandrel prestressed concrete continuous rigid frame bridge
**Main span:** 290m
**Location:** Liupanshui City, Guizhou Province
**Completion:** August 2013
**Owner(s):** Guizhou Expressway Group Co., Ltd.
**Designer(s):** CCCC Second Highway Consultants Co., Ltd.
**Constructor(s):** Guizhou Road & Bridge Group Co., Ltd., CCCC Second Harbor Engineering Company, Ltd.

# 马鞍山长江大桥
## Ma'anshan Bridge over Yangtze River

马鞍山长江大桥位于马鞍山长江段江心洲，是安徽省马鞍山市内连接和县和雨山区的过江通道。大桥分为左汊桥、右汊桥两部分，跨江主体桥梁长11.209km，桥面宽33.0m，按双向六车道高速公路布置。

马鞍山长江大桥的主桥（左汊桥）为三塔两跨连续钢箱梁悬索桥，主跨跨径为2×1080m。钢箱梁宽度为38.5m、高度为3.5m，中塔处梁与塔固结，梁高从3.5m过渡至5.0m。主缆跨径布置为360m+1080m+1080m+360m，主跨垂跨比1/9，采用91根⌀5.2预制平行钢丝索股，每根主缆154股。吊索纵向间距16m，采用平行钢丝索股。中塔为钢-混凝土混合的门式框架结构，上塔柱为钢结构，高度为127.8m；下塔柱为预应力混凝土结构，高度为37.5m。边塔为钢筋混凝土门式框架结构，高度为165.3m。中、边塔均采用钻孔灌注桩基础。锚碇为沉井基础重力式结构。

马鞍山长江大桥中塔采用钢与混凝土混合结构和塔梁固结体系，有效解决了三塔悬索桥主缆与鞍座间的抗滑移问题的同时兼顾了主梁的刚度需求。

Ma'anshan Bridge over Yangtze River is located in the Jiangxinzhou of Ma'anshan Yangtze River section. It is a cross-river passage connecting Hexian County and Yushan District in Ma'anshan City, Anhui Province. The bridge is divided into two parts: the left branch bridge and the right branch bridge. The main bridge across the river is 11.209km long and the deck is 33.0m wide. It is designed as dual-way six-lane expressway.

The main bridge (left branch bridge) is a three-tower two-span continuous steel box girder suspension bridge with main spans of 2×1,080m. The steel box girder has a width of 38.5m and a depth of 3.5m. The girder depth is increased from 3.5m to 5.0m approaching the mid-tower and fixed with it. The span arrangement of the main cables is 360m+1,080m+1,080m+360m, and the sag span ratio of the main cables is 1/9. Each main cable consists of 154 parallel wire bundles, and each bundle includes 91 ⌀5.2 prefabricated steel wires. The hangers placed along the bridge at each 16m are made with parallel wire bundles. The mid-tower is a steel-concrete hybrid portal frame structure composed of a 127.8m high steel structure above the deck and a 37.5m high prestressed concrete structure below the deck. The towers in side spans are portal frame shape reinforced concrete structures with a depth of 165.3m. Both the middle and side towers are supported by bored piles. The anchorage blocks are gravity anchorages with caissons.

The main feature of the bridge is the development of a new system to fix the girder with the mid-tower composed of a steel structure and a concrete structure. The new system not only solved the anti-slipping problem between the main cable and the cable saddle effectively, but also ensured the rigidity of the girder.

桥　　名：马鞍山长江大桥
桥　　型：三塔两跨吊连续钢箱梁悬索桥
主跨跨径：2×1080m
桥　　址：安徽省马鞍山市
建成时间：2013年12月
建设单位：安徽省高速公路总公司
设计单位：安徽省交通规划设计研究院有限公司，中铁大桥勘测设计院集团有限公司
施工单位：中铁大桥局集团有限公司，中交第二公路工程局有限公司，中交第二航务工程局有限公司

**Name:** Ma'anshan Bridge over Yangtze River
**Type:** Three-tower double-suspended-span suspension bridge with continuous steel box girder
**Main span:** 2×1,080m
**Location:** Ma'anshan City, Anhui Province
**Completion:** December 2013
**Owner(s):** Anhui Provincial Expressway Corporation
**Designer(s):** Anhui Transport Consulting & Design Institute Co., Ltd., China Railway Major Bridge Reconnaissance & Design Institute Co., Ltd.
**Contractor(s):** China Railway Major Bridge Engineering Group Co., Ltd., CCCC Second Highway Engineering Co., Ltd., CCCC Second Harbor Engineering Company Ltd.

中国桥梁 1949—2024 | BRIDGES IN CHINA

# 东水门长江大桥

## Dongshuimen Bridge over Yangtze River

**Name:** Dongshuimen Bridge over Yangtze River
**Type:** Double-tower single-cable-plane steel truss girder cable-stayed bridge
**Main span:** 445m
**Location:** Chongqing City
**Completion:** March 2014
**Owner(s):** Chongqing City Construction Investment ( Group ) Co., Ltd.
**Designer(s):** China Merchants Chongqing Communications Technology Research and Design Institute Co., Ltd., T. Y. Lin International Engineering Consulting (China) Co., Ltd.
**Contractor(s):** China Railway Major Bridge Engineering Group Co., Ltd.

桥　　名：东水门长江大桥
桥　　型：双塔单索面钢桁梁斜拉桥
主跨跨径：445m
桥　　址：重庆市
建成时间：2014 年 3 月
建设单位：重庆市城市建设投资（集团）有限公司
设计单位：招商局重庆交通科研设计院有限公司，林同棪国际工程咨询（中国）有限公司
施工单位：中铁大桥局集团有限公司

东水门长江大桥位于重庆市嘉陵江和长江的交汇处，跨越长江连接渝中区和南岸区。大桥全长 1.125km。主桥采用双层交通模式，上层为双向四车道城市快速路，桥面宽度 24m，下层为双线城市轨道交通。

东水门长江大桥的主桥为双塔单索面钢桁梁斜拉桥，采用半漂浮结构体系，跨径布置为 222.5m+445m+190.5m。主梁采用双桁片式三角形钢桁架结构，钢桁梁高度为 13m，主要杆件均为焊接箱形截面。上下层桥面均采用正交异性钢桥面板，桥面板与双桁片之间形成板桁组合结构。桥塔高度为 182m，桥面以上高度 109m。主塔两侧设置 9 对斜拉索，索面设在桥面中心线。塔柱立面呈梭形，截面周边为同半径的圆弧轮廓。南北两塔的高度分别为 172.61m 和 162.49m，采用牛腿式构造支承主梁。斜拉索采用稀疏式布置，全桥仅有 36 根斜拉索，单根拉索为 139 股平行钢绞线，最大拉力达到 14500kN。

东水门长江大桥提出了一种利用主梁自身刚度、辅以稀疏单索面支承的部分斜拉桥结构，解决了双桁片板桁结合主梁的单索面超大吨位拉索的锚固难题，开发了钢锚箱、侧拉板、剪力钉及横向预应力组合受力的索-塔锚固构造技术。

Dongshuimen Bridge over Yangtze River is located at the meeting point of the Jialing River and the Yangtze River in Chongqing, connecting Yuzhong District and Nan'an District across the Yangtze River. The total length of the bridge is 1.125km. The main bridge has double decks in vertical including expressway and railway. The upper deck is a four-lane urban expressway in dual directions with a deck width of 24m and the lower deck is designed as dual-line urban railway.

Dongshuimen Bridge over Yangtze River is a steel truss girder cable-stayed bridge with two pylons and single cable plane. The semi-floating structural system is adopted, and the spans are arranged as 222.5m+445m+190.5m. The main girder is a double-truss triangular steel structure with the depth of 13m, and main members of the truss girder are of the welded box section. Both upper and lower decks adopt orthotropic steel plate. A plate truss composite structure is formed between the bridge deck and bouble trusses. The main pylons are 182m high, and 109m above the deck. Nine couples of stay cables are anchored to the pylon, and the cable plane is located along the centerline of the deck. The pylons are designed in the shape of spindles, and external contours of the pylons adopt arcs with the same diameter. The heights of the north and south towers are 172.61m and 162.49m respectively, and the corbel structures are designed to support the main girder. Only 36 stay cables are sparsely arranged in the whole bridge. One single cable has 139 parallel strands and the maximum tension reaches 14,500kN.

A partially supported cable-stayed bridge structure with main girder stiffened and sparse single-plane cables supported was proposed for the bridge, which solved the anchorage problem of the single-plane cables with super large force to the main girder of double-truss combined with the decks. The cable-pylon anchorage technology composed of steel anchorage box, side tension plate, shear studs and transverse prestressing was developed.

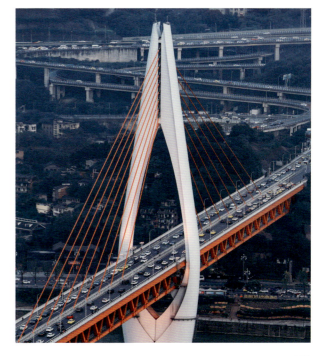

# 沪昆高铁北盘江特大桥
## Shanghai-Kunming High-speed Railway Bridge over Beipan River

沪昆高铁北盘江特大桥位于贵州省安顺市关岭布依族苗族自治县与黔西南布依族苗族自治州晴隆县交界处,跨越北盘江,为沪昆客运专线铁路贵州西段的重点工程,是世界上跨度最大的高速铁路混凝土拱桥,也是当时世界上跨度最大的混凝土拱桥。大桥全长721.25m,桥面宽度13.4m,按双线高速铁路布置,设计时速为350km/h。

沪昆高铁北盘江特大桥主桥为上承式钢筋混凝土拱桥,主跨跨径445m,矢跨比1/4.45。主桥钢筋混凝土拱圈采用等高、中段等宽近拱脚段变宽的单箱三室结构,内设钢管混凝土空间桁架式劲性骨架。钢管弦杆内灌注C80混凝土,拱脚与拱座固结。拱上建筑采用全空腹式构造,中间段为预应力混凝土连续梁、两端各连预应力混凝土T构过渡跨,腹孔墩为钢筋混凝土双柱式框架结构。拱圈劲性骨架采用缆索吊装、拉索扣挂悬臂拼装施工方法。

沪昆高铁北盘江特大桥的桥面系结构采用了多跨连续梁接T构的全连续长联结构体系,一联长度达到599.6m。在拱跨范围内不设缝,提高了列车高速行驶的安全性和舒适性;针对高速铁路特大跨径混凝土拱桥的特点,提出了结构变形高精度分析方法和整体位移控制标准;研发了导风屏障、桥面变形实时智能监测等装置,建立了智能化运行保障系统。

Shanghai-Kunming High-speed Railway Bridge over Beipan River is located at the junction of Guanling Buyizu & Miaozu Autonomous County in Anshun City and Qinglong County in Qianxinan Buyizu & Miaozu Autonomous Prefecture, Guizhou Province. It is the world's longest span high-speed railway concrete arch bridge, which is also the world's longest span concrete arch bridge when completed. The bridge is 721.25m in length and 13.4m in width. It is a dual-track high-speed railway bridge with a design speed of 350km/h.

The main bridge is a top supported reinforced concrete arch bridge with a main span of 445m and a rise-span ratio of 1/4.45. The reinforced concrete arch is designed as a single box with three cells and constant height, and constant width in the middle gradually increasing to the arch springing. The arch has a stiffening skeleton by concrete-filled steel tube truss with chords filled with C80 concrete. The arch springing are fixed with the abutments. The arch spandrel is open. The middle deck spans are prestressed concrete continuous bridges, and both ends are prestressed concrete T rigid frame spans. The piers for the decks are reinforced concrete double-column frames. The stiffening skeletons of arches are erected by cable hoisting and cantilever construction method by temporary stays.

The bridge deck is a long multi-span continuous beam connected to T rigid frame with a length of 599.6m without expansion joint in the arch span to improve the safety and comfort of high-speed train. According to the characteristics of long-span concrete arch bridge of high-speed railway, the high precision analysis method of structural deformation and the overall displacement control standard has been put forward. A wind barrier system and a real-time intelligent monitoring device for bridge deck deformation have been developed, and an intelligent operation guarantee system has been established.

桥　名：沪昆高铁北盘江特大桥
桥　型：上承式钢筋混凝土拱桥
主跨跨径：445m
桥　址：贵州省安顺市、黔西南布依族苗族自治州
建成时间：2016年12月
建设单位：沪昆铁路客运专线贵州有限公司
设计单位：中铁二院工程集团有限责任公司
施工单位：中铁广州工程局集团有限公司

**Name:** Shanghai-Kunming High-speed Railway Bridge over Beipan River
**Type:** Top supported reinforced concrete deck arch bridge
**Main span:** 445m
**Location:** Anshun City and Qianxinan Buyizu & Miaozu Autonomous Prefecture, Guizhou Province
**Completion:** December 2016
**Owner(s):** Shanghai-Kunming Railway Passenger Dedicated Line Guizhou Co., Ltd.
**Designer(s):** China Railway Eryuan Engineering Group Co., Ltd.
**Contractor(s):** China Railway Guangzhou Engineering Group Co., Ltd.

# 港珠澳大桥

## Hong Kong-Zhuhai-Macao Bridge

港珠澳大桥跨越珠江口伶仃洋，东起香港国际机场附近的香港口岸人工岛，西接大屿山岛12km长的香港连接线，一直到珠海和澳门口岸人工岛29.6km长的主线，再往西至珠海洪湾立交13.4km长的珠海连接线。桥梁全长55km，是世界上最长的跨海桥隧工程。

港珠澳大桥主线工程由6.7km沉管隧道和22.9km跨海桥梁组成。跨海桥梁从东到西设置了青州航道桥、江海直达船航道桥和九洲航道桥三座通航孔桥以及深、浅水区非通航孔桥。青州航道桥是一座双塔双索面钢箱梁斜拉桥，主跨458m；江海直达船航道桥是一座三塔单索面钢箱梁斜拉桥，两个主跨各258m；九洲航道桥是一座双塔单索面钢-混凝土组合梁斜拉桥，主跨298m；深水区非通航孔桥为110m跨径钢箱连续梁桥，采用独柱墩整幅梁；浅水区非通航孔桥为85m跨径预应力混凝土连续梁桥，采用独柱墩双幅梁。

为了降低深水区非通航孔桥的阻水率，减少环境负面影响，有效保护中华白海豚栖息地，港珠澳大桥采用装配化埋床式全预制墩身和承台（埋入海床），研发了结构构造、设计方法和施工方案，将预制整体承台和墩柱下放到复合桩上，通过临时围堰允许承台在干燥的环境中与桩连接，避免了在海洋环境中湿接施工，缩短了施工时间，并达到耐久性和高质量的施工目标。九洲航道桥和江海直达船航道桥分别采用风帆式和海豚式桥塔，建筑造型优美、标志性强。

港珠澳大桥获得了国际桥梁与结构工程协会杰出结构奖。

Hong Kong-Zhuhai-Macao Bridge crosses the Lingdingyang Bay at the mouth of the Pearl River. It starts from the artificial island of Hong Kong Port near Hong Kong International Airport in the east, connecting Lantau Island in the west and becomes a 12km long connection line in Hong Kong. The 29.6km long main line runs westward to the artificial island of Zhuhai and Macao Port, and extends further westward to the Hongwan Interchange in Zhuhai, which is a 13.4km long connection line in Zhuhai. The bridge has a total length of 55km, and is the longest sea-crossing bridge and tunnel project in the world.

The main line of Hong Kong-Zhuhai-Macao Bridge consists of a 6.7km immersed tunnel and a 22.9km sea-crossing bridge. The sea-crossing bridge is composed of three navigation channel bridges, including Qingzhou Channel Bridge, Jianghai Direct Ship Channel Bridge and Jiuzhou Channel Bridge from east to west, as well as non-navigation channel bridges in deep and shallow water areas. Qingzhou Channel Bridge is a double-tower double-plane steel box girder cable-stayed bridge with a main span of 458m. Jianghai Direct Ship Channel Bridge is a single cable plane three-tower steel box girder cable-stayed bridge with two main spans of 258m each. Jiuzhou Channel Bridge is a double-tower single cable plane steel-concrete composite girder cable-stayed bridge with a main span of 298m. The non-navigation channel bridges in deep water area are 110m span steel box continuous girder bridges, which consist of single column pier and single box girder, while the non-navigation channel bridges in shallow water area are 85m span prestressed concrete continuous girder bridges, which consist of single column pier and dual girders.

In order to reduce the water blocking rate of non-navigation channel bridges in deep-water area, and to restrain the negative impact on the environment and effectively protect the habitat of Chinese white dolphins, fully prefabricated and embedded pier shafts and pile caps (buried in the seabed) were proposed, designed and developed. The fully prefabricated pile caps and pier columns were placed on composite piles, then the pile caps were connected to the piles in a dry environment by temporary cofferdams. Thus, the wet joint construction in the marine environment has been avoided, and the construction time was shortened, and the construction objectives of durability and high quality have been achieved. Jiuzhou Channel Bridge and Jianghai Direct Ship Channel Bridge adopt sail style and dolphin style bridge towers respectively, with beautiful architectural shape and strong visual impact.

The Project of Hong Kong-Zhuhai-Macao Bridge has won the Outstanding Structure Award of International Association for Bridge and Structural Engineering.

桥　　名： 港珠澳大桥
桥　　型： 斜拉桥，连续梁桥，简支梁桥等
桥梁长度： 全长55km，主跨跨径458m
桥　　址： 香港特别行政区、珠海市和澳门特别行政区
建成时间： 2018年10月
建设单位： 港珠澳大桥管理局
设计单位： 中交公路规划设计院有限公司，中铁大桥勘测设计院集团有限公司，丹麦COWI公司等
施工单位： 中国交通建设股份有限公司，中铁大桥局集团有限公司，广东省长大公路工程有限公司等

**Name:** Hong Kong-Zhuhai-Macao Bridge
**Type:** Cable-stayed bridge, continuous girder bridge, simply supported girder bridge, etc.
**Length:** Total length 55km, main span 458m
**Location:** Hong Kong, Zhuhai City and Macao
**Completion:** October 2018
**Owner(s):** Hong Kong-Zhuhai-Macao Bridge Authority
**Designer(s):** CCCC Highway Co., Ltd., China Railway Major Bridge Reconnaissance & Design Institute Co., Ltd., COWI, etc.
**Contractor(s):** China Communications Construction Company Limited, China Railway Major Bridge Engineering Group Co., Ltd., Guangdong Provincial Changda Highway Engineering Co., Ltd., etc.

# 南沙大桥

## Nansha Bridge

南沙大桥位于广东省珠江水域，西接广州市南沙区，东连东莞市沙田镇，由坭洲水道桥、大沙水道桥两座悬索桥及连接线组成。大桥全长12.89km，桥面按双向八车道高速公路布置。

南沙大桥的坭洲水道桥为双塔两跨吊钢箱梁悬索桥，主跨跨径1688m。钢箱梁全宽47.9m、高度为4m。主缆跨径布置为658m+1688m+520m，横向间距为42.1m，主跨垂跨比1/9.5，采用127根ϕ5预制平行钢丝索股，每根主缆252股，标准强度1960MPa。吊索纵向标准间距12.8m。桥塔采用钢筋混凝土门式框架结构，设上、中、下三道横梁，塔高260m，基础采用群桩，锚碇为重力式结构。大桥纵向采用静力限位-动力阻尼约束体系，竖向和横向采用碟形弹簧与动力阻尼组合的新型减震抗风支座。

南沙大桥的大沙水道桥为双塔单跨吊钢箱梁悬索桥，主跨跨径1200m。钢箱梁断面与坭洲水道桥相同。主缆跨径布置为360m+1200m+480m，主跨垂跨比1/9.5，主缆采用169股127ϕ5.2预制平行钢丝索股，标准强度1770MPa。桥塔采用钢筋混凝土门式框架结构，设上、下两道横梁，塔高193.1m，基础采用群桩，锚碇为重力式结构。

南沙大桥的坭洲水道桥大规模采用了我国自主研发的1960MPa级镀锌铝钢丝主缆，主缆外缠S形截面钢丝，并配置了新型空气除湿系统。南沙大桥吊索还采用了成套减振装置，可以控制吊索振动。

Nansha Bridge, located on the Pearl River Waterway of Guangdong Province, starts from Nansha District of Guangzhou City in the west and ends at Shatian Town of Dongguan City in the east. Nansha Bridge consists of two suspension bridges-Nizhou Waterway Bridge, Dasha Waterway Bridge and approach bridges. The total length of Nansha Bridge is 12.89km with eight traffic lanes in dual direction.

Nizhou Waterway Bridge of Nansha Bridge is a double-tower double-suspended-span suspension bridge with steel box girder, and the main span length is 1,688m. The steel box girder is designed with a 47.9m width and a 4m central depth. The span of the main cable is 658m+1,688m+520m, and the spacing between cables is 42.1m. The sag span ratio is 1/9.5. Both main cables are prefabricated with 252 parallel wire bundles, and each bundle includes 127 $\phi$ 5 steel wires with standard strength 1,960MPa. The longitudinal spacing between hangers is 12.8m. The towers are portal frame reinforced concrete structures with three crossbeams. The towers are 260m high and supported by group pile foundations. Both anchorages are gravity-type. The bridge adopts a longitudinal restraint system including the movement restrainers for static loads and viscous dampers for dynamic loads. A new seismic-reduction and wind-resistant bearing, which combines disc springs and viscous dampers, is applied in the vertical and transverse directions.

Dasha Waterway Bridge of Nansha Bridge is a double-tower single-suspended-span suspension bridge with steel box girder, and the main span length is 1,200m. The same steel box girder is applied as Nizhou Waterway Bridge. The span of the main cable is 360m+1,200m+480m. The sag span ratio is 1/9.5. Both main cables are prefabricated with 169 parallel wire bundles, and each bundle includes 127 $\phi$ 5.2 steel wires with standard strength 1,770MPa. The towers are portal frame reinforced concrete structures with two crossbeams. The towers are 193.1m high and supported by group pile foundations. Both anchorages are gravity-type.

The 1,960MPa Al-Zn alloy coated steel wires developed by China were applied in Nizhou Waterway Bridge. The main cables are wrapped with S-shaped cross-sectional steel wire and equipped with a new armor coating and dehumidification system. Vibration reduction devices were systematically used for the hangers of Nansha Bridge to control the vibration of hangers.

**Name:** Nansha Bridge
**Type:** Double-tower double-suspended-span suspension bridge with steel box girder, double-tower single-suspended-span suspension bridge with steel box girder
**Main span:** Nizhou Waterway Bridge 1,688m, Dasha Waterway Bridge 1,200m
**Location:** Guangzhou City and Dongguan City, Guangdong Province
**Completion:** April 2019
**Owner(s):** Guangdong Province Traffic Group Co., Ltd.
**Designer(s):** CCCC Highway Consultants Co., Ltd., Guangdong Communication Planning & Design Institute Group Co., Ltd.
**Contractor(s):** CCCC Second Highway Engineering Co., Ltd., CCCC Second Harbor Engineering Company Ltd., Poly Changda Engineering Co., Ltd.

# 北京新首钢大桥

Beijing New Shougang Bridge

桥　　名：北京新首钢大桥
桥　　型：双塔双索面斜拉-刚构组合桥
主跨跨径：280m
桥　　址：北京市
建成时间：2019年9月
建设单位：北京市公联公路联络线有限责任公司
设计单位：北京戈建建筑设计顾问有限责任公司，
　　　　　北京市市政工程设计研究总院有限公司
施工单位：北京城建集团有限责任公司

北京新首钢大桥位于北京长安街西延长线上，横跨永定河，东起石景山区古城大街，横穿首钢工业园区，西连门头沟区石担路。全桥总长1.354km，桥面按双向八车道城市主干路布置。

主桥为双塔双索面斜拉-刚构组合桥，中线与河道中线斜交角为57.4°，主跨跨径为280m。主梁采用分离式变截面全焊接钢箱结构，中间设间距3m的横梁，顶板行车道部分采用正交异性桥面板构造。主跨梁高从10.51m渐变至3.3m，宽度从54.9m到47m再到53.7m逐渐变化。一高一矮钢桥塔分别设在大桥两端，均采用外倾拱形、三维空间扭曲形态的构造。高塔的桥面以上高度约112m，与主梁和桥墩固结；矮塔的桥面以上高度约66m，与主梁固结，在梁底设单向活动支座。斜拉索采用竖琴式渐变索距的空间布置方式，塔上索间距2.90m~7.26m，梁上索间距3.76m~14.4m，112根拉索承担超过300000kN的钢箱梁。主桥采用支架施工方法，克服了温度变化下钢塔段倾斜角度不同、姿态不同带来的高空测量难度和塔段制造、吊装、运输、焊接中的难题。

北京新首钢大桥桥型新颖独特、自然和谐，既简洁优雅又富于变化，从整体到细节注重艺术、工程、结构和技术的融合。

Name: Beijing New Shougang Bridge
Type: Double-tower double-cable-plane cable-stayed rigid-frame composite bridge
Main span: 280m
Location: Beijing City
Completion: September 2019
Owner(s): Beijing Gonglian Highway Connection Line Co., Ltd.
Designer(s): Nicolas Godelet Architects & Engineers, Beijing General Municipal Engineering Design & Research Institute Co., Ltd.
Contractor(s): Beijing Urban Construction Group Co., Ltd.

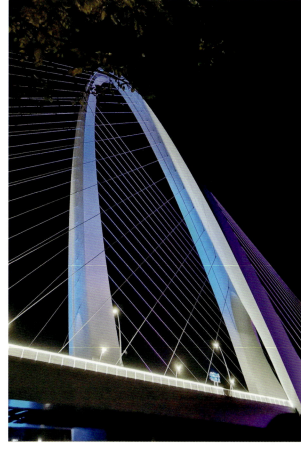

Beijing New Shougang Bridge, crossing the Yongding River, is located in the westward extended line of Chang'an Street in the Capital of China, which starts from the Gucheng Avenue in Shijingshan District at the east, goes through Shougang Industrial Park, ends westward at Shidan Road in Mentougou District. The whole bridge has a total length of 1.354km, and eight driving lanes in dual directions.

The main bridge is a cable-stayed rigid-frame composite bridge with double inclined towers and double cable planes. The skew angle between the center lines of the bridge and the river is 57.4°. The main span length is 280m. The main girder uses separated fully-welded steel boxes with varying cross sections and orthotropic bridge deck. Transverse beams are set inside the main girder at an interval space of 3m. The depth of the main girder varies gradually from 10.51m to 3.3m, and the width from 54.9m to 47m then to 53.7m. Two steel towers stand, one tall and one short, at each end of the main span. Two arched towers incline to each side span and possess a three-dimensional twisted spatial configuration. The tall tower is about 112m high above the bridge deck, and is rigidly fixed with the main girder and the bridge pier. The short tower is 66m high above the bridge deck and is rigidly fixed with the main girder, but connected to the bridge pier through one-direction movable supports. The cables are arranged in a way of harp with gradually-changed spaces. The cable spacing changes from 2.90m to 7.26m on the towers and from 3.76m to 14.4m on the main girder. Totally 112 cables carry the steel box deck over 300,000kN. The construction of the main bridge on scaffoldings overcomes the difficulty of the measurement high above the deck caused by different inclination angles and height of the steel tower sections under temperature changes, and the problems in manufacturing, hoisting, transportation and welding of the tower sections.

Beijing New Shougang Bridge has a neoteric and unique type, which is of natural harmony. It is concise and elegant as well as rich in variation. From the whole to the details, it is characterized by the integration of art, engineering, structure and technology.

# 平塘大桥
## Pingtang Bridge

| | |
|---|---|
| 桥　名： | 平塘大桥 |
| 桥　型： | 三塔双索面钢-混凝土组合梁斜拉桥 |
| 主跨跨径： | 2×550m |
| 桥　址： | 贵州省黔南布依族苗族自治州 |
| 建成时间： | 2019年12月 |
| 建设单位： | 贵州省公路开发有限责任公司 |
| 设计单位： | 贵州省交通规划勘察设计研究院股份有限公司 |
| 施工单位： | 中铁二十局集团有限公司，珠海市中港路桥建设有限公司等 |

**Name:** Pingtang Bridge
**Type:** Three-tower double-cable-plane steel-concrete composite girder cable-stayed bridge
**Main span:** 2×550m
**Location:** Qiannan Buyizu & Miaozu Autonomous Prefecture, Guizhou Province
**Completion:** December 2019
**Owner(s):** Guizhou Highway Development Group Co., Ltd.
**Designer(s):** Guizhou Transportation Planning Survey & Design Academe Co., Ltd.
**Contractor(s):** China Railway 20th Bureau Group Corporation Limited, Zhuhai Zhonggang Road & Bridge Construction Co., Ltd., etc.

　　平塘大桥位于贵州省黔南布依族苗族自治州，跨越漕渡河大峡谷，是余庆—安龙高速公路（黔高速S62）重要节点。大桥全长2.135km，主桥宽度30.2m，按双向四车道高速公路布置，设计时速为80km/h。

　　平塘大桥主桥为三塔双索面钢-混凝土组合梁斜拉桥，跨径布置为249.5m+2×550m+249.5m，采用半漂浮结构体系。主梁采用双工字形钢梁与混凝土桥面板组合梁，由工字形纵梁、横梁、小纵梁形成的平面钢框架和预制桥面板结合成型。桥塔为折线H形钢筋混凝土结构，三座桥塔的高度分别为145.2m、149.2m及145.2m，均采用挖孔嵌岩桩基础。主梁在中塔的塔梁间设横向固定支座和纵向限位装置、边塔处采用竖向支承和纵向阻尼器，并在塔梁相交处设横向抗风挡块。斜拉索采用双索面扇形布置方式，每座桥塔布有22对空间索，拉索在钢梁上采用锚拉板构造锚固，在桥塔上采用钢锚梁与混凝土锚块结构锚固。

　　平塘大桥为三塔结构形式并处在山区深谷风复杂的环境中。设计中通过采用空间桥塔及增加顺桥向中塔刚度等措施提高了结构整体刚度。通过在塔梁间设置合理的支座、限位装置及阻尼器等，满足了结构在活载、风及温度作用下的受力和变形要求。

Pingtang Bridge is located in Qiannan Buyizu & Miaozu Autonomous Prefecture of Guizhou Province, crossing the Grand Canyon of Caodu River, as an important node of Yuqing-Anlong Expressway (Guizhou Expressway S62). The total length of the bridge is 2.135km, and the total width of the main bridge is 30.2m. The bridge deck is a dual-way four-lane expressway with a design speed of 80km/h.

The main bridge is a three-tower double-cable plane steel-concrete composite girder cable-stayed bridge adopting semi-floating structural system. The span arrangement is 249.5m+2×550m+249.5m. The main girder is composed of double I-shaped steel beams and concrete deck, including prefabricated deck and steel frame formed by I-shaped longitudinal beams, transverse beams and secondary longitudinal beams. The tower is reinforced concrete structure with H-shaped and a broken contour line. Three main towers are 145.2m, 149.2m and 145.2m high, respectively, and the foundations are excavated rock-socketed piles. Transverse fixed supports and longitudinal restrainer are equipped between the middle tower and the main girder, while vertical supports and longitudinal dampers are arranged at two side towers, and transverse wind-resistant blocks at the intersection of towers and girder are installed. The stay cables are fan-shaped with double cable planes, and each tower has 22 pairs of spatial cables. The cables are anchored on the steel main beams by tension plate anchorage, and anchored on towers by steel anchorage beams and concrete anchorage blocks.

The bridge with three towers is located in a complex mountainous environment with deep valley wind. In the design, the overall stiffness of the bridge has been improved by using spatial towers and increasing the longitudinal stiffness of the middle tower. By setting reasonable supports, movement constraint devices and dampers between the towers and the girder, the stress and deformation requirements of the structure under live load, wind and temperature have been met.

# 重庆鹅公岩轨道大桥

## Chongqing Egongyan Rail Transit Bridge

鹅公岩轨道大桥位于重庆市九龙坡区，跨越长江水道，南起南岸区，北至九龙坡区。大桥全长1.65km，桥面设双线轨道及人行道。

为保证相邻的既有鹅公岩大桥的运营安全并保持二者造型统一，鹅公岩轨道大桥主桥采用双塔五跨连续钢-混凝土混合梁自锚式悬索桥，主跨跨径为600m，建成时为世界主跨跨度最大的自锚式悬索桥。大桥主缆锚固段和锚跨段采用预应力混凝土箱梁，锚跨梁高4.5~10m，宽17m；其余部分采用钢箱梁，梁高4.5m，宽22m。主缆跨径布置为210m+600m+210m，主跨垂跨比为1/10，采用127根$\phi$5.3锌铝合金镀层预制平行钢丝索股，每根主缆92股，标准强度为1860MPa。吊索纵向间距15m，采用$\phi$7平行钢丝束索股。桥塔采用钢筋混凝土门式框架结构，桥塔下部采用灌注嵌岩桩基础。大桥主梁与主塔连接处采用竖向支承及纵向阻尼约束，与桥墩连接处采用竖向支承及横向限位约束。

重庆鹅公岩轨道大桥采用"先斜拉后悬索"的施工方法，满足了自锚式悬索桥"先梁后缆"的施工要求，避免了在航道水域设置临时支撑。还采用了研发的"多点同步步履式顶推施工技术"，解决了边跨钢箱梁体量大、无法水路运输的难题。

| | |
|---|---|
| Name: | Chongqing Egongyan Rail Transit Bridge |
| Type: | Double-tower five-span continuous steel-concrete hybrid girder self-anchored suspension bridge |
| Main span: | 600m |
| Location: | Chongqing City |
| Completion: | December 2019 |
| Owner(s): | Chongqing Rail Transit (Group) Co., Ltd. |
| Designer(s): | Shanghai Municipal Engineering Design Institute (Group) Co., Ltd. and T.Y. Lin International Engineering Consulting (China) Co., Ltd. |
| Contractor(s): | China Railway Construction Bridge Engineering Bureau Group Co., Ltd. |

Egongyan Rail Transit Bridge is located in Jiulongpo District of Chongqing City and crosses the Yangtze River Waterway. The bridge starts from Nan'an District in the south and ends at Jiulongpo District in the north, having a total length of 1.65km with rail transit lines in dual direction and pedestrian walkways.

In order to keep the consistency in the bridge appearance and ensure the operational safety considering the existing adjacent E'gongyan Bridge, the main bridge of E'gongyan Rail Transit Bridge is a double-tower five-span continuous steel-concrete hybrid girder self-anchored suspension bridge with a main span length of 600m, which is the world's longest self-anchored suspension bridge at the time of completion. The prestressed concrete box girder is used at the anchorage sections and the side spans, with a 4.5~10m depth and a 17m width, while steel box girder is adopted in other sections, with a depth of 4.5m and a width of 22m. The span of the main cable is 210m+600m+210m. The sag span ratio is 1/10. Both main cables are prefabricated with 92 parallel wire bundles, and each bundle includes 127 $\phi$5.3 steel wires with Zn-Al alloy coating and standard strength of 1,860MPa. The hangers are made of $\phi$7 steel wires, having a longitudinal spacing of 15m. The towers are portal frame reinforced concrete structures, supported by rock-embedded bored pile foundations. Vertical bearings and longitudinal damping devices are set for the girder at the tower, vertical bearings and transverse movement restraint devices are set for the girder at the pier.

The construction method of "cable-staying before suspension" was adopted, satisfying the construction requirements of "deck before cable" for self-anchored suspension bridges and also avoiding temporary supports built in the navigation waterway. A steel-box girder-erection construction technique called multi-point synchronous walking-pedrail launching construction technology was developed to address the challenge incurred by the unavailability of shipping transportation due to long steel box girder volume in the side span.

BRIDGES IN CHINA

2020

中 国 桥 梁

# 攀登与超越
CLIMBING AND SURPASSING

2024

# 引　言

"十三五"期间，中国经济实力、科技实力、综合国力和人民生活水平跃上了新的大台阶，全面建成了小康社会，中华民族伟大复兴向前迈出了新的一大步。"十四五"交通规划提出了要加大高速公路、铁路、航空港口等交通基础设施建设投资，提升农村公路和县域道路的通达性，完善城市交通体系，为桥梁和交通基础设施持续发展注入新的活力。

到 2020 年，中国已经建成的公路和铁路桥梁的数量分别达到了 91 万座和 9 万座，双双超越美国，成为世界第一。在全世界已经建成的跨径前十的各类桥型中，梁桥有 5 座、拱桥有 7 座、斜拉桥有 7 座、悬索桥有 6 座在中国。在交通运输部提出的平安百年品质工程号召下，中国桥梁界在延续跨海大桥和大跨度桥梁建设的同时，更加注重桥梁技术创新、桥梁品质提升和桥梁环境友好，争取引领世界桥梁品质和技术发展。

在跨海大桥建设方面，先后建成了平潭海峡公铁两用大桥、深中通道和澳门第四条跨海大桥等；在大跨度悬索桥建设方面，先后建成了五峰山长江大桥和瓯江北口大桥等；在大跨度斜拉桥建设方面，先后建成了沪苏通长江公铁大桥和南京江心洲长江大桥等，后者获得了国际桥梁与结构工程协会杰出公路和铁路桥梁奖；在大跨度拱桥建设方面，相继建成了平南三桥和天峨龙滩特大桥等，两次刷新了拱桥跨径的世界纪录。

在最近的 5 年里，中国又建成了一大批高品质的跨海大桥，大跨度悬索桥、斜拉桥和拱桥。本章选取了中国跨海大桥 6 座，大跨度悬索桥 3 座、斜拉桥 2 座和拱桥 3 座。拱桥的跨径两次创造了世界纪录，跨海大桥、大跨度悬索桥和斜拉桥的品质有了极大的提升，标志着中国向桥梁强国迈进了一大步。

# INTRODUCTION

During the "Thirteenth Five-Year Plan" period, China's economic strength, technological prowess, comprehensive national power, and living standard all reached new levels, culminating in the comprehensive achievement of a more prosperous society, and marking a significant step forward in the great rejuvenation of the Chinese nation. The "Fourteenth Five-Year" transportation plan proposed increased investment in the construction of transportation infrastructure such as highways, railways, ports, and airports. It also emphasized improving the accessibility of rural roads and county-level road networks and perfecting urban transportation systems. These initiatives injected new vitality into the continuous development of transportation infrastructure and bridges.

Until 2020, China had built 910,000 highway bridges and 90,000 railway bridges, surpassing the United States to become the leader in bridge construction of the world. Among the top ten longest-span bridges of various types that have been built worldwide, China is home to five girder bridges, seven arch bridges, seven cable-stayed bridges, and six suspension bridges. In response to the call for a "Safe and High-Quality Centennial Project" by the Ministry of Transport, the Chinese bridge community, while continuing to build large sea-crossing and long-span bridges, has placed greater emphasis on bridge technology innovation, quality enhancement, and environmental friendliness, aiming to lead global bridge quality and technological development.

In the field of sea-crossing bridge construction, this period saw a series of significant achievements including the completion of the Pingtan Strait Highway and Railway Bridge, the Shenzhen-Zhongshan Link, and the Fourth Sea-crossing Bridge of Macao. Examples of long-span suspension bridge projects include the Wufengshan Bridge over the Yangtze River and the Beikou Bridge over the Ou River. Notable long-span cable-stayed bridges include the Shanghai-Suzhou-Nantong Highway and Railway Bridge over the Yangtze River and the Nanjing Jiangxinzhou Bridge over the Yangtze River, the latter of which received the Outstanding Highway and Railway Bridge Award by IABSE. The Third Pingnan Bridge and the Tian'e Longtan Bridge both set new world records for arch bridge spans.

In the past five years, China has built a large number of high-quality sea-crossing bridges, long-span suspension bridges, cable-stayed bridges, and arch bridges. This chapter highlights six sea-crossing bridges, three long-span suspension bridges, two cable-stayed bridges, and three arch bridges, two of which set world span records. The quality of sea-crossing bridges, long-span suspension bridges, and cable-stayed bridges has greatly improved, marking a significant step forward in China's journey to becoming a leading nation in bridge engineering.

# 沪苏通长江公铁大桥

## Shanghai-Suzhou-Nantong Highway and Railway Bridge over Yangtze River

沪苏通长江公铁大桥是江苏省连接苏州市和南通市的跨越长江的公铁两用通道。大桥全长11.072km，其中公铁合建桥梁长6.989km。大桥采用双层桥面构造，上层为双向六车道的通锡高速公路，设计速度100km/h；下层为双向四线铁路，分别为设计速度200km/h的沪苏通铁路和设计速度250km/h的通苏嘉甬高速铁路。

主航道桥为双塔三索面钢桁梁斜拉桥，跨径布置为140m+462m+1092m+462m+140m。主梁采用钢箱-桁架双层组合钢梁结构，横向三主桁。塔柱采用钻石形钢筋混凝土结构，承台顶以上塔高330m；斜拉索为扇形布置，采用2000MPa级高强度平行钢丝。主塔采用沉井基础。桥塔自重在塔底截面的最大轴力中所占比例较高，为了减小桥塔截面尺寸、降低桥塔自重并减小基础规模，设计方案采用了高强度高性能混凝土。采用超高主塔多索面钢锚梁整体组拼安装技术，保证了钢锚梁和索道管精度，提高了安装效率。同时，研制的18000kN步履式架梁起重机解决了大节段钢桁梁高空多杆件对接难题。

沪苏通长江公铁大桥是中国自主设计建造、世界上首座跨度超千米的公铁两用斜拉桥。

Shanghai-Suzhou-Nantong Highway and Railway Bridge over Yangtze River spans Suzhou City and Nantong City in Jiangsu Province across the Yangtze River. The total length of the bridge is 11.072km, of which 6.989km is built as the road rail joint part. The bridge adopts a double-deck structure. The upper deck is a two-way six-lane expressway, namely Nantong-Wuxi Highway with a design speed of 100km/h, and the lower deck is a two-way four-track railway, namely the Shanghai-Suzhou-Nantong Railway with a design speed of 200km/h and the Nantong-Suzhou-Jiaxing-Ningbo High-speed Railway with a design speed of 250km/h.

The main channel bridge is a double-tower three-cable-plane steel truss girder cable-stayed bridge, with a span arrangement of 140m+462m+1092m+462m+140m. The main girder adopts a steel box-truss double-layer combined structure, and three main trusses transversely. The tower is a diamond-shaped reinforced concrete structure, and its height above the top of the bearing platform is 330m. Stay cables are designed with a fan-shape arrangement, using 2,000MPa grade high-strength parallel steel wires. The tower uses a caisson foundation. The self-weight of the bridge tower accounts for a relatively large proportion of the axial force on the tower bottom section, and the designer adopted high-strength and high-performance concrete to reduce the cross-sectional size of the bridge tower, the self-weight of the bridge tower and the scale of the caisson foundation.

桥　名：沪苏通长江公铁大桥
桥　型：双塔三索面钢桁梁斜拉桥
主跨跨径：1092m
桥　址：江苏省苏州市、南通市
建成时间：2020年7月
建设单位：沪苏通长江公铁大桥建设部
设计单位：中铁大桥勘测设计院集团有限公司
施工单位：中铁大桥局集团有限公司

**Name:** Shanghai-Suzhou-Nantong Highway and Railway Bridge over Yangtze River
**Type:** Double-tower three-cable-plane steel truss girder cable-stayed bridge
**Main span:** 1,092m
**Location:** Suzhou City and Nantong City, Jiangsu Province
**Completion:** July 2020
**Owner(s):** Construction Headquarters of Husutong Yangtze River Bridge
**Designer(s):** China Railway Major Bridge Reconnaissance & Design Institute Co., Ltd.
**Contractor(s):** China Railway Major Bridge Engineering Group Co., Ltd.

The overall assembly and installation technology of the multi-cable plane steel anchor beam of the ultra-high main tower was adopted to ensure the accuracy of the steel anchor beam and the cableway pipe. This kind of application improved installation efficiency. Moreover, through the development of 18,000kN of walking beam cranes, the problem of high-altitude multi-member docking of large-segment steel trusses was solved.

Shanghai-Suzhou-Nantong Highway and Railway Bridge over Yangtze River is designed and built by China as the first highway and railway cable-stayed bridge with a span over 1,000m.

# 平潭海峡公铁两用大桥
## Pingtan Strait Highway and Railway Bridge

| | |
|---|---|
| 桥 名: | 平潭海峡公铁两用大桥 |
| 桥 型: | 斜拉桥，连续刚构桥，简支梁桥 |
| 桥梁长度: | 全长 16.323km，最大跨径 532m |
| 桥 址: | 福建省福州市 |
| 建成时间: | 2020 年 12 月 |
| 建设单位: | 福建铁路有限公司 |
| 设计单位: | 中铁大桥勘测设计院集团有限公司，中铁第四勘察设计院集团有限公司 |
| 施工单位: | 中铁大桥局集团有限公司，中国铁建大桥工程局集团有限公司 |

**Name:** Pingtan Strait Highway and Railway Bridge
**Type:** Cable-stayed bridge, continuous rigid frame bridge and simply supported girder bridge
**Length:** Total length 16.323km, main span 532m
**Location:** Fuzhou City, Fujian Province
**Completion:** December 2020
**Owner(s):** Fujian Railway Co., Ltd.
**Designer(s):** China Railway Major Bridge Reconnaissance & Design Institute Co., Ltd., China Railway Siyuan Survey and Design Group Co., Ltd.
**Contractor(s):** China Railway Major Bridge Engineering Group Co., Ltd., China Railway Construction Bridge Engineering Bureau Group Co., Ltd.

平潭海峡公铁两用大桥是福州至平潭铁路、长乐至平潭高速公路的关键控制性工程，是中国第一座公铁两用跨海大桥，桥梁全长 16.323km。线路北起松下收费站，上跨元洪航道、鼓屿门水道、大小练岛水道和北东口水道，南至苏澳收费站。

平潭海峡公铁两用大桥上层桥面为双向六车道高速公路，设计速度 100km/h；下层桥面为双线铁路，设计速度 200km/h。四座通航孔桥中，除了北东口水道桥为 2×168m 双主跨连续刚构桥之外，其余三座通航孔桥统一采用双塔双索面钢桁架－混凝土混合梁斜拉桥，主跨分别为 532m、364m 和 336m。非通航孔桥和引桥根据墩高、水深及地质条件分别采用跨径 88m 和 80m 的简支钢桁组合梁桥，跨径为 64m、48m 和 40m 的预应力混凝土箱梁桥。

平潭海峡公铁两用大桥是连接福州城区和平潭综合实验区的快速通道，远期规划是连接北京和台北的陆路通道，对促进两岸经贸合作和文化交流等具有重要意义。桥梁设计和施工中克服了风大、浪高、水深、流急等极端不利条件，研发了两孔同步架设和"多孔连做"节段拼装等创新技术，成功实现了中国铁路桥梁从内陆走向海洋。

Pingtan Strait Highway and Railway Bridge is a critical control project for the Fuzhou—Pingtan Railway and the Changle—Pingtan Expressway. With a total length of 16.323km, it is the first sea-crossing highway and railway bridge in China. The bridge starts from Songxia toll station in the north, crossing the Yuanhong Waterway, the Guyumen Waterway, the Daxiaoliandao Waterway and the Beidongkou Waterway, reaching Su'ao toll station in the south.

The upper deck of the bridge is designed to carry dual way six-lane highway traffic with the design speed of 100km/h, while the lower deck is designed to carry double track railway with the design speed of 200km/h. Among the four navigation channel bridges, Yuanhong Waterway Bridge, Guyumen Waterway Bridge and Daxiaoliandao Waterway Bridge are steel truss and concrete hybrid girder cable-stayed bridges with double pylons and double cable planes, with the main

spans of 532m, 364m and 336m, respectively, except that Beidongkou Waterway Bridge is a continuous rigid frame bridge with two main spans of 168m. Non-navigation channel bridges and approach bridges are simply supported steel truss composite girders with span lengths of 88m and 80m, and prestressed concrete box girders with span lengths of 64m, 48m and 40m, respectively, according to pier height, water depth and geological conditions.

Pingtan Strait Highway Railway Bridge is the fast track connecting Fuzhou City and Pingtan Comprehensive Experimental Zone. Long-term planning is a part of land passage connecting Beijing and Taipei, which is of great significance to promote cross-strait economy and trade cooperation and cultural exchanges. In the design and construction of the bridge, extreme unfavorable conditions such as strong wind, high waves, deep water and rapid flow were overcome, and innovative technologies such as simultaneous erection of two spans and segmental assembly of double spans were developed. The successful construction of Pingtan Strait Highway and Railway Bridge marks the growth of China railway bridges from inland to the ocean.

# 五峰山长江大桥
## Wufengshan Bridge over Yangtze River

五峰山长江大桥是连镇高速铁路、江宜高速公路共同跨越长江的公铁两用通道,全长6.41km,上层设双向八车道高速公路,下层设双向四线高速铁路,是世界上第一座高速铁路悬索桥。

五峰山长江大桥主桥为双塔单跨吊钢桁梁悬索桥,主跨跨径为1092m。钢桁梁立面采用华伦桁式,横断面采用带副桁的直主桁式,主桁中心桁宽30m,桁高16m,节间距14m,材质为Q370qE钢。主缆跨径为350m+1092m+350m,垂跨比为1/10,采用127ϕ5.5预制平行钢丝索股,每根主缆352股,标准强度为1860MPa。吊索采用标准强度1770MPa的镀锌高强钢丝,纵向间距14m。桥塔采用钢筋混凝土门式框架结构,桥塔基础为桩基础。北塔高203m,南塔高191m。北锚碇采用大型沉井基础,南锚碇采用不等深圆形地下连续墙基础。大桥每个主塔及桥墩处主桁下均设有竖向刚性支座、纵向活动支座,在两主塔处钢梁底设纵向液压阻尼器。

五峰山长江大桥钢桁梁架设施工采用自主研发的9000kN缆载起重机及两节间大节段钢梁整体安装技术,提高了架设安全性,加快了施工进度。

Wufengshan Bridge over Yangtze River is a passageway for Lianyungang-Zhenjiang High-speed Railway and Jiangdu-Yixing Expressway across the Yangtze River, with a total length of 6.41km, and is the first high-speed railway suspension bridge in the world. Eight expressway lanes in dual directions are set on the upper level of the deck and four high-speed railway tracks in dual directions are set on the lower level of the deck.

The main bridge of Wufengshan Bridge over Yangtze River is a double-tower single-suspended-span suspension bridge with a main span of 1,092m. The stiffening girder is designed as a Warren truss type, with the cross section adopting straight main trusses and subsidiary trusses. The central width between the main trusses is 30m; the truss depth is 16m and the section spacing is 14m; Q370qE grade steel is used. The span of the main cable is 350m+1,092m+350m. The sag-to-span ratio is 1/10. Both main cables are prefabricated with 352 parallel wire bundles, and each bundle consists of 127 ϕ 5.5 steel wires with standard strength of 1,860MPa. The hangers are also made with parallel wire bundles with standard strength of 1,770MPa, and the longitudinal spacing between hangers is 14m. The towers are portal frame reinforced concrete structures, supported by pile foundation. The height of the northern tower and southern tower are 203m and 191m, respectively. The north anchorage is supported by a caisson foundation, and the south anchorage is supported by a circular diaphragm wall foundation with various depths. Vertical rigid bearings and longitudinal movable bearings are set for the steel girder at each tower and pier; hydraulic dampers are set longitudinally for the steel girder at the two towers.

A 9,000kN cable-carrying crane and the installation technique for large-size steel truss girder segments of two intersections were developed for the girder erection of Wufengshan Bridge over Yangtze River, improving the erection safety and facilitating the construction progress.

| | |
|---|---|
| 桥　　名： | 五峰山长江大桥 |
| 桥　　型： | 双塔单跨单吊钢桁梁悬索桥 |
| 主跨跨径： | 1092m |
| 桥　　址： | 江苏省镇江市 |
| 建成时间： | 2020 年 12 月 |
| 建设单位： | 中国铁路上海局集团有限公司 |
| 设计单位： | 中铁大桥勘测设计院集团有限公司 |
| 施工单位： | 中铁大桥局集团有限公司，中交第二航务工程局有限公司 |

**Name:** Wufengshan Bridge over Yangtze River
**Type:** Double-tower single-suspended-span suspension bridge with steel truss girder
**Main span:** 1,092m
**Location:** Zhenjiang City, Jiangsu Province
**Completion:** December 2020
**Owner(s):** China Railway Shanghai Group Co., Ltd.
**Designer(s):** China Railway Major Bridge Reconnaissance & Design Institute Co., Ltd.
**Contractor(s):** China Railway Major Bridge Engineering Group Co., Ltd., CCCC Second Harbor Engineering Company Ltd.

平南三桥

The Third Pingnan Bridge

平南三桥位于广西壮族自治区贵港市平南县，跨越浔江，是当时世界上跨度最大的拱桥。大桥全长1.035km，桥面宽36.5m，按双向四车道一级公路布置，两侧设非机动车道和人行道。

平南三桥的主桥为中承式钢管混凝土拱桥，主跨跨径575m，矢跨比1/4。大桥横向采用双拱肋构造，为桁式钢管混凝土结构，每个拱肋由4根直径1.4m的钢管混凝土弦杆、钢管腹杆及横连杆组成。拱肋横向通过多道风撑相连，拱脚与拱座固结。桥面系采用钢-混凝土组合结构、全漂浮体系，纵向采用电涡流阻尼器，由吊杆、拱肋横撑及端墩支承。拱肋采用缆索吊运、斜拉扣挂悬臂拼装施工，拱肋弦管错边量在2mm以内。为了避免粉质黏土、强透水卵石及含溶洞岩层等不利地质条件影响，平南三桥的北台拱座基础、地基采用"圆形地下连续墙＋卵石层注浆加固"方案，基础置于卵石层顶面。扣索采用一次张拉不调索力技术，提高了拱段拼装速度。

平南三桥运用了真空辅助四级连续泵送灌注拱肋弦管C70自密实无收缩混凝土技术，彻底克服了管内混凝土脱空、脱粘的顽疾。首创了力主动控制技术代替传统的刚度控制，利用卫星定位、智能张拉等技术，把吊扣塔顶部偏位自动控制在20mm内，实现了吊扣塔大幅度瘦身。

The Third Pingnan Bridge is located in Pingnan County, Guigang City, Guangxi Zhuang Autonomous Region, across the Xun River, and was the world's longest span arch bridge at that time. The main bridge is 1,035m in length and 36.5m in width. It is a dual-way four-lane first-class highway with non-motor lanes and sidewalks on both sides. The design speed is 60km/h.

The main bridge is a half-through concrete-filled steel tube arch bridge. The main span is 575m and the rise-span ratio is 1/4. The main bridge adopts double arch ribs which include four concrete-filled steel tubes with diameters of 1.4 meters, with vertical and transverse steel tube connectors. The arch ribs are laterally connected by multiple wind bracings, and the arch feet are fixed to the arch seats. The deck adopts full floating system and steel-concrete composite girders, longitudinally incorporating an eddy current damper and supported by hangers, transverse connectors and end piers. The arch ribs were erected by cable hoisting and cantilever construction with temporary stays, and the amount of the matching error of the arch ribs was within 2mm. The abutment foundations adopted a scheme of circular underground continuous wall and pebble layer grouting strengthening to avoid the influence of unfavorable geological conditions such as silty clay, strongly permeable pebble and karst cave rock formation. The technology of one-time tensioning of temporary cable without adjusting was adopted to improve the assembling speed of the arch rib segments.

The steel tube chords were filled with C70 self-compacting non-shrinkage concrete adopting the technique of vacuum-assisted four-stage continuous pumping, which effectively overcomes the stubborn problem of voiding and debonding of the concrete inside the steel tubes. The bridge was constructed using force active control instead of traditional stiffness control for the first time. It also utilized satellite positioning, intelligent tensioning, and other advanced technologies. As a result, the top movement of the temporary tower was automatically controlled within 20mm, reducing the size of the tower.

| | |
|---|---|
| 桥 名： | 平南三桥 |
| 桥 型： | 中承式钢管混凝土拱桥 |
| 主跨跨径： | 575m |
| 桥 址： | 广西壮族自治区贵港市 |
| 建成时间： | 2020年12月 |
| 建设单位： | 广西交通投资集团有限公司 |
| 设计单位： | 四川省公路规划勘察设计研究院有限公司，广西交通设计集团有限公司 |
| 施工单位： | 广西路桥工程集团有限公司 |

**Name:** The Third Pingnan Bridge
**Type:** Half-through concrete filled steel tube arch bridge
**Main span:** 575m
**Location:** Guigang City, Guangxi Zhuang Autonomous Region
**Completion:** December 2020
**Owner(s):** Guangxi Communications Investment Group Corporation Ltd.
**Designer(s):** Sichuan Highway Planning, Survey, Design and Research Institute Ltd., Guangxi Communications Design Group Co., Ltd.
**Contractor(s):** Guangxi Road and Bridge Engineering Group Co., Ltd.

# 南京江心洲长江大桥

## Nanjing Jiangxinzhou Bridge over Yangtze River

| | |
|---|---|
| 桥　　名： | 南京江心洲长江大桥 |
| 桥　　型： | 三塔双索面双主跨组合梁斜拉桥 |
| 主跨跨径： | 2×600m |
| 桥　　址： | 江苏省南京市 |
| 建成时间： | 2020 年 12 月 |
| 建设单位： | 南京市公共工程建设中心 |
| 设计单位： | 中交公路规划设计院有限公司 |
| 施工单位： | 中交第二航务工程局有限公司 |

南京江心洲长江大桥（又名南京长江第五大桥）位于江苏省南京市的长江水道之上，是连接浦口区与建邺区的过江通道。桥梁总长 4.4km，主桥长 1796m，桥面为双向六车道城市主干道，设计速度 100km/h。

主桥为三塔双索面双主跨组合梁斜拉桥，半漂浮结构体系，跨径布置为 80m+218m+2×600m+218m+80m。主梁采用轻型钢-混凝土组合结构。塔柱采用钢-混凝土组合结构，其纵向为钻石形、横向为独柱式，中塔高 175.4m，南、北边塔高 167.7m。斜拉索共 240 根，中央双索面扇形布置。

大桥使用粗集料活性粉末混凝土桥面板，改善了传统钢桥面沥青铺装材料和工艺缺陷，且能有效预防钢材疲劳开裂。纵向的钻石形索塔具有较大的纵向刚度，并采用钢壳混凝土组合结构，提升了工厂化制造水平，并实现现场无污染管控。主塔、桥面、桥墩的建设还采用了预制拼装工法，实现了建造过程的高效环保。

南京江心洲长江大桥获得了国际桥梁与结构工程协会杰出公路和铁路桥梁奖。

**Name:** Nanjing Jiangxinzhou Bridge over Yangtze River
**Type:** Three-tower double-cable-plane double-main-span composite girder cable-stayed bridge
**Main span:** 2×600m
**Location:** Nanjing City, Jiangsu Province
**Completion:** December 2020
**Owner(s):** Nanjing Public Project Construction Center
**Designer(s):** CCCC Highway Consultants Co., Ltd.
**Contractor(s):** CCCC Second Harbor Engineering Company Ltd.

Nanjing Jiangxinzhou Bridge over Yangtze River (also known as the Fifth Nanjing Bridge over Yangtze River) is located across the Yangtze River Waterway in Nanjing, Jiangsu Province. It is a crossing passageway connecting Pukou District and Jianye District. The total length of the bridge is 4.4km, the length of the main bridge is 1,796m, and the bridge deck is a dual-way six-lane urban arterial road with the design speed of 100km/h.

The main bridge is a three-tower double-cable-plane double-main-span composite girder cable-stayed bridge with a semi-floating structural system. Its span arrangement is 80m+218m+2×600m+218m+80m. The main beam adopts a light steel-concrete composite structure. The towers are longitudinally diamond-shaped, transversely single-column steel-concrete composite structure, with a height of 175.4m for the middle tower and 167.7m for the south and north towers. The bridge adopts a fan-shaped arrangement with central double cable planes including 240 cables.

The bridge utilizes the coarse aggregate active powder concrete bridge deck, which can effectively prevent the risk of steel fatigue cracking and can solve the defects of traditional steel bridge deck asphalt pavement materials and processes. Besides, the use of steel shell concrete composite towers with a large longitudinal stiffness improves the level of factory manufacturing and realizes pollution-free control on site. Moreover, the construction of the main tower, bridge deck, and piers adopts the prefabricated assembly method to achieve efficient and environmental protection in the construction process.

The Project of Nanjing Jiangxinzhou Bridge over Yangtze River won the Road and Rail Bridge Award of International Association for Bridge and Structural Engineering.

# 藏木雅鲁藏布江大桥
## Zangmu Bridge over Yarlung Zangbo River

藏木雅鲁藏布江大桥位于西藏自治区山南市，横跨雅鲁藏布江，是川藏铁路拉萨至林芝段关键控制性工程，主跨跨径430m，是世界上跨度最大的铁路钢管混凝土拱桥。大桥全长525.1m，桥面宽度18m，按双线铁路布置。

藏木雅鲁藏布江大桥为中承式钢管混凝土拱桥，矢跨比1/3.84。大桥横向采用各内倾4.6°的双拱肋结构，其间设多道一字形、米字形等钢管横撑；拱肋为采用耐候钢的桁式钢管混凝土结构，每个拱肋由4根直径为1600~1800mm的渐变钢管混凝土弦杆、箱形和H形截面腹杆及横连杆组成，拱脚与拱座固结；桥面结构为单箱双室预应力混凝土连续箱梁，由吊杆和边墩支承。钢管拱肋采用缆索吊装、斜拉扣索悬臂拼装施工方法。

藏木雅鲁藏布江大桥处于高寒、大温差、强紫外线等高原环境，采用耐候钢材料，避免了在雪域高原地区开展涂装维护工作；新型风屏障将横风进行导流，使透风率减小至50%以下；采用了摩擦摆支座＋电涡流阻尼器组合减隔震技术，以减小拱圈和桥墩的地震作用力；大桥主钢管采用变管径技术，钢管直径由1.8m变为1.6m，减轻自重约15%。研制了管内高稳定性、自密实、无收缩混凝土，解决了在高海拔、大温差复杂环境下，管内大体积混凝土易出现的脱空和不密实的难题。提出的大型钢构件空中姿态调整技术，降低了高原峡谷强风环境下拱肋吊装施工风险。

Zangmu Bridge over Yarlung Zangbo River, located in Shannan City, Tibet Autonomous Region, spans the Yarlung Zangbo River. It is the key landmark project of the Lhasa-Nyingchi section of the Sichuan-Tibet Railway and is the world's longest concrete-filled steel tube railway arch bridge in terms of span with a main span of 430m. The total length of the bridge is 525.1m. The width of the bridge deck is 18m, and is arranged as the two-track railway.

The bridge is a half-through concrete-filled steel tube arch bridge with a rise-span ratio of 1/3.84. The bridge has double arch ribs with inward inclination of 4.6°, and multiple transverse and crossing steel tube bracings are set between the ribs. Each rib is a truss of weathering resistant steel and is composed of four concrete-filled steel tube chords with diameters changing from 1,600 to 1,800mm, box-shaped and H-shaped vertical, diagonal connectors and transverse connectors. The arch feet and the arch seats are fixed. The deck is a single-box double-cell prestressed concrete continuous box girder supported by suspenders and side piers. The steel truss arch ribs are erected by cable hoisting and cantilever method with temporary towers and stays.

Zangmu Bridge over Yarlung Zangbo River is located in a plateau environment with frigid, large temperature differences, and strong ultraviolet radiation. The use of weathering resistant steel materials avoids painting and maintenance in the snowy plateau area. The new type of wind barrier can diversify the crosswind so that the ventilation rate was reduced to less than 50%. Seismic isolation technology utilizing a combination of friction pendulum bearings and eddy current dampers reduced the seismic force on the arch and abutments. The main steel rib of the bridge adopted the technology of variable diameter, and the diameter of the steel tube varied from 1.8m to 1.6m, which reduced the self-weight by about 15%. A high stability, self-compacting, non-shrinkage concrete was developed to solve the problems of concrete voids and lack of compactness of large volume concrete in high altitude, large temperature difference environments. The proposed position adjustment technology for large steel components reduced the construction risk of arch rib lifting under the strong wind environment of the plateau canyon.

**Name:** Zangmu Bridge over Yarlung Zangbo River
**Type:** Half-through concrete filled steel tube arch bridge
**Main span:** 430m
**Location:** Shannan City, Tibet Autonomous Region
**Completion:** June 2021
**Owner(s):** Tibet Railway Construction Co., Ltd.
**Designer(s):** China Railway Eryuan Engineering Group Co., Ltd.
**Contractor(s):** China Railway Guangzhou Engineering Group Co., Ltd.

# 舟岱大桥

## Zhoushan-Daishan Bridge

宁波舟山港主通道舟岱大桥是浙江省舟山市连接定海区与岱山县的跨海通道。大桥主线位于灰鳖洋海域，南起烟墩互通，穿马目山后设南通航孔桥跨越长白西航道、主通航孔桥跨越舟山中部港域西航道和北通航孔桥跨越岱山南航道，并设长白海上互通及其接线连接长白岛，主线北止双合互通，桥梁全长28km。

舟岱大桥桥面为双向四车道高速公路，设计速度100km/h。南通航孔桥为主跨390m的双塔双索面钢箱梁斜拉桥，主通航孔桥为主跨2×550m的三塔双索面钢箱梁斜拉桥，北通航孔桥为主跨260m的钢-混凝土混合梁连续刚构桥，深水区非通航孔桥为跨径70m的预应力混凝土连续箱梁桥，采用整孔预制和架设，近岸区非通航孔桥为跨径62.5m的预应力混凝土节段预制拼装箱梁桥。陆域段桥梁采用墩梁全预制一体化绿色拼装技术，海域段主通航孔桥承台采用"内层钢套箱整体安装＋外层钢套箱逐块安装"快速施工工艺；钢管桩沉桩采用北斗卫星导航定位基准服务系统实现沉桩精度校核，预制墩身拼装大规模采用新型自锚式预应力体系。

舟岱大桥全线建成彻底结束岱山海上悬岛时代，对推进浙江海洋强省建设、长三角一体化发展和扎实推动高质量发展建设共同富裕示范区，具有重要意义。

Zhoushan-Daishan Bridge is a sea-crossing passageway connecting Dinghai District and Daishan County in Zhoushan City, Zhejiang Province. The main bridge is located in the Huibieyang Sea area, starting from Yandun Interchange in the south, passing through Mamu Mountain, with the south navigation channel bridge crossing the west navigation channel of Changbai, the main navigation channel bridge crossing the west channel of Zhoushan Central Port Region and the north navigation channel bridge crossing the south channel of Daishan. The main bridge also connects Changbai Island with Changbai Sea Interchange, finally ends at Shuanghe Interchange in the north, with a total length of 28km.

The deck of the bridge is designed to carry dual way four-lane highway traffic with the design speed of 100km/h. The south navigation channel bridge is a double-tower double-cable-plane steel box girder cable-stayed bridge with a main span of 390m. The main navigation channel bridge is a three-tower double-cable-plane steel box girder cable-stayed bridge with two 550m main spans. The north navigation channel bridge is a continuous rigid frame steel concrete hybrid bridge with a main span of 260m. The non-navigation channel bridge in the deep water area consists of 70m span prestressed concrete continuous box girders, which were prefabricated and erected on site. The non-navigation channel bridge in the nearshore area is composed of 62.5m span of prestressed concrete precast segmental box girders. In order to significantly

桥　　名：舟岱大桥
桥　　型：斜拉桥、连续刚构桥、简支梁桥、连续梁桥
桥梁长度：全长28km，主跨跨径2×550m
桥　　址：浙江省舟山市
建成时间：2021年12月
建设单位：宁波舟山港主通道项目工程建设指挥部
设计单位：浙江数智交院科技股份有限公司，中交公路规划设计院有限公司
施工单位：浙江交工集团股份有限公司，中铁大桥局集团有限公司，中国交通建设集团有限公司等

reduce the environmental impact of bridge construction activities, fully prefabricated piers and girders with "green" assembly technology had been adopted in the land area. The rapid construction technology of "integral installation of inner steel boxed cofferdam plus segmental installation of outer steel boxed cofferdam" had been developed for the pile caps of the main navigation bridge in the sea area. Beidou satellite navigation and positioning reference service system had been used to verify the accuracy of steel pipe pile driving. A new type of self-anchored prestressing system was adopted to assemble the precast pier on a large scale.

The completion of the Zhoushan-Daishan Bridge has completely ended the era of Daishan as an island far from the mainland, which is of great significance for promoting the construction of a strong marine province of Zhejiang, the integrated development of the Yangtze River Delta and solidly promoting the high-quality development and construction of a common prosperity demonstration zone.

**Name:** Zhoushan-Daishan Bridge
**Type:** Cable-stayed bridge, continuous rigid frame bridge, simply supported girder bridge and continuous girder bridge
**Length:** Total length 28km, main span 2×550m
**Location:** Zhoushan City, Zhejiang Province
**Completion:** December 2021
**Owner(s):** Ningbo Zhoushan Port Main Channel Project Engineering Construction Headquarters
**Designer(s):** Zhejiang Institute of Communications Co., Ltd., CCCC Highway Consultants Co., Ltd.
**Contractor(s):** Zhejiang Communications Construction Group Co., Ltd., China Railway Major Bridge Engineering Group Co., Ltd., China Communications Construction Group Co., Ltd., etc.

# 凤凰黄河大桥

## Phoenix Bridge over Yellow River

| | |
|---|---|
| 桥　　名： | 凤凰黄河大桥 |
| 桥　　型： | 三塔六跨组合梁自锚式悬索桥 |
| 主跨跨径： | 2×428m |
| 桥　　址： | 山东省济南市 |
| 建成时间： | 2022年1月 |
| 建设单位： | 济南城市建设集团有限公司 |
| 设计单位： | 上海市政工程设计研究总院（集团）有限公司 |
| 施工单位： | 中交第二航务工程局有限公司，中铁十二局集团有限公司 |

凤凰黄河大桥位于山东省济南市，跨越黄河连接起步区、高新区和历城区，全长6.683km，设双向八车道及两条轻轨线路。

凤凰黄河大桥主桥为三塔六跨空间索面自锚式悬索桥，主跨跨径为2×428m。组合梁宽61.7m，中心梁高4m，采用正交异性组合桥面板。主缆跨径为171.5m+428m+428m+171.5m，中跨垂跨比为1/6.15，边跨垂跨比为1/15.6，采用127∅6.2预制平行钢丝索股，每根主缆61股，标准强度为1960MPa。吊索标准纵向间距9m，采用平行钢丝束索股。中塔塔高126.0m，边塔塔高116.1m。桥塔下部采用钻孔灌注桩基础，桩直径为2.0m，桩长100m。大桥主梁在桥塔、边墩处设竖向支座和横向钢阻尼器，并在桥塔处设纵向液体黏滞阻尼器。

凤凰黄河大桥主桥设计采用上部钢结构、下部钢-混凝土组合结构的A形塔柱，协调优化了结构刚度和主缆抗滑系数的要求，并设置刚性三角桁架中央扣，改善桥塔受力。采用超宽闭口钢箱梁，交通同层布置，降低了接线道路布置的难度；在机动车道及缆吊区铺设纤维钢筋混凝土桥面板，改善了箱梁受力性能，提高了结构耐久性。

Phoenix Bridge over Yellow River, located in Ji'nan City of Shandong Province, connects Qibu District, Gaoxin District and Licheng District crossing the Yellow River. The bridge has a total length of 6.683km with dual-way 8 traffic lanes, and 2 light rails.

The main bridge of Phoenix Bridge over Yellow River is a three-tower six-span self-anchored suspension bridge with a spatial cable system with the main spans of 2×428m. The composite girder width is 61.7m, the center girder depth is 4m. The orthotropic composite slab is applied in the deck system.

The span of the main cable is 171.5m+428m+428m+171.5m. The sag to span ratios are 1/6.15 in the main spans and 1/15.6 in the side spans, respectively. Both main cables are prefabricated with 61 parallel wire bundles, and each bundle includes 127$\phi$6.2 steel wires with standard strength of 1,960MPa. The hangers are also made of parallel wire bundles, and the longitudinal standard spacing between hangers is 9m. The height of the middle tower and side tower are 126.0m and 116.1m, respectively. The towers are supported by bored piles of 2.0m diameter and 100m height. Vertical bearings and transverse steel dampers were set for the girder at the middle tower and at the side towers, respectively. In addition, longitudinal viscous dampers were set for the main girder at the towers.

The main bridge adopts A-shaped tower with steel structures for the upper part and steel-concrete composite structures for the lower part. The design involves coordinating and optimizing the structural stiffness and the anti-slip safety factor of the main cable. A rigid triangular-truss central buckle was set to further improve the mechanical condition of the tower. The bridge adopts an ultra-wide steel box girder that allows the highway and railway to be arranged on the same deck level, easing the arrangement of approach bridges. The fiber-concrete layer was applied on the traffic lanes and the anchorage area of cables and hangers of the deck, improving the mechanical performance and durability of the girder.

**Name:** Phoenix Bridge over Yellow River
**Type:** Three-tower six-span self-anchored suspension bridge
**Main span:** 2×428m
**Location:** Ji'nan City, Shandong Province
**Completion:** January 2022
**Owner(s):** Ji'nan City Construction Group Co., Ltd.
**Designer(s):** Shanghai Municipal Engineering Design Institute (Group) Co., Ltd.
**Contractor(s):** CCCC Second Harbor Engineering Company Ltd., China Railway 12th Bureau Group Co., Ltd.

# 瓯江北口大桥

## Beikou Bridge over Ou River

瓯江北口大桥位于浙江省温州市瓯江北汊入海口，上层高速公路接甬台温高速公路，全长7.9km；下层一级公路南接国道G228线灵昆段，北连国道G228线乐清段，全长3.9km，均为双向六车道。

主桥为三塔四跨吊悬索桥，主跨跨径为2×800m。主缆跨径为230m+800m+800m+348m，垂跨比为1/10。加劲梁采用板桁组合钢桁架，主桁采用华伦式结构，桁高12.5m，两片主桁中心间距36.2m。吊杆纵向间距10m，采用平行钢丝束索股。中塔采用A形混凝土中塔，设沉井基础，塔高145.5m。南北塔采用混凝土门式塔，设钻孔灌注桩基础，塔高分别为143.5m和147.5m。南、北锚均采用重力锚。大桥加劲梁在边塔设置纵向黏滞阻尼器，桥塔及边墩处设置竖向支座，加劲梁上、下弦节点与塔柱间设置横向抗风支座。

为了提高大桥作为多塔连跨悬索桥的结构刚度，采用了刚性的混凝土中塔和板桁组合加劲梁。其中，在中塔的塔顶鞍座内设置了多个摩擦板，以通过增加接触面积来提高摩擦力，解决了中塔鞍座内主缆抗滑移的问题；板桁组合加劲梁采用"缆载起重机+分体式液压提升"架设方法及"缆载起重机荡移卸船+滑移系统"工艺，解决了跨中缆梁相交段吊装及边跨加劲梁转运的难题。中塔采用防撞能力强、刚度大、经济性更优的倒圆角矩形沉井基础，来满足中塔基础所受弯矩大、船撞力大及基岩埋深大的需求。

Beikou Bridge over Ou River is located in the north branch estuary of Ou River in Wenzhou City, Zhejiang Province. The expressway on the upper level of the deck connects the Ningbo-Taizhou-Wenzhou expressway and has a total length of 7.9km. The first-class highway on the lower level of the deck starts from the Lingkun section of the G228 national highway in the south and ends at the Yueqing section of the G228 national highway in the north, having a total length of 3.9km. Six traffic lanes in dual directions are set for both the expressway and the first-class highway.

The main bridge is a three-tower four-suspended-span two-main-span suspension bridge with the main spans of 2×800m. The span arrangement of the main cable is 230m+800m+800m+348m. The sag-to-span ratio is 1/10. The steel truss with orthotropic deck stiffening girder is

applied. The Warren truss is 12.5m deep and the distance between the center lines of the two main trusses is 36.2m. The hangers are also made of parallel wire bundles, and the longitudinal spacing between hangers is 10m. The A-shaped concrete middle tower is 145.5m high and supported by a caisson foundation. The northern and southern towers are portal framed reinforced concrete structures supported by bored piles, with 143.5m and 147.5m heights, respectively. Gravity-type anchorages are used for both the northern and southern banks. Viscous dampers are set for the girder at the side towers; vertical bearings are set for the girder at the towers and piers; transverse wind-resistant bearings are set between the upper, lower chords and the towers.

In order to enhance the structural stiffness, a rigid concrete middle tower and steel truss with orthotropic deck stiffening girder were designed and applied. Multiple friction plates were set inside the saddle on the middle tower top to increase the contact area for overcoming the anti-slip problem of the main cable crossing the saddle. An erection method that used cable cranes and separated hydraulic synchronous lifting had been developed to address the girder erection problem in the middle span where the main cable is under the upper deck level, and a construction technique that combines the swing-unloading and the sliding system had been developed to address the girder transporting problem in the side span. Based on the feature that the foundation of the middle tower is subjected to large bending moments, large ship collision forces and has deep bedrock, the middle tower adopts the chamfered rectangular open caisson foundation, which has a better anti-collision ability, higher stiffness and better economic performance.

桥　　名：瓯江北口大桥
桥　　型：三塔四跨吊钢桁梁悬索桥
主跨跨径：2×800m
桥　　址：浙江省温州市
建成时间：2022年5月
建设单位：温州瓯江口大桥有限公司
设计单位：浙江数智交院科技股份有限公司，中铁大桥勘测设计院集团有限公司
施工单位：中铁大桥局集团有限公司，中交一公局集团有限公司，中交第二航务工程局有限公司

**Name:** Beikou Bridge over Ou River
**Type:** Three-tower four-suspended-span suspension bridge with steel truss girder
**Main span:** 2×800m
**Location:** Wenzhou City, Zhejiang Province
**Completion:** May 2022
**Owner(s):** Wenzhou Ou River Bridge Co., Ltd.
**Designer(s):** Zhejiang Institute of Communications Co., Ltd., China Railway Major Bridge Reconnaissance & Design Institute Co., Ltd.
**Contractor(s):** China Railway Major Bridge Engineering Group Co., Ltd., China First Highway Engineering Co., Ltd., CCCC Second Harbor Engineering Company Ltd.

# 金门大桥

**Kinmen Bridge**

桥　　名：金门大桥
桥　　型：五塔六跨预应力混凝土箱梁斜拉桥
桥梁长度：全长5.4km，主跨跨径4×200m
桥　　址：金门县烈屿乡至金门本岛
建成时间：2022年10月
建设单位：国登营造股份有限公司
设计单位：台湾世曦工程顾问股份有限公司
施工单位：台湾世曦工程顾问股份有限公司，东丕营造股份有限公司

金门大桥是连接金门县大金门和小金门的首座跨海大桥。大桥西起金门县烈屿乡（小金门）后头湖埔路，东到金门本岛（大金门）金宁乡湖下慈湖路，全长5.4km，包括主桥、左右边桥、左右引桥及两岛立交等。主桥宽18.8m，采用双向四车道标准，设计速度60km/h。

主桥为五塔六跨斜拉桥，跨径布置为125m+4×200m+125m，主塔采用曲线形混凝土墩柱，每座桥塔设置11对斜拉索，单索面扇形布置，中间3塔采用塔墩梁固结体系，两边各1塔采用半漂浮体系，主梁采用预应力混凝土箱梁。左右边桥为三跨预应力混凝土连续箱梁桥，跨径布置为110m+150m+100m。左右引桥和两岛立交采用35~50m跨径预应力混凝土简支箱梁桥。

桥梁所处深槽地段花岗岩岩层深度变化剧烈，采用钢围堰现浇基础，主梁则采用预制节段悬臂拼装施工。

Kinmen Bridge is the first cross-sea bridge connecting the Greater Kinmen Island and Lesser Kinmen Island in Jinmen County. The bridge starts from Houtou Hupu Road in Lieyu Township of Jinmen County (Lesser Kinmen) in the west and ends at Huxia Cihu Road in Jinning Township, Jinmen Island (Greater Kinmen) in the east. The total length of the bridge is 5.4km, including the main bridge, left and right side bridges, left and right approach bridges, and two overpasses on both islands. The bridge adopts a dual-way four-lane standard with a total width of 18.8m and a design speed of 60km/h.

The main bridge is a five-tower six-span cable-stayed bridge with the span arrangement of 125m+4×200m+125m. The main towers are curved concrete columns, and each tower is equipped with 11 pairs of stay cables, with single cable plane fan-shaped layout. The middle three towers adopt tower-pier-beam fixed system, and both side towers adopt semi-floating structural system. The main girder is prestressed concrete box girder. The left and right side bridges are three span prestressed concrete continuous box girders, with the spans of 110m+150m+100m. The left and right approach bridges and the overpasses in two islands adopt prestressed concrete simply supported box girder with the spans of 35m to 50m.

The bridge is located in a deep groove section with drastic changes in the depth of the granite rock stratum, and a cast-in-place foundation with steel cofferdam was used. The main girder was constructed by precast segmental cantilever method.

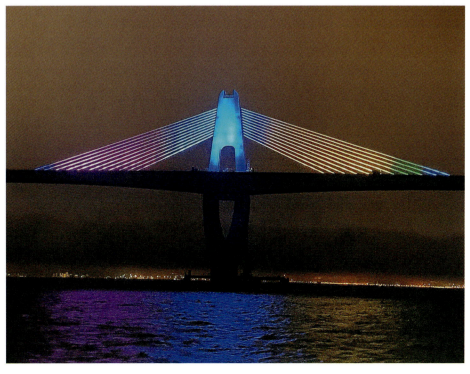

**Name:** Kinmen Bridge
**Type:** Five-tower six-span prestressed concrete cable-stayed bridge
**Length:** Total length 5.4km, main span 4×200m
**Location:** Lieyu County and Jinmen Island, Jinmen County
**Completion:** October, 2022
**Owner(s):** Guodeng Construction Co., Ltd.
**Designer(s):** Taiwan Shixi Engineering Consulting Co., Ltd.
**Contractor(s):** Taiwan Shixi Engineering Consulting Co., Ltd., Taiwan Dongpi Construction Co., Ltd.

# 天峨龙滩特大桥
## Tian'e Longtan Bridge

| | |
|---|---|
| 桥　　名：天峨龙滩特大桥 | **Name:** Tian'e Longtan Bridge |
| 桥　　型：上承式钢筋混凝土拱桥 | **Type:** Reinforced concrete arch bridge |
| 主跨跨径：600m | **Main span:** 600m |
| 桥　　址：广西壮族自治区河池市 | **Location:** Hechi City, Guangxi Zhuang Autonomous Region |
| 建成时间：2023 年 12 月 | **Completion:** December, 2023 |
| 建设单位：广西交通投资集团有限公司 | **Owner(s):** Guangxi Communications Investment Group Corporation Ltd. |
| 设计单位：广西交通设计集团有限公司 | **Designer(s):** Guangxi Communications Design Group Co., Ltd. |
| 施工单位：广西路桥工程集团有限公司 | **Contractor(s):** Guangxi Road and Bridge Engineering Group Co., Ltd. |

天峨龙滩特大桥位于广西壮族自治区河池市天峨县，跨越龙滩水库库区，为南丹至天峨高速公路的重要工程，主跨跨径600m，是世界上已建和在建桥梁中跨度最大的拱桥。大桥全长 2488.55m，桥面宽 24.5m，按双向四车道高速公路布置。

天峨龙滩特大桥主桥为上承式钢筋混凝土拱桥，矢跨比 1/4.8。主桥采用分离式平行双等宽变高混凝土箱肋拱，拱肋之间设多道箱形截面横向联系，拱肋内设置了钢管混凝土弦杆与钢腹杆组成的桁式劲性骨架，拱脚与拱座固结；主桥桥道梁采用 3 联 4×40m 预应力混凝土连续 T 梁，T 梁高 2.5m。拱肋劲性骨架采用缆索吊运、斜拉扣索悬臂拼装施工。

天峨龙滩特大桥设计中，因为大大增强了劲性骨架，从而减少了外包混凝土浇筑过程中的应力和变形，外包混凝土分 3 环、8 工作面、36 次浇筑，瞬时拉应力控制在 1MPa 内，防止了裂缝产生，混凝土中配置横强纵弱的普通钢筋，使拱肋混凝土的应力水平与跨径400m级拱桥持平。按线弹性理论应力、挠度叠加法计算值与实测值完全吻合。针对天峨龙滩特大桥桥址处于复杂陡峭山区，破碎的强风化泥质砂岩、顺层坡、局部裂隙发育等复杂地质情况，采用基底注浆、低温升抗裂混凝土等技术，为大体积基础施工提供了强有力支持。

Tian'e Longtan Bridge is located in Tian'e County, Hechi City, Guangxi Zhuang Autonomous Region, across the Longtan Reservoir, which is an important project of the Nandan-Tian'e Highway, and has the largest span among all existing or under-construction arch bridges in the world with a main span of 600m. The total length of the bridge is 2,488.55m, the width of the bridge deck is 24.5m, and it is arranged as a four-lane dual carriageway highway.

The main bridge is a reinforced concrete arch bridge with a rise-span ratio of 1/4.8. The main arch is composed of two parallel equal-width and variable-depth box ribs and multiple box-shaped lateral connections between the ribs. There are rigid frames made up of concrete-filled steel tube chords and steel truss webs embedded in each arch rib, and the arch feet and the arch seats are fixed. The main bridge deck adopts three 4×40 meters prestressed concrete continuous T-beam with the depth of 2.5m. The rigid frames in arch ribs were erected by cable hoisting and cantilever construction with temporary stays.

The greatly enhanced rigid frame reduces the stress and deformation during the casting of outside concrete. The outside concrete was cast in 3 rings, 8 working faces and 36 times, and the tensile stress was controlled within 1MPa, which prevented cracks. The design principle of using strong transverse and weak longitudinal reinforcement was utilized, thus the concrete stress degree of the arch ribs is equivalent to that of the 400m-span arch bridges. Calculated values according to the theoretical stress and deflection by superposition and linear elasticity were in complete agreement with the measured values. Aiming at the complex geological situation that the bridge site is in a complex and steep mountainous area, with broken strongly weathered muddy sandstone, dip slopes, and local fissure development, it adopted technologies such as base grouting and low temperature rise anti-cracking concrete, which provided strong support for the construction of the large-volume foundation.

# 深中通道
## Shenzhen-Zhongshan Link

深中通道位于广东珠江入海口，连接深圳市、中山市和广州市，是集"桥、岛、隧、水下互通"于一体的世界级跨海集群工程。深中通道全长24km，采用双向八车道高速公路标准建设，设计速度100km/h。海底隧道长6.8km，其中沉管段长5km，由32个管节及1个最终接头组成，隧道两端各设置一座人工岛；海上桥梁长17.2km，包括伶仃洋大桥、中山大桥及非通航孔桥等。

伶仃洋大桥为双塔三跨钢箱梁悬索桥，主缆跨径布置为580m+1666m+580m，垂跨比为1/9.65，钢箱梁总宽49.7m，梁高4m；桥塔采用H形门式造型，塔高270m；大桥通航净高76.5m，桥面高度91m，位于强台风频发的开阔海域，通过优化整体钢箱梁的综合气动外形，可满足颤振检验风速83.7m/s；锚碇基础采用"锁扣钢管桩＋工字形板桩＋平行钢丝索"自平衡柔性围堰筑岛＋"横向8字形地下连续墙"，实现了深厚海相淤泥地质、全离岸海中大型锚碇快速建造技术，并大幅降低了阻水率；为解决主缆全寿命周期内"高温、高湿、高盐"环境下的腐蚀疲劳问题，研制了6mm直径2060MPa高强锌铝镁（稀土）合金镀层主缆钢丝。中山大桥采用双塔三跨钢箱梁斜拉桥，主跨580m，主塔高213.5m。海上非通航孔桥长约11.4km，共有钢箱梁138跨、混凝土箱梁155跨，梁体跨径大、吨位重，架设精度要求高。

深中通道伶仃洋大桥在整体式钢箱梁抗风技术、钢桥面U肋焊接接头细节构造、高耐久主缆钢丝、海相软基地区锚碇建造、混凝土索塔工业化建造等方面进行了技术创新。

Shenzhen-Zhongshan Link is located at the Pearl River estuary in Guangdong, connecting Shenzhen, Zhongshan and Guangzhou and is a world class sea-cross group project integrating "bridge, island, tunnel and underwater interchange". Shenzhen-Zhongshan Link has a total length of 24km, constructed according to the dual-way eight-lane highway standards with the design speed of 100km/h. The undersea tunnel is 6.8km long, of which the immersed tube is 5km long, consisting of 32 segments and 1 final joints. Artificial islands were built at two ends of the tunnel. Bridges oversea are 17.2km long, including the Lingdingyang bridge, Zhongshan bridge and non-navigation channel bridges, etc.

Lingdingyang Bridge is a double-tower three-span steel box girder suspension bridge, with a span arrangement of 580m+1,666m+580m, rise-span ratio of 1/9.65. The stiffening steel box girder has a total width of 49.7m and depth of 4m. The bridge tower adopts the H shape, with the height of 270m. The deck level of the bridge is 91m with the navigational height of 76.5m, located in the open sea area with frequently strong typhoons. By optimizing the comprehensive aerodynamic shape of the whole steel box girder, it can meet with the flutter checking speed of 83.7m/s. The foundation of anchorages adopted self-balancing flexible cofferdam with " steel pipe piles with locking buckle + I-shaped piles + parallel steel wire" to build island and "transverse 8-shaped diaphragm wall", which realized the rapid construction of large-scale anchorages in the deep sea silt geology and the full offshore sea, and reduced the water blocking rate. In order to solve the problem of corrosion and fatigue in the environment of "high temperature, high humidity, and high salt" during the whole life cycle of the main cable, 6mm diameter 2,060MPa high-strength zinc-aluminum-magnesium (rare earth) alloy coated main cable steel wire had been developed. Zhongshan Bridge adopts a double-tower three-span steel box girder cable-

stayed bridge, with a main span of 580m, and the height of the main tower is 213.5m. The non-navigation channel bridge over the sea is about 11.4km long, with a total of 138 spans of steel box girders, 155 spans of concrete box girders. The box girders have characteristics of long span, heavy weight, and high precision requirements for construction.

Lingdingyang Bridge has carried out technological innovations in the wind-resistant technology of the integral steel box girder, the detailed structure of U-rib welded joints on the steel deck, highly durable main cable steel wires, the construction of anchorages in the marine soft soil area, and the industrialized construction of concrete towers, etc.

桥　　名：深中通道
桥　　型：双塔三跨吊钢箱梁悬索桥，双塔三跨钢箱梁斜拉桥
桥梁长度：全长 24km，主跨跨径 1666m
桥　　址：广东省深圳市，中山市和广州市
建成时间：2024 年 6 月
建设单位：广东省交通集团有限公司，深中通道管理中心
设计单位：中交公路规划设计院有限公司，中交水运规划设计院有限公司，上海市隧道工程轨道交通设计研究院，中铁大桥勘测设计院集团有限公司等
施工单位：中交第二航务工程局有限公司，保利长大工程有限公司，中交第二公路工程局有限公司，中铁大桥局集团有限公司等

**Name:** Shenzhen-Zhongshan Link
**Type:** Double-tower three-suspended-span steel box girder suspension bridge, double-tower three-span steel box girder cable-stayed bridge
**Length:** Total length 24km, main span 1,666m
**Location:** Shenzhen，Zhongshan and Guangzhou, Guangdong Province
**Completion:** June 2024
**Owner(s):** Shenzhen-Zhongshan Link Administration Center of Guangdong Provincial Communication Group Co., Ltd.
**Designer(s):** CCCC Highway Consultants Co., Ltd., China Communication Planning and Design Institute for Water Transportation Co., Ltd., Shanghai Tunnel Engineering & Rail Transit Design and Research Institute, China Railway Major Bridge Reconnaissance & design Institute Co.,Ltd.etc.
**Contractor(s):** CCCC Second Harbor Engineering Company Ltd., Poly Changda Engineering Co., Ltd., CCCC Second Highway Engineering Co.,Ltd., China Railway Major Bridge Engineering Group Co., Ltd., etc.

# 澳门第四条跨海大桥

## The Fourth Sea-crossing Bridge of Macao

| | |
|---|---|
| 桥　　名： | 澳门第四条跨海大桥 |
| 桥　　型： | 钢桁梁桥 |
| 主跨跨径： | 280m |
| 桥　　址： | 澳门特别行政区 |
| 建成时间： | 2024年6月 |
| 建设单位： | 澳门特别行政区政府公共建设局 |
| 设计单位： | 林同棪国际工程咨询(中国)有限公司 |
| 施工单位： | 中国铁建大桥工程局集团有限公司，中国土木工程集团有限公司，澳马建筑集团有限公司等 |

　　澳门第四条跨海大桥起自澳门新城区填海A区东侧，与港珠澳大桥口岸人工岛连接，跨越外港航道和内港航道，与澳门新城区填海E区相连，桥梁全长3.085km。

　　澳门第四条跨海大桥桥面宽48.4m，设双向八车道，中间两车道为电车专用道，设计速度为80km/h。全桥共设置两个通航孔，为两联钢桁-钢箱组合结构连续钢桁梁桥，跨径布置为202.5m+280m+202.5m，分为中间钢桁梁主体部分和两侧悬臂翼缘，中间核心箱室与两片主桁架紧密结合。钢桁架内倾形成整体，显著改善桁架结构横向稳定性。两侧悬臂翼缘形成梁板单元，可实现与主结构分离单独安装，有助于降低对施工吊装设备的要求。由于航道与桥梁斜交，桥墩优化为独柱式结构，顶部设双支座，承台与桩基布置更为紧凑。边跨钢梁主体结构与两侧悬臂翼缘分开安装，先利用22000kN浮式起重机分四大节段从过渡墩向主墩方向安装边跨钢梁主体结构，然后再利用轨道梁面起重机逐段安装两侧悬臂翼缘；中跨钢梁采用10000kN桥面步履式架梁起重机逐节段悬臂架设，由两个主墩向跨中对称施工，最后在跨中合龙。

　　澳门第四条跨海大桥是连接澳门半岛和氹仔岛之间的又一通道，并且连接港珠澳大桥，对完善澳门地区的陆路交通具有重要的意义。

The Fourth Sea-crossing Bridge of Macao begins on the east side of Reclamation Area A in the New Town of Macao. It connects to the artificial island of the Hong Kong-Zhuhai-Macao Bridge Boundary Crossing Facilities, crosses the Outer Harbour Channel and the Inner Harbour Channel, and connects to Reclamation Area E in the New Town of Macao. The total bridge is 3.085km in length.

The Fourth Sea-crossing Bridge of Macao has a deck width of 48.4m. It has dual way eight lanes and two middle lanes for trams. The design speed is 80km/h. There are two navigational spans in the bridge, which are continuous steel truss bridges with the span arrangement of 202.5m+280m+202.5m. It consists of the main part of the middle steel truss girder and two cantilevered side flanges, with the middle core box cell and the two main trusses closely combined. The steel truss is inclined inward to improve the lateral stability of the structure. The flanges on both sides are cantilevered and form a girder unit that can be installed independently of the main structure. This reduces the requirement for construction lifting equipment. The piers are optimized as a single column structure with double bearings at the top due to the skew crossing of the channel and the bridge. Additionally, the bearing and pile foundation are arranged more compactly. The main structure of the side span steel girder and both sides of the cantilever flange were installed separately. The installation process involved using a 22,000kN floating crane to install the side span steel girder main structure in four major segments from the transition pier to the direction of the main pier. Then, the rail crane on the deck was used to install both sides of the cantilever flange by segments. The steel girder of the middle span was erected by segmental balanced cantilever method using a 10,000kN deck-travelling crane, starting from the two main piers towards the middle of the spans. The segments were then joined at the midspans.

The Fourth Sea-crossing Bridge of Macao serves as a connection between the Macao Peninsula and Taipa Island. It also links to the Hong Kong-Zhuhai-Macao Bridge, which greatly improves land transportation in the region.

**Name:** The Fourth Sea-crossing Bridge of Macao
**Type:** Steel truss girder bridge
**Main span:** 280m
**Location:** Macao Special Administrative Region
**Completion:** June 2024
**Owner(s):** Direção dos Serviços de Obras Públicas do Governo da Região Administrativa Especial de Macau
**Designer(s):** T. Y. Lin International Engineering Consulting (China) Co., Ltd.
**Contractor(s):** China Railway Construction Bridge Engineering Bureau Group Co., Ltd., China Civil Engineering Construction Corporation, Companhia de Construção e Engenharia OMAS, Limitada, etc.

# 黄茅海跨海通道

## Huang Mao Hai Link

黄茅海跨海通道东起珠海市平沙镇，西接江门市斗山镇，横跨珠江口崖门入海口黄茅海水域，路线全长31.1km，跨海段长14.5km，设置2座通航孔桥，黄茅海大桥和高栏港大桥。

黄茅海跨海通道为双向六车道高速公路，设计速度100km/h。黄茅海大桥为三塔双索面斜拉桥，跨径布置为100m+280m+720m+720m+280m+100m；主梁采用分体式钢箱梁，梁高4.0m，斜拉索横向间距45.9m；桥塔采用混凝土独柱塔，断面为圆形、圆端形变截面，桥塔基础采用变截面群桩基础；斜拉索采用平行钢丝拉索，设置20根中央辅助索；支承体系采用竖向全漂浮体系，中塔塔梁连接采用纵向弹性索与横向抗风支座，边塔塔梁连接采用纵向阻尼与横向抗风支座，辅助墩和过渡墩采用竖向支座。高栏港大桥为独柱塔双塔双索面斜拉桥，跨径布置为110m+248m+700m+248m+110m，主梁为分体式钢箱梁。中引桥为全长1600m的钢箱梁桥，跨径布置为6×100m+5×100m+5×100m，下部结构采用整幅式TY复合墩；东引桥和西引桥采用40m跨径的预应力混凝土小箱梁桥及60m跨径的预应力混凝土节段梁桥。

黄茅海跨海通道工程融入平安百年品质工程理念，提出了全寿命周期建设要求，确保桥梁的强度和耐久性，组成大湾区跨海跨江通道群，加快形成世界级交通枢纽，让粤港澳大湾区发展更加均衡。

Huang Mao Hai Link crosses from the east of Pingsha Town in Zhuhai City to the west of Doushan Town in Jiangmen City, over the Pearl River Yamen estuary into the Huang Mao Sea. The total length of the link is 31.1km, with a sea-crossing section covering 14.5km, featuring two navigational spans, Huang Mao Hai Bridge and Gao Lan Gang Bridge. The Huang Mao Hai Link is a dual-way six lanes highway, designed for the speed of 100km/h.

Huang Mao Hai Bridge, is a three-tower cable-stayed bridge with a single-column tower and two cable planes, and the span arrangement of 100m+280m+720m+720m+280m+100m. The main girder adopts a 4.0m depth separate steel box girder, with cables spacing of 45.9m transversely. The towers consist of single-column concrete structure with variable circular cross-section. The bridge tower foundation utilizes a variable section group pile foundation. The stay cables adopt parallel steel wires, and 20 cross cables are set up. The bridge system employs a vertical full-floating system, connecting the middle tower and the deck with longitudinal elastic cables and transverse wind resistance support. The connection of the side tower and the deck features longitudinal damping and transverse wind resistance support, while the auxiliary and transition piers adopt vertical bearing. Gao Lan Gang Bridge is a two-tower cable-stayed bridge with single-column tower and two cable planes, with a span arrangement of 110m+248m+700m+248m+110m. The main deck is a separate steel box girder. The middle approach bridge is a 1600m long steel box girder bridge with span arrangement of 6×100m+5×100m+5×100m, and the substructure adopts entire width TY composite pier. The eastern and western approach bridges incorporate 40m span prestressed concrete small box girder bridge and 60m span prestressed concrete segmental bridge.

Huang Mao Hai Link incorporates the concept of "Safe and sound for hundred years" and puts forward the whole life cycle construction requirements to ensure the strength and durability of the bridge, which forms a group of cross-sea and cross-river links in the Guangdong-Hong Kong-Macao Greater Bay Area, accelerates the formation of a world-class transportation hub and fostering more balanced regional growth in the Greater Bay Area.

桥　　名：黄茅海跨海通道
桥　　型：三塔双索面斜拉桥，双塔双索面斜拉桥
桥梁长度：全长31.1km，主跨跨径2×720m
桥　　址：广东省珠海市至江门市
建成时间：2024年12月
建设单位：黄茅海跨海通道管理中心
设计单位：广东省交通规划设计研究院股份有限公司，中交公路规划设计院有限公司，北京交科公路勘察设计研究院有限公司
施工单位：中交第二航务工程局有限公司，中交路桥建设有限公司，中铁大桥局集团有限公司，保利长大公路工程有限公司等

**Name:** Huang Mao Hai Link
**Type:** Three-tower double-cable-plane cable-stayed bridge, double-tower double-cable-plane cable-stayed bridge
**Length:** Total length 31.1km, main span 2×720m
**Location:** Zhuhai City to Jiangmen City, Guangdong Province
**Completion:** December 2024
**Owner(s):** Huang Mao Hai Link Management Center of Guangdong Provincial Communication Group Company Limited.
**Designer(s):** Guangdong Communication Planning & Design Institute Group Co.,Ltd., CCCC Highway Consultants Co., Ltd., Jiaoke Transport Consultants Ltd.
**Contractor(s):** CCCC Second Harbor Engineering Company Ltd., Road & Bridge International Co., Ltd., China Railway Major Bridge Engineering Group Co.,Ltd., Poly Changda Engineering Co., Ltd., etc.

# 后 记

2024年，是中华人民共和国成立75周年。为了庆祝新中国成立75周年，经过编辑委员会、编写组和出版社三方的共同努力，特编辑出版《中国桥梁 1949—2024》画册。

本画册遴选出了中国桥梁各个发展时期的共计75座桥梁。其中，1949年到1979年学习与探索时期的桥梁14座，包括中国第一座预应力混凝土铁路桥梁和公路桥梁、特大桥梁武汉长江大桥和南京长江大桥以及梁桥和拱桥的经济桥型和施工技术代表桥梁等；1980年到1999年跟踪与自主时期的桥梁13座，包括代表中国自主建设里程碑的上海南浦大桥、创造世界跨径纪录的斜拉桥、混凝土梁桥和混凝土拱桥等；2000年到2009年发展与图强时期的桥梁15座，包括创造世界长度纪录的跨海大桥，上海卢浦大桥、重庆石板坡长江大桥复线桥和苏通长江公路大桥等跨径创造世界纪录的桥梁等；2010年到2019年创新与提高时期的桥梁19座，包括武汉二七长江大桥和泰州长江大桥等世界最大跨度双主跨斜拉桥和悬索桥、提升桥梁技术水平和品质的港珠澳大桥等；2020年到2024年攀登与超越时期的桥梁14座，包括体现桥梁技术创新的天峨龙滩特大桥和南京江心洲长江大桥、体现品质提升的瓯江北口大桥和黄茅海跨海通道等、体现环境友好的深中通道和澳门第四条跨海大桥等。

75年来，中国桥梁工程发展取得了举世瞩目的成就，成为推动国际桥梁技术进步和科技创新的新动力，从"跟跑者"到"并跑者"再到"领跑者"。希望这本画册的出版发行，能够成为中华人民共和国成立75年来桥梁建设事业发展的珍贵记录，让国际桥梁界同行更加了解中国的桥梁建设，推动中国从桥梁大国走向桥梁强国。

# AFTERWORD

In 2024, marking the 75th anniversary of the founding of the People's Republic of China, a special effort was made to celebrate this significant milestone. This effort produced this album *Bridges in China 1949-2024*. It was compiled and published as a result of the collaborative efforts of the Editorial Committee, the Compilation Board, and the publishing house.

The album *Bridges in China 1949-2024* features a total of 75 bridges from various development periods of the bridges in China. It includes: 14 bridges from the Learning and Searching period (1949-1979), including China's first prestressed concrete railway and highway bridges, major bridges like the Wuhan Bridge over the Yangtze River and the Nanjing Bridge over the Yangtze River, and representative bridges of economical beam and arch types and construction techniques; 13 bridges from the Chasing and Independence period (1980-1999), including milestones of China's independent construction like the Shanghai Nanpu Bridge, and bridges that set world records for span length among cable-stayed bridges, concrete beam bridges, and concrete arch bridges; 15 bridges from the Development and Strengthening period (2000-2009), featuring sea-crossing bridges that set world records for total length, and world-record span length bridges including the Shanghai Lupu Bridge, the Chongqing Shibanpo Parallel Bridge over the Yangtze River, and the Sutong Highway Bridge over the Yangtze River; 19 bridges from the Innovation and Improvement period (2010-2019), including the world's longest spanning double-main-span cable-stayed and suspension bridges such as the Wuhan Erqi Bridge over the Yangtze River and the Taizhou Bridge over the Yangtze River, as well as bridges that improved technological and quality standards such as the Hong Kong-Zhuhai-Macao Bridge; 14 bridges from the Climbing and Surpassing period (2020-2024), showcasing bridges that exemplify technological innovation such as the Tian'e Longtan Bridge and the Nanjing Jiangxinzhou Bridge over the Yangtze River, quality enhancements such as the Beikou Bridge over the Ou River and the Huang Mao Hai Link, and environmental friendliness such as the Shenzhen-Zhongshan Link and the Fourth Sea-crossing Bridge of Macao.

Over the past 75 years, the development of bridge engineering in China has achieved globally recognized successes, becoming a new force driving the advancement of international bridge technology and innovation, evolving first from a follower to a parallel runner, and now to a leader. We hope that the publication and distribution of this album will serve as a valuable record of the progress made in bridge construction since the founding of the People's Republic of China 75 years ago. The aim of this album is to provide the international bridge community with a deeper understanding of China's bridge construction achievements and to promote China's transition from a major bridge-building country to a powerful bridge-building nation.

图书在版编目（CIP）数据

中国桥梁 . 1949—2024 / 葛耀君主编 . — 北京：人民交通出版社股份有限公司, 2024.3
ISBN 978-7-114-19424-5

Ⅰ. ①中… Ⅱ. ①葛… Ⅲ. ①桥—中国—画册 Ⅳ.
①U448-64

中国国家版本馆 CIP 数据核字 (2024) 第 014194 号

本书由人民交通出版社股份有限公司独家出版发行。未经著作权人书面许可，本书图片及文字任何部分，不得以任何方式和手段进行复制、转载或刊登。版权所有，侵权必究。

Copyright © 2024

All rights reserved. No part of this publication may be reproduced, stored in a retrieval system, or transmitted in any form or by any means, electronic, mechanical, photocopying, recording or otherwise, without the prior written permission of the copyright holder. Printed in China.

*Zhongguo Qiaoliang*

| | |
|---|---|
| 书　　名： | 中国桥梁 1949—2024 |
| 著 作 者： | 葛耀君 |
| 责任编辑： | 卢俊丽 |
| 责任校对： | 赵媛媛 |
| 责任印制： | 刘高彤 |
| 出版发行： | 人民交通出版社股份有限公司 |
| 地　　址： | （100011）北京市朝阳区安定门外外馆斜街3号 |
| 网　　址： | http://www.ccpcl.com.cn |
| 销售电话： | （010）59757973 |
| 总 经 销： | 人民交通出版社股份有限公司发行部 |
| 经　　销： | 各地新华书店 |
| 印　　刷： | 北京雅昌艺术印刷有限公司 |
| 开　　本： | 965×635　1/8 |
| 印　　张： | 26.5 |
| 字　　数： | 270千 |
| 版　　次： | 2024年3月　第1版 |
| 印　　次： | 2024年3月　第1次印刷 |
| 书　　号： | ISBN 978-7-114-19424-5 |
| 定　　价： | 389.00元 |

（有印刷、装订质量问题的图书，由本公司负责调换）